SERVING THE SERVANT

Also by Danny Goldberg

In Search of the Lost Chord:
1967 and the Hippie Idea

Bumping into Geniuses:
My Life Inside the Rock and Roll Business

How the Left Lost Teen Spirit

SERVING THE SERVANT

REMEMBERING KURT COBAIN

DANNY GOLDBERG

First published in Great Britain in 2019 by Trapeze,
an imprint of The Orion Publishing Group Ltd
Carmelite House, 50 Victoria Embankment,
London EC4Y 0DZ

An Hachette UK company

1 3 5 7 9 10 8 6 4 2

A CIP catalogue record for this book is
available from the British Library.

ISBN (Hardback): 978 1 409 18278 8
ISBN (Trade paperback): 978 1 409 18279 5
ISBN (eBook): 978 1 409 18281 8

Typeset by Born Group

Printed in Great Britain by CPI Group (UK) Ltd, Croydon, CR0 4YY

MIX
Paper from
responsible sources
FSC
www.fsc.org FSC® C104740

www.orionbooks.co.uk

For my brother, Peter, and sister, Rachel, and our parents, Victor and Mimi Goldberg, who loved books, records, and their children

CONTENTS

INTRODUCTION

One afternoon in the fall of 2011, during the brief flowering of Occupy Wall Street, I visited ground zero of the movement in Zuccotti Park. As I was leaving, a short, tattooed teenage boy with a pierced eyebrow shyly asked me if I would take a picture with him. Celebrities were often visiting the encampment in those days and I said I was pretty sure he had me mixed up with someone else, but the boy shook his head and answered, "I know who you are. You used to work with Kurt Cobain."

I couldn't help but wonder if he had even been alive when Kurt killed himself seventeen years earlier. What was it about Kurt's music that endured long enough to get through to him? Every one of us who worked with Kurt has had these kinds of experiences with fans from time to time. It's as if encountering someone who knew Kurt gets them closer to a spirit that makes them feel less alone.

Not everything about Kurt's legacy is that tender, though. In death, as in life, he is full of contradictions. When I started writing this book, I typed the name "Kurt Cobain" into the search box on Amazon. In addition to posters, guitar picks, books, vinyl, videos, and T-shirts, there were "Dark Oval Lens Kurt Cobain Inspired Nirvana Sunglasses," a Kurt Cobain fleece throw blanket, a Kurt Cobain pocket lighter, a facsimile of Kurt's Washington State driver's license, a stainless steel pillbox with a picture of Kurt playing the guitar on it, and a "Kurt Cobain Unplugged Action Figure." My favorite is a bumper sticker that reads, "I'm not talking to myself, I'm talking to Kurt Cobain." If there was one that said he was speaking to me I would definitely have ordered it.

I embark on this project knowing that Kurt was a compulsive reader of his own press. He complained about rock writers who wanted to psychoanalyze him and resented it when they described his art as if it were merely a refracted commentary on his personal life, but he did hundreds of interviews to help refine the image he wanted to project.

His artistic legacy and tragic suicide created a persona that functions like a Rorschach test. Many who knew Kurt emphasize those aspects of his life that reinforce their particular notion of who they think he was. I am no exception. I owe much of my career to him and was one of his managers and a friend. In my office, I often stare at a framed photo of the two of us in which there is a sparkle in his eyes, the essence of which I keep trying to remember.

The memory thing is an issue. I've forgotten a lot of details. Just as I was about to get in touch with Courtney Love, to help me with my recollections, I heard from her because she wanted the same kind of help from me for her memoir. Twenty-five years is a long time. None of us are getting any younger. For me, one of the biggest issues is that sometimes it's hard to tell where public history ends and where personal memory begins. So many of the facts of Kurt's life have been documented in books, movies, You-Tube clips, boxed sets, and articles. The internet, which barely existed during Kurt's life, has sites with set lists from almost every show Nirvana played, and in many cases with transcripts of the band's onstage banter between songs.

I've been able to reconstruct some events from my files and have been helped enormously by talking to others whom I knew when I worked with Kurt. I found that many people with whom I reconnected had both large gaps in their memory and a few vivid hardwired recollections that they have retained for years as relics of both Kurt's life and their own. Similarly, some periods of my own memory are a vague impressionistic mush, but I have almost cinematic clarity for a handful of moments. However, even some of these stories have become semi-mythical after years of retelling, and I found numerous instances where one person's cherished anecdote clashed with mine or with another's.

In addition to the effect he had on millions of fans, Kurt deeply touched hundreds of people personally in his short life. Even after a quarter of a century, bitter feelings linger between some of those who were close to him early in his career and those, like me, who worked with him later; and between those who have negative feelings about Courtney and those, like me, who are fond of her. Most of the people I encountered when I worked with Kurt and Nirvana were eager to share their memories, but a few were not, because even after all this time their feelings about his life and death were still too raw.

I understand those who want to stay quiet. For the first couple of decades after his suicide I avoided books and films about Kurt. Recently, I binged on most of them. Several accounts focus on his parents' divorce, his subsequent unhappy childhood, and his tenacious struggle for recognition as a musician in the Northwest during the late 1980s. Kurt did tell me at various times about his sense of abandonment by his parents and the sense of isolation he felt as a kid, but I have little to add to that historical record of his early life and I didn't seek out people whom I didn't know from my work with Kurt. He and I didn't enter each other's lives until shortly before Nirvana started to work on *Nevermind,* the album that made them an international phenomenon when it was released in September 1991.

This is a subjective description of the time I was connected to him, the last three and a half years of his life, when Kurt Cobain did the work he is most remembered for. I view his artistry as being far more than a collection of Nirvana's greatest hits and believe that he belongs on the highest tier of the rock-and-roll hierarchy. He was also generous to other musicians and thoughtful about his role as a public figure. On a personal level he was kind to me both tangibly and in ways I cannot express.

Many of those who were closest to Kurt remain furious at him for killing himself. I respect their feelings but that's not where I'm coming from. I miss him and I will always wonder if there was something I could have done to prevent his early death. Yet as far as I can tell, neither medical science nor spiritual traditions nor great philosophers understand why some people take their own lives and others do not. As I've worked my way through the bittersweet process of remembering his life and art, the story I've increasingly been telling myself is that his suicide was not a moral failing but the result of a mental illness that neither he nor anyone around him was able to successfully treat or cure. (I do not use the word "illness" the way a doctor would but as a stand-in for a force that I believe was beyond anyone's control.)

I did not play music with Kurt or share his deep connection to punk rock culture, nor did I take drugs with him. However, I worked for him on the principal creative project of his life, a body of work that reinvented rock and roll in global popular culture and, for many of his fans, redefined masculinity as well.

Despite the squalor of his low points and the grotesque reality of his death, mine is a largely romantic view of Kurt's creative and idealistic sides. On at least one occasion in the past, this impulse to focus on his positive legacy was tone-deaf to the grief some of his other friends experienced. I gave the final eulogy at the private funeral that Courtney pulled together after his body was found. In *Nirvana: A Biography* British rock journalist Everett True described his reaction to it: "Danny Goldberg had given a speech at Kurt's funeral service that had made me realize precisely why the singer had finally given up. This speech had no grounding in reality, no relation to any man I've known. In it, Kurt was referred to as, 'An angel that came to earth in human form, as someone who was too good for this life and that was why he was only here for such a short time.' Bull-fucking-shit! Kurt was as pissy and moody and belligerent and naughty and funny and dull as the rest of us."

Not long after his book was published, at a music business conference in Australia, Everett and I spent time together and found that we had a lot more in common than either of us expected when it came to our feelings about Kurt. Even so, I know that Everett's negative reaction to my eulogy was shared by several others.

As I see it, various perspectives each contain part of the truth. Kurt had splits in his personality. He was a depressive, a junkie, *and* a creative genius. He could be bitterly sarcastic or despairing, but he also had a deeply romantic streak and confidence in the excellence of his art. Kurt was a slob and maintained a goofy sense of humor. He liked the same junk food that he ate as a kid, and he liked to wear pajamas during the day. Yet his slacker affect often obscured a highly sophisticated intellect.

Mark Kates, who was one of the Geffen Records executives closest to Kurt, spoke for many when he told me in a voice choked with emotion, "Two things that often are forgotten about Kurt:

First, that he was very funny. Second, that he was incredibly smart."

Kurt had contempt for those who disrespected him, and he could be grumpy and unpleasant when he was in pain, but most of the time he exuded a graciousness rare in geniuses or stars. He was (dare I say it?) a nice guy most of the time.

The photo of Kurt and me that I keep looking at was taken on March 6, 1992, at a concert by two of his favorite bands, Mudhoney and Eugenius, at the Palace in Los Angeles. Nirvana's breakthrough album, *Nevermind*, had come out the previous September, and in the ensuing five and a half months the band had experienced one of the most meteoric explosions of popularity in musical history. They had uniquely combined the punk rock energy and antiestablishment ethos of the Sex Pistols with pop melodies at the moment when that was exactly what much of the global rock audience wanted. Kurt tended to be self-deprecating in interviews and he would often compare the pop side of his songwriting to the Bay City Rollers, the Knack, or Cheap Trick, but I think he was always emulating the Beatles.

In the weeks since the album's initial single, "Smells Like Teen Spirit," had first been played on the radio there had been a surreal and abrupt transition between the band's austere punk rock origins and the new reality. They traveled in airplanes instead of vans and slept in hotels instead of on friends' couches. Most strangers who looked at them now saw them as celebrities rather than as derelicts.

Twenty years earlier, Bruce Springsteen had become famous quickly when *Born to Run* got him on the covers of *Time* and *Newsweek*, but even the Boss had to wait several more years (till *The River*) to have a pop hit and a number one album. For Nirvana, critical acclaim and pop success happened all at once, and the phenomenon was all the more remarkable because they had emerged from the insular world of punk rock, which up until that moment had faced indifference from most American rock fans.

Musicians have more individual cultural power than other artists. Except for a handful of auteurs, actors are dependent on other people's scripts. Even the biggest movie stars, novelists, and painters can't meet their audience in adoring groups of thousands on a nightly basis or get into their fans' heads every day the way a hit song does. Hence the power of the phrase "rock star." Because he was that rare rock star who stood for something more than sex appeal or entertainment, Kurt was viewed by many journalists and fans as a savant. It was a mind-fuck, but it had its compensations. He was proud of what the band had accomplished, and it was a relief that for the first time in his life he had enough money to live comfortably.

This particular night, Kurt was enjoying being a mere fan again. Mudhoney was one of his favorite Seattle bands and he was friends with their lead singer, Mark Arm. Kurt also had befriended Eugene Kelly of Eugenius (originally called Captain America before Marvel Comics forced them to jettison the name). Kelly had written "Molly's Lips," a song Nirvana covered on an early single, for Kurt's previous group, the Vaselines. A year earlier Kurt had looked up to Arm and Kelly, but now he was like their more successful younger brother, magnanimously cheering them on.

Despite the powerful impact of MTV, which played Nirvana videos several times a day, Kurt wasn't hassled by members of the crowd. Perhaps it was because at five feet eight inches tall and slightly hunched over from scoliosis, he blended into the background, or because he dressed the same as he had when he was broke, in torn jeans and Converse sneakers, or that he had no entourage or security hovering around him. However, I suspect that a number of fans that night did recognize Kurt but knew he'd rather be left alone to enjoy the music along with them.

Kurt had recently gotten out of rehab and as far as I could tell he was clean. His eyes were clear, a dramatic contrast to the depressing opaque heroin gaze I'd first seen when Nirvana performed on *Saturday Night Live* a couple of months earlier. Kurt and Courtney had both gone into treatment and it seemed to have worked. I swear that, for the moment, he was happy.

During a break in the show we were standing in an uncrowded corner of the balcony where people with passes could go, and Kurt spotted a photographer, put his arm over my shoulder, and said with a warm grin, "Let's take a picture," as if he knew it was a moment I'd want to remember.

Courtney was several months pregnant and she and Kurt had just moved into a new apartment on Alta Loma Terrace in the Hollywood Hills. At the last minute, Kurt decided to host a party at the new place after the concert. He was playing with the idea of being a grown-up and, for the moment, getting off on it. The apartment was hard to find. It was barely visible from the road, in a weird structure that required an outside tram to get to the front door. It was a time before most people had GPS and Kurt hadn't given out driving directions, so very few people showed up, but the vibe was great anyway. It was such a relief to see Kurt and Courtney feeling good about themselves for a moment. This oasis of peace would not last very long. The following week, Courtney would begin a series of interviews with Lynn Hirschberg for a profile in *Vanity Fair* that would come to torment the couple when it was published several months later and reverberate negatively for years to come.

I was forty years old when I met Kurt Cobain, and he was twenty-three. If he were still alive we would both be middle-aged guys today, but at the time I was old and he was young. Kurt was still at that stage of a rock career when most of the songs are about how you felt as a teenager. I was a jaded veteran of twenty years in the rock-and-roll business. I had a kid, a mortgage, and a corporate job. The year before, I'd had a career peak when I'd been thanked at the Grammys by Bonnie Raitt after she won album of the year. Kurt's persona had been forged in the antiestablishment world of Northwest punk rock, a culture that had contempt for conventional showbiz rituals like awards shows.

Kurt had a sophisticated sense of how to synthesize every aspect of rock and roll. He wrote the music *and* the lyrics for Nirvana. He was the lead singer *and* the lead guitarist. (In most rock bands two or more members shared these responsibilities, such as Jagger and Richards in the Rolling Stones, and Plant and Page in Led Zeppelin. Other than Kurt, Jimi Hendrix had been the only member of a superstar band who did both.) Kurt controlled every detail of the production of Nirvana's recordings. He personally designed the album covers and even many of the T-shirts, and came up with the ideas for the music videos.

Nevermind has sold over fifteen million copies, but it is not mere commercial accomplishment that accounts for Kurt's enduring mystique, nor can a list of his musical attributes. He was an excellent guitarist, but he was no Hendrix. His voice was uncorrupted by artifice or inhibition and conveyed both vulnerability and power, but rock has produced many great singers. He was a compelling live performer, but others were more theatrical. He was the rare songwriter who could combine pop song structure with hard rock, but the Rolling Stones had pulled that off periodically over the years. He was a much better lyricist than he admitted but not at the level of Bob Dylan or Leonard Cohen. He was a moralist but not a crusader.

Kurt's admiration for the Beatles included the holistic relationship that the band, especially John Lennon, had with a mass audience. As I perceived it, Kurt defined the entire breadth of his public life as art, including every live performance, every interview, and every photo. For all of his misgivings about fame, he used it very effectively. He was one of a handful of artists in the history of rock and roll who communicated simultaneously in multiple cultural languages, including the energy of hard rock, the integrity of punk rock, the infectious familiarity of hit songs, and the inspirational appeal of social consciousness. In addition, during the early nineties, Kurt carried what Allen Ginsberg, speaking of Bob Dylan decades earlier, had called "the bohemian torch of enlightenment and self-empowerment."

But the misty look I see in people's eyes—the look that kid at Occupy Wall Street had—is based on something else, a unique empathy Kurt had for other people, especially outcasts. He made many of his fans feel that there was a force in the universe that accepted them. They felt that they actually knew him and that, somehow, he knew them.

As I see it, the antecedent for Kurt's level of connection to teenage angst is found not in the rock-and-roll canon but in the fiction of J. D. Salinger, particularly *The Catcher in the Rye*. Like that classic fifties novel, Kurt's art gave dignity to underdogs and did so in a way that cracked the code of mass culture so that millions could share in it. The Reagan era that spawned his generation of punk rock is long gone, encased in amber, but twenty-five years after his death, Kurt's poetic, unfiltered understanding of adolescent pain still motivates young people to wear Nirvana T-shirts and to believe they are making some kind of statement by doing so.

Kurt was much more than the sum of his demons. A drawing in his journals depicts "the many moods of Kurdt Cobain: Baby, Pissy, Bully, Sassy." (In those days, he was still trying out various spellings of his name.) In a *Spin* magazine piece commemorating the tenth anniversary of Kurt's death, John Norris referred to him as "punk, pop-star hero, victim, junkie, feminist, geek avenger, wiseass."

Kurt's longtime bandmate and friend Krist Novoselic reminded me recently, "Kurt could be sweet and the most beautiful person and he made the most touching, beautiful gestures to me, but Kurt could also be really mean and vicious."

To me, Kurt sometimes came across as a bemused wise man from outer space, but he could also be a focused control freak, a vulnerable victim of physical pain or social rejection, a duplicitous junkie, a loving father and husband, or a kindly friend. He could be paranoid one minute and preternaturally self-confident the next; the sensitive outsider, a self-deprecating regular guy, the quiet but powerful center of attention, a shrewd self-promoter, or a despairing man-child for whom life often seemed meaningless. Kurt conveyed a lot of his feelings without talking. I have vivid memories of some of his expressions: anguished, amused, bored, pissed off, and nurturing. These were all amplified by his piercing blue eyes.

As the years have gone by, the aspect of Kurt I've been most preoccupied with is his role as an artist. As a kid his family assumed he would be a graphic artist when he grew up, and he never stopped drawing or sculpting. However, Kurt had an acute self-awareness about the level of his visual talents. "I was the best artist in Aberdeen," he told me with a rueful smile once, "but I never thought I would have stood out as an artist in a big city." Instead, the creative idiom that was his primary obsession was music. In this realm he *knew* he was exceptional. By the time I met Kurt, he radiated a quiet conviction about the quality of his work that was validated by everyone around him, including other artists.

I assume that most people reading this book are Nirvana fans but I periodically run into people who don't get what the fuss is about. That's the nature of music. Nothing appeals to everyone and we all have a significant bias in favor of whatever we loved in high school.

The closest thing I can come up with as a quantitative measurement of Kurt's impact is from statistics available on the music streaming service Spotify, which launched in 2008, fourteen years after Kurt's death. Here is a list of the worldwide streams, since Spotify began, of the most popular songs by Kurt's peers as well as some artists who came right before or after Nirvana. (Numbers are as of May 2018.)

Madonna, "Material Girl"	56 million
Prince, "Kiss"	80 million
N.W.A, "Straight Outta Compton"	113 million
Pearl Jam, "Alive"	116 million
Bruce Springsteen, "Dancing in the Dark"	126 million
Soundgarden, "Black Hole Sun"	139 million
2Pac, "Ambitionz az a Ridah"	144 million
U2, "With or Without You"	210 million
Foo Fighters, "Everlong"	210 million
R.E.M., "Losing My Religion"	229 million
Radiohead, "Creep"	257 million
Dr. Dre, "Still D.R.E."	275 million
Green Day, "Basket Case"	282 million
Michael Jackson, "Billie Jean"	353 million
Guns N' Roses, "Sweet Child O' Mine"	358 million
Nirvana, "Smells Like Teen Spirit"	387 million

Just sayin'.

The title *Serving the Servant* is an homage to a song Kurt wrote for the *In Utero* album in the wake of Nirvana's sudden commercial triumph. It's often remembered for its first line, "Teenage angst has paid off well," a self-deprecating reflection on the massive success of the previous album. Kurt also made it clear that some of the lyrics were an attempt to clarify his relationship with his estranged father, Don (whom I met for the first and only time at Kurt's funeral). To me, the title represents the reality of working with Kurt—he was the servant of a muse that only he could see and hear but whose energy he transmuted into a language that millions could identify with. The job of those of us who worked for him was to facilitate that work to the extent we were capable of doing so.

ONE

GOLD MOUNTAIN ENTERTAINMENT

I first encountered Kurt in November 1990 in Los Angeles. He and the other members of Nirvana, Krist Novoselic and Dave Grohl, met with me and my younger partner John Silva in the office of our management company, Gold Mountain Entertainment, on Cahuenga Boulevard West, not far from Universal City.

The first words Kurt ever said to me were an emphatic "Absolutely not" when I asked the band if they wanted to stay on Sub Pop, the underfunded but highly regarded Seattle-based indie label that had released their first recordings, including their debut album, *Bleach*, which had done well enough in the punk subculture that major record companies were now trying to lure the band away.

He had been silent during the first fifteen minutes of that meeting and Krist had done most of the talking. Kurt's firm answer about Sub Pop was my first indication of the dynamic within the band. Dave was a virtuoso rock drummer who would take the band to a much higher musical level than had his predecessors. Krist had formed the band with Kurt a few years earlier and shared his political and cultural ideas. The three members played music brilliantly together and had a collective vision of how the band fit into both the punk and rock worlds, but Kurt had the final word.

During rock and roll's early years the role of manager was often associated with venality and incompetence. Elvis Presley's manager, Colonel Tom Parker, was widely perceived as a manipulator who took advantage of his famous client, infantilizing Elvis while feathering his own nest wildly out of proportion to his value. The Beatles' first manager, Brian Epstein, was beloved by the band and was the first businessperson to recognize how special they were, but in retrospect he was unsophisticated about maximizing their income and power.

In subsequent years the word "manager" in the music business came to mean various things depending on the practitioner and on the artist. For actors, agents often provide some of the kinds of career guidance that managers do for musicians and singers. However, in the music business "booking agents" are responsible solely for the important but narrowly focused job of arranging live appearances and rarely have much to do with record companies, music publishers (which are the entities that own or administer songwriting copyrights), or media strategy, which are all overseen by managers. Music managers also serve as the liaison between the artist and their lawyers and accountants as well as booking agents, especially when balancing tour options for various parts of the world. Mark Spector, who has managed Joan Baez for several decades, describes the job as "the buck stops here."

In some cases, managers also play the roles of personal adviser and sounding board. My initial introduction to the job came while watching the Bob Dylan documentary *Dont Look Back*, in which Dylan's manager Albert Grossman was filmed gleefully negotiating higher concert fees. More importantly to a teenage viewer, Grossman was also shown to be in on the jokes Dylan cracked at the expense of unhip civilians. (*Dont Look Back* was also one of Kurt's favorite films.)

I wound up briefly working for Grossman in the early seventies and later in the decade did publicity for his Bearsville label. He had the air of someone who was the keeper of many hip secrets. Dylan's song "Dear Landlord" is believed to be about Grossman, especially the line "If you don't underestimate me, I won't underestimate you." In service of his clients (including The Band and Janis Joplin), Grossman changed the power dynamics on behalf of artists relative to record companies, talent agencies, concert promoters, and the media. For example, it was Grossman who told Columbia Records that they couldn't shorten Dylan's six-minute-long "Like a Rolling Stone" to the Top 40 radio–friendly length stations usually insisted on, and it became a hit single anyway.

Another of my early role models was Andrew Loog Oldham, whose name popped out at me when I read the liner notes on early Rolling Stones albums like *December's Children (And Everybody's)*. In those days Oldham not only managed the Stones, he also produced their albums.

My mentor in the music business was Led Zeppelin's manager, Peter Grant, whom I worked for in my early twenties. Grant took Grossman's pro-artist attitude to the next level. An intimidating, three-hundred-pound former professional wrestler with a cockney accent, Grant successfully insisted on Zeppelin's getting a much bigger piece of the economic pie than any musical artist before them. Prior to this, most concert promoters paid artists 50 percent of the net profits for their concerts. Grant insisted on 90 percent and the business was changed forever. I soon internalized Grant's attitude, which was: *Fuck everyone else. What the band wants is all that matters.*

The word "manager" is somewhat misleading. It can sound as if we are somehow in charge of our clients when in reality it's the opposite. It's a service profession and the artist is the boss. Several years after Kurt's death I became friends with Oldham (who says that Grossman was one of his role models as well) and we compared notes about the similarities and differences between managing the Rolling Stones in the mid-sixties and Nirvana in the nineties. Oldham's Delphic take on the job is, "An accomplished manager is only that when he has an act that hustles him as much as he hustles the act."

One of the managers I admire the most is Kenny Laguna, who has brilliantly guided Joan Jett's career for more than a quarter of a century. Kenny once spoke to me about the highs and lows of being a manager, "It's a funny profession. One day I'm talking to Senator Schumer about Joan doing something for the State Department, and the next day I'm trying to find a way of getting a cat urine stain out of her Oriental rug."

Since even the best artists are prone to insecurity, managers are predisposed to cast everything in the best light to their clients. Sometimes this can lead to counterproductive sugarcoating. There is a scene in the Dixie Chicks documentary *Shut Up & Sing* where the group asks their manager Simon Renshaw if the outcry about Natalie Maines's criticism of President George W. Bush at the outset of the Iraq War will hurt their career. He calmly assures them that the crisis will quickly blow over. (It didn't. The right-wing echo chamber haunted them for the next year.) I would have said exactly the same thing in that situation. After all, they were about to go onstage.

Of course, there are exceptions. If a client is doing something unethical or self-destructive there is an obligation to try to dissuade them, but the default position is to be an advocate. The managers I wanted to emulate had an idealized version of their clients inside their heads, which they projected to both the artist and the rest of the world. After seeing a concert by a client, a friend once said to me, "I guess you wouldn't tell him that the show is too long," to which I replied, "I wouldn't even tell that to *myself.*"

In the mid-eighties, when I was in my mid-thirties, I formed my management company Gold Mountain (an Anglicization of "Goldberg"). Our first clients were Belinda Carlisle and Bonnie Raitt. By 1990, we were doing well enough that I wanted to broaden the roster to include artists that appealed to younger audiences. I was aware that punk culture was growing in popularity and moving beyond the limited province of rock critics and college radio. Since I had paid scant attention to punk since the seventies, I hired John Silva, who was then in his twenties and already managing critically acclaimed bands such as House of Freaks and Redd Kross. Silva had a music nerd's obsession with fanzines and vinyl seven-inches. He knew many tastemakers in the punk subculture that had evolved in the previous decade, and earlier in his life he had briefly been roommates with the legendary punk singer Jello Biafra. Silva also had an extraordinary work ethic and ambition that dovetailed perfectly with mine.

A few months after our partnership began we started managing Sonic Youth, who had recently signed to Geffen Records' new imprint DGC Records. Having only worked with indie labels up until that point, the band chose us as a team to help them navigate the commercial music business as they prepared for the release of their first major-label album, *Goo*.

Sonic Youth had been releasing EPs and albums for eight years and during that time had become one of the most respected and influential artists in the indie music world. Lead guitarist Thurston Moore, who had boyish looks, a lanky six-foot-six-inch frame, and a shrewd intellect, was influenced as much by the unique guitar tunings of avant-garde composer Glenn Branca as he was by punk rock. In 1981 Moore married bassist and singer Kim Gordon, who had previously been an art student and who viewed the punk world through a similar intellectual prism. Guitarist and singer Lee Ranaldo and drummer Steve Shelley shared with their bandmates a love of multiple musical genres. Collectively they combined a subversive commitment to punk rebellion with a grace and intelligence that made them beloved in virtually every corner of the fractious indie world.

I soon came to realize that Kim and Thurston had their fingers on a musical pulse that was otherwise inaccessible to me, so I hung around them whenever I could. They saw their role in the community as being not only artists but curators. Nirvana was the latest in a long line of bands who had grown their audiences because Sonic Youth had brought them on tour. Kurt saw the Sonic Youth guitarist as one of his mentors. In his journals there are several entries where he scribbled a reminder to himself to "call Thurston." When Silva had first mentioned Nirvana to me, I was hesitant to take them on because I was always worried about the investment of time it usually took to develop newer artists before they could afford to pay us anything. At Silva's urging Thurston called to suggest that I make an exception to my rule, and thank God I listened to him.

It was not until June 1991, three months before *Nevermind*

was released, that I finally saw Nirvana play, when they opened for Dinosaur Jr. at the Hollywood Palladium. I had seen hundreds of shows over the years and was usually blasé about them, but this time I was transfixed. Although most people were there to see the headliner, Kurt connected very deeply with the audience. He didn't resort to conventional theatrics, but it felt to me as if he was able to convey his inner spirit in a way that created instant intimacy. To this day, I cannot describe exactly what he did, only how it felt. It was a particular form of rock-and-roll magic I'd never witnessed before. Although I had no idea of the dimensions of the commercial tsunami soon to come, I knew that I was very, very fortunate to be working with Nirvana.

At the time, Gold Mountain was a midsized management company with a staff of around twenty-five people and several dozen clients. For many of them I performed a primarily administrative role, but with a few I developed a personal connection. I now realized that Kurt was going to be much more important to me than I'd originally expected. As I drove home after the concert, I analogized my blossoming admiration for Kurt to Peter Grant's single-minded commitment to Jimmy Page. I was excited.

In the years since his death I am often asked variations on the question "What was Kurt really like?" Sometimes the best I could do was to see him through a glass darkly, connecting with some parts of him and blocked from others. There were moments I could get through to him remarkably easily and other times I felt impelled to walk on eggshells around his emotions. In addition to the kaleidoscopic qualities mentioned earlier, there was always a side of Kurt that was hidden, some of it the artistic genius that he literally couldn't explain and some of it a despair rooted in pain that was too unbearable to expose.

Yet most day-to-day business issues were informed by the fact that from the time we started working with Nirvana there was an almost instant understanding between Silva, myself, and the band about the balance they wanted to achieve between appealing to existing fans and attracting new ones. We had no idea that the latter category would run into the millions, but the recent successes of Jane's Addiction and Faith No More made it clear that there were at least hundreds of thousands of rock fans who, while oblivious to punk rock, were nonetheless yearning for something musically and culturally distinct from the "hair bands" and heavy metal artists popular at the time. This was a new, young audience drawn both to emotionally accessible music and countercultural values. There were dozens of small decisions that would be made over the course of the next year to achieve this balance, but Kurt and I rarely felt the need to get into long conversations about it. We had an almost immediate click into a shared attitude, and although Kurt would later articulate a lot of his thinking in interviews, in private a lot was conveyed to me by half-completed sentences, eye rolls, grimaces, or smiles.

In his journals Kurt wrote, "Punk rock says nothing is sacred. I say art is sacred." Nevertheless, he made it clear to me that he still had a deep emotional connection to many aspects of punk and cared what people in the subculture thought of him.

I had been in the music business in New York in the 1970s when the Ramones and other artists created the first wave of punk rock. I had started as a rock critic but soon found my talents lay more in PR. My journalist friends were obsessed with the punk scene at CBGB and I liked the energy and some of the music, but my heart was in making a place for myself in the mainstream music business, and once I got a job working for Zeppelin's Swan Song label I paid little attention to punk.

Now I had to do my best to catch up. I knew that any understanding of Kurt's art could not be complete without the context of the culture that inspired him as a teenager, that embraced him in his early twenties, and from which he internalized a set of values he would refer to as "Punk Rock 101" in his suicide note.

TWO

PUNK ROCK 101

In 1993, Kurt told journalist Robert Hilburn, "I was a seriously depressed kid. Every night at one point I'd go to bed bawling my head off. I used to try to make my head explode by holding my breath, thinking if I blew up my head, they'd be sorry. There was a time when I never thought I'd live to see twenty-one." In his book *Come as You Are: The Story of Nirvana*, Michael Azerrad quotes Kurt's reflection on his childhood: "I used to think I was adopted, that they found me on a spaceship. I knew there were thousands of other alien babies dropped off and I've met a few of them. One day we'll find out what we're supposed to do."

Kurt's alienation as a teenager was magnified by having to grow up in the conservative logging town of Aberdeen, Washington, where his artistic sensibilities made him an outcast. The one Aberdeen band that had a following in the national punk pantheon was the Melvins, and they had an incalculable influence on

Nirvana's early career—personally and musically. In those days, punk bands rarely drew more than a hundred people to a show and it was easy for fans to hang out with the group afterward. The Melvins' lead singer, Buzz Osborne (a.k.a. King Buzzo), turned Krist Novoselic on to the indie band Flipper, and when I spoke to Krist in 2018 he still glowed when recalling the epiphany of hearing their album *Generic* as a teenager.

Kurt first saw the Melvins perform in 1984, when he was sixteen years old. Shortly afterward, Buzz made Kurt a punk compilation tape that included songs by Black Flag and Flipper. Kurt was mesmerized and for months would lip-synch to the songs every single day. He told British writer Jon Savage that although he had enjoyed some of the melodies of mainstream rock bands like Led Zeppelin and Aerosmith, most of the lyrics were one dimensional: "A lot of it was sexism, the way they wrote about their dicks and having sex. That bored me." Listening to punk rock, Kurt found his calling. Those songs expressed how he felt socially and politically. It was a huge relief that, in some respects at least, he was not alone. There was another world on *this* planet and he was determined to be part of it. Buzz soon introduced Kurt to Krist. The next year Melvins drummer Dale Crover played with Nirvana on their first demos. (A few years after that, Buzz introduced Dave Grohl to Nirvana.)

Punk fans are passionate about the music they love, and there are Talmudic arguments among aficionados about the merits of different artists and what is or isn't punk, discussions that I remain unqualified to address. What follows is the dumbed-down way that I, as an interloper from a different generation, was able to absorb some of what had inspired Kurt in his formative years.

The punk rock culture of the seventies in New York and the one that revolved around the Sex Pistols in London were only of peripheral interest to Kurt. He and Krist were galvanized in high school by a subsequent iteration of punk and other indie rock that flowered in America in the 1980s. Although that movement was commercially limited, it took on the role of a secular religion to its fans, the center of which was a group of artists that the mainstream music business largely ignored.

Between 1980 and '81—a few years before Buzz made that mix tape for Kurt—Flipper and Hüsker Dü released their first singles; Mission of Burma and Minor Threat released their first EPs; the Minutemen, the Dead Kennedys, and the Replacements released their first albums; Henry Rollins joined Black Flag; and Sonic Youth and the Butthole Surfers were formed. All of these bands had albums that appeared on the many "Top Fifty" album lists that Kurt repeatedly made in his journals in an attempt to sketch out Nirvana's inspirations. There were numerous times I heard him naming these artists with such a tone of admiration that it sounded like a catechism. Unlike old-school rock groups who had formed in the sixties or seventies, these punk bands did not consider commercial success necessary to validate their work and viewed popular music with a jaundiced eye.

Black Flag was one of the first such bands that Kurt saw in person, and like most of their contemporaries they played fast and loud. Greg Ginn of Black Flag created SST Records to release the band's music but over the course of the eighties SST became a home for dozens of artists that Kurt loved. Ray Farrell worked at SST for years and was hired by Geffen Records a year before Nirvana went there. When they first met, Kurt wistfully told Farrell, "I would have killed to be on SST."

SST bands couldn't get booked in clubs that relied on mainstream rock-and-roll audiences because they didn't have visibility in the conventional rock media that influenced talent buyers. Thus, SST and other indie labels like the Dead Kennedys' Alternative Tentacles had to find different venues, including VFW halls that hadn't previously featured live music. Young promoters emerged and created an alternative touring circuit that cultivated the subculture that Nirvana would later enter.

Krist remembers Nirvana's early tours in this circuit with great affection. "We had nothing else going on. We had this van and we would just cruise down the highway. We went to Florida, went to Canada. We were happy as clams. We would just get paid a few hundred bucks every night, and that was plenty of money."

In addition to the music, the wider punk culture was also an inspiration to Kurt. Because most of the artists he loved received virtually no exposure on commercial radio stations and their records weren't carried at chain record stores, they usually had to be found at small independent record shops, which became a second home to a lot of punk fans. These stores also sold inexpensively produced punk fanzines, which had a distinct aesthetic and espoused various antiestablishment values. Among the most influential were *Flipside*, which began publishing in 1977, and *Maximum Rocknroll*, which started in 1982. (Mass publications ignored or marginalized eighties punk at the time, as did *Rolling Stone*. This created a vacuum initially filled by *Creem*, which Kurt subscribed to as a teenager, and later by *Spin* when it was launched in 1985.)

Other than fanzines, the primary media that connected punk to its small but passionate fan base were college radio stations. College airplay was compiled in a tip sheet called *CMJ* (*College Media Journal*). *CMJ* created the *New Music Report* in 1982, which became an important curator for emerging artists in the indie/punk underground.

The music in the scene diversified over the course of the eighties. "It was punk if you did it your own way," says Farrell. Some evoked the lyrical minimalism of the Ramones, but as the eighties proceeded, an increasing group of punk rockers injected a wider variety of musical influences and biting social and political consciousness into their lyrics. Among the latter, Fugazi's Ian MacKaye and the Dead Kennedys' Jello Biafra were important role models for the political side of Kurt's persona.

As the eighties unfolded, the solidarity that indie artists felt with one another as outsiders replaced musical style as the binding force of the community. That was the context in which Sonic Youth, whose aesthetic owed more to the New York art scene than it did to the Sex Pistols, could emerge as mentors in the community. What this diverse group of punk rockers had in common were values that Kurt would later inject into his corner of the mainstream rock culture: making music that was personal, supporting other artists in the community, and maintaining an egalitarian relationship with the audience.

One of the paradoxes of my relationship with Kurt was that I was associated with two of the cultural forces that a lot of punks demonized: hippies and major labels.

The word "hippie" meant different things to different people at different times. By the eighties, long hair on men, which was rebellious in the sixties, had become part of the uniform of conventional macho rock culture. Hence the pejorative "hair band." There were even some punk shows at which guys with long hair were physically attacked by drunken fans who used the word "hippie" as an epithet.

Some of Kurt's heroes were more open-minded. They realized that while external symbols could quickly become passé or be coopted, there was a through-line of sincere bohemian idealism in meaningful art of every generation, and that included the early hippie culture. Greg Ginn of Black Flag saw over seventy-five Grateful Dead shows. Ian MacKaye of Fugazi saw the *Woodstock* movie sixteen times. Mark Arm recorded Bob Dylan's "Masters of War" as a single to protest the first Gulf War. Mike Watt of the Minutemen cited Creedence Clearwater Revival as a political band (in part because of the anti-war song "Fortunate Son") and said that the shirts worn by Creedence prefigured the popularity of flannel as a "regular guy" uniform for punks in the eighties. Prior to forming Nirvana, Kurt and Krist had a Creedence cover band. (However, while I initially assumed that Green River, Mark Arm's band before Mudhoney, was an homage to the Creedence album of the same name, it was actually a reference to the serial killer operating in Seattle at that time.)

Kurt identified at different times with both hippies and hippie haters. Shortly before *Nevermind* was released, John Rosenfelder, a young promo guy whom we all called Rosie, earnestly told him that there was enthusiasm for "Smells Like Teen Spirit" among some of the stoner college radio guys steeped in psychedelics. Kurt sneeringly replied, "I want a tie-dyed T-shirt made with the blood of Jerry Garcia." On other occasions, however, Kurt nostalgically remembered drinking beer in front of Jimi Hendrix's grave in Seattle.

The song "Territorial Pissings" on *Nevermind* begins with a phrase lifted from the sixties song "Get Together," the most successful version of which was performed by the Youngbloods. In a fierce, garbled voice that seems to mock the hippie anthem Krist sings, "Come on people now / smile on your brother / everybody get together / try to love one another right now." Many rock critics described the intro as a signal that Nirvana was mocking the peace-and-love era.

However, Krist told me they did not mean to impugn the ideals of the song but were bitterly commenting on the *abandonment* of those ideals by the majority of baby boomers as they got older and more influential. The most complete answer Kurt gave in public about "Get Together" was in an interview in Brazil's *O Globo*: "The song speaks of people who join together to be cool and try something new, the ideal contrast to the macho men I'm portraying in 'Territorial Pissings.' We didn't want to be offensive to the guy who wrote it. The idea of being positive and causing change in society and the world was appropriated by the media, who turned it into something ridiculous, a caricature."

There was no ambiguity in Kurt's ritual smashing of his guitar onstage, which became a feature of many Nirvana shows early in the band's career. He was openly mimicking the Who's Pete Townshend, who originated the practice onstage in 1964 after the band played *their* sixties anthem "My Generation." Drummer Keith Moon often followed suit by toppling over his drum kit, an action that Dave Grohl gleefully copied at the end of many Nirvana shows.

Instrument destruction fit in perfectly with the anarchic strains of punk rock, but Kurt's preoccupation with the Beatles was much more unusual for artists in the subculture Nirvana emerged from. As Thurston Moore reminded me, the members of Nirvana would often coyly refer to "the B-word," as if listening to the Fab Four was a guilty pleasure. When it came to attitudes about a mass audience, most punk rockers were more like poets or avant-garde classical musicians than mainstream rockers.

Nirvana's mixed signals about the sixties counterculture, one of Kurt's many ingenious cultural straddles, led British writer Jon Savage to claim that the very name Nirvana was "a sarcastic commentary on hippie pieties," although Kurt's explanations for the name were invariably respectful of its spiritual provenance.

There were plenty of "Fuck Woodstock" T-shirts at the UK's Reading Festival when Nirvana headlined it. However, Kurt and Krist both told me that they admired sixties radicals like Abbie Hoffman and Timothy Leary and lamented the fact that their generation didn't have similar countercultural thought leaders. Moreover, while the members of many punk bands shaved their heads or wore a Mohawk, the guys in Nirvana had the kind of long hair that would have fit right in at Woodstock.

For Christmas 1991 I gave Kurt and Courtney a bound facsimile edition of the entire eighteen-month life of the *San Francisco Oracle*, the quintessential San Francisco hippie paper. Shortly thereafter, Kurt did an interview in which he pointed out that the Haight-Ashbury community had realized that hippie symbolism had been drained of meaning as early as 1967, alluding to a "Death of Hippie" march that the *Oracle* had prominently covered.

Viewed through my baby-boomer eyes, punk rebellion sometimes seemed like a mere iteration of the adolescent angst popularized in the fifties movie *The Wild One*. The protagonist, Johnny Strabler, played by Marlon Brando, is asked what he is rebelling against, and the leather-clad motorcyclist sullenly replies, "Whaddaya got?" Similarly, there was a cohort of punk fans for whom unfocused anger, tribal solidarity with other punks, and a shared taste in music were all there was. However, many of the currents of punk rock that inspired Kurt also had a specific political subtext. In 1980, decades before Donald Trump emerged as the voice of angry older white males, Black Flag anticipated their fear in the song "White Minority" ("We're gonna be a white minority . . . We're gonna feel inferiority").

Kurt's teenage years coincided with Ronald Reagan's presidency from 1981 to '89, which was a catalyst for a lot of the rage of the American punk culture of that era, similar to the way the anti-war movement had influenced the sixties counterculture and opposition to Margaret Thatcher's conservatism had motivated the Clash and others in the British punk movement.

To the kind of young people who were attracted to punk rock, Reagan's homespun style epitomized retro Hollywood phoniness. First Lady Nancy Reagan made the simplistic "Just Say

No" antidrug campaign the centerpiece of her national identity, which exacerbated the drug war. While her husband was overseeing the dismantling of many programs that helped the poor, Mrs. Reagan spent $200,000 on new china for the White House. Reagan was elected by huge majorities. Embattled punks in the eighties, having no mass culture of "resistance" against the administration to plug into, created one themselves. DOA released a song called "Fucked Up Ronnie." The Minutemen wrote "If Reagan Played Disco," and there was a hardcore band called Reagan Youth. In 1983, Biafra's group, the Dead Kennedys, organized a Rock Against Reagan tour. Two years later Thurston characterized Sonic Youth's *Bad Moon Rising* album as "a rejection of the smiley face façade of Reagan's 'Morning in America' reelection campaign." In 1991, after *Nevermind* was released, Kurt said, "The Reagan years have definitely set us back to where the average teenager feels kind of lost and there isn't much hope."

Reagan's vice president and successor, George H. W. Bush, presided over the Gulf War, which seemed to many in the punk culture like a conflict that was launched primarily to protect the interests of oil companies. Kurt and Krist felt isolated when the war had a 90 percent approval rating and spawned ubiquitous yellow ribbons, ostensibly to symbolize support for the troops, but often expropriated by hawks as signifying support of the war itself.

One thing that brought together most people in the music world, myself included, was opposition to then senator Al Gore's wife, Tipper, and other "Washington wives" who organized an effort to ban the sale of albums with profane lyrics to minors. Many of the artists whom Nirvana admired were targeted. The Dead Kennedys album *Frankenchrist* included a poster reproduction of Swiss surrealist H. R. Giger's painting *Penis Landscape*. ("This picture is like Reagan America on parade," Biafra proudly said.) The poster and the album that contained it were the subject of an obscenity prosecution by the Los Angeles district attorney and successfully defended by the Southern California affiliate of the ACLU, whose foundation board I chaired.

There were those in the punk community who conflated the very existence of corporate record companies with conservative politics. I asked Michael Azerrad about the significance of Reagan to the eighties punk movement and he jokingly replied, "He was totally a major-label president." By the end of Kurt's life *I* was such an executive, and like most of my peers I detested Reagan's policies, but I knew that Azerrad was adopting the voice of a typical punk fan at the time and his formulation reminded me of the tightrope Kurt had walked.

In an interview for France's *Best* magazine the year after *Nevermind* came out Kurt said, "I had a tendency to reason in terms of 'us' against 'them.' Since we've been part of a big business, I realize that things unfortunately aren't that simple. We meet people in huge companies that sincerely love music and are trying to make things evolve. That being said, I understand how kids who like underground think we're sellouts. I used to reason exactly like them."

Even though the Kurt I met was unambiguous about wanting Nirvana to sign with a major label, the mystique of indies had been a huge part of his coming of age as an artist and he never lost his respect for indie culture.

Without the existence of labels such as SST (formed in 1978), Alternative Tentacles (1979), Dischord (1980), Epitaph (1980), Touch and Go (1981), K (1982), Homestead (1983), C/Z (1985), Sub Pop (1988), and Matador (1989), a lot of the music that inspired Kurt would not have been able to find an audience. And when Nirvana was trying to get a record deal, it was to such indies that Kurt sent cassettes and letters. Beyond the fact that he admired the music on those labels, they were usually the only plausible options in those days for a punk-influenced band.

Not surprisingly, there was a defiant tribalism prevalent among many in the indie world. Because these were shoestring operations that paid little or no artist advances, they were rarely in a position to acquire long-term contracts. Thus major labels, in addition to their cultural orthodoxy, could represent an existential threat to the indies by swooping in to sign their most promising artists after the smaller labels had the foresight to put them on the map. (Hüsker Dü, for example, made their first three albums on SST and then signed with Warner Bros. in 1986.)

I understood that the only way that many of the young people at indies could make progress in the music business was by delegitimizing previous generations. Musical trends are created by teenagers. A "generation" in music usually spans around four years, the length of time it takes to get through high school. There are always a few opportunities for smart, ambitious people in their early twenties who can credibly claim that their elders "don't get it." I had benefited from a similar formulation as a long-haired hippie type contrasting myself to "straight" older guys when I wormed my way into the business in the late sixties.

Nevertheless each artist has their own set of goals and indie fundamentalism wasn't for everyone. By the time I met Kurt, he had already concluded that while some aspects of indie pride were legitimate, some attitudes were informed by an inverse snobbery that could be lame. When it served his purpose, Kurt would point out that by 1990, records by REM, the Stooges, the Ramones, Patti Smith, and the Sex Pistols had been released in the United States on major labels with no adverse effect on those artists' music or credibility.

The big signifier for Nirvana was Sonic Youth. Thurston Moore told me in 2018 what the band's rationale was for signing with Geffen: "We noticed that Hüsker Dü's music hadn't changed when they signed to Warner. On the independent labels we dealt with, SST Records, Blast First Records, and Neutral Records, if there was accounting, it was always somewhat suspect. With Geffen, we would get an advance that would allow us to be able to pay our rents, get health insurance, have a slightly better lifestyle, and maybe, just maybe, not have to work day jobs. We felt like we could negotiate a contract that would make sense."

Sonic Youth were secure enough in their place in the subculture to ignore carping from indie fundamentalists. Thurston still bristles at the fact that punk musician and indie-label champion Steve Albini wrote a piece "drawing up scenarios about how an artist systematically gets ripped off on a major label." Thurston says, "He was so crude in his description. He ended his piece, 'If you're gonna fuck a pig don't be surprised if you get shit on your dick.' I wrote a letter in response to Steve saying, 'That's a very interesting scenario. There's only one thing you didn't mention in your example of a band getting butt-fucked by corporate labels. They must be really *stupid.*'"

By contrast Thurston says, "We went to every meeting. We knew what we were getting into. We knew where the money was coming from . . . who was spending what. I didn't feel like we were signing to a 'bluesman's contract,' as Albini put it. We were talking to a bank. We didn't feel like we were selling out. We were buying in."

But even Thurston was occasionally torn between adherence to indie ideology and the way he functioned in the real world. In the documentary *1991: The Year Punk Broke*, filmed *after* Sonic Youth were already signed to Geffen, he is shown telling young German fans, "I think we should destroy the bogus capitalist process that is destroying youth culture. The first step is to destroy the record companies."

Krist Novoselic was two years older than Kurt and was the one person who went on the entire journey with him from Aberdeen to worldwide adulation. Krist knew how talented and sensitive Kurt was. Almost a foot taller than Kurt at six foot seven, Krist seemed to me like the big brother Kurt never had but minus the sibling rivalry.

When I contacted him for this book Krist repeatedly mused, "It's always good to talk about Kurt." Now in his fifties, balding and gray, Krist retains an almost childlike innocence and idealism about music and politics, and he still exudes an earnest, protective attitude about his bandmate. "Some people thought that Kurt was lazy because he didn't want to go to work to go clean toilets as a janitor, but when it came to art and music, he wasn't lazy. He worked really hard."

Kurt was one of only a handful of lead guitarists who played a left-handed guitar with normal stringing, so he had few role models as a musician. (Kurt was almost entirely self-taught and never learned to read music.) Some guitarists (including Duane Allman and David Bowie) who were otherwise left-handed played guitar with their right hand. Kurt, like Jimi Hendrix, wrote with his right hand but played guitar with his left.

Krist recalls that from the moment they met, Kurt was constantly writing and rewriting lyrics and composing music. Kurt was almost as prolific a visual artist as he was musically. Krist remembers, "I went to his apartment in Aberdeen one day and he had drawn these pornographic cartoons involving Scooby-Doo. They were really good! Kurt was always sculpting, painting, and drawing. He could have gone to art school. He went to Olympia because there was nothing happening in Aberdeen." Courtney concurs: "He had to go to Olympia to be exposed to people he respected who were into different kinds of music besides the Melvins and Black Sabbath."

Olympia is fifty miles east of Kurt's hometown, with a larger population of around fifty thousand, and it is the home of the Evergreen State College, a progressive school that doesn't give grades. Underground cartoonists Lynda Barry and *Simpsons* creator Matt Groening had gone to Evergreen. So would Tobi Vail and Kathleen Hanna of the band Bikini Kill, Carrie Brownstein of Sleater-Kinney, Sub Pop founder Bruce Pavitt, and Calvin Johnson, founder of K Records, who also sang and played guitar in the influential local band Beat Happening.

Olympia's central role in the punk scene of the eighties was fueled by Evergreen's radio station, KAOS, which had a policy requiring that 80 percent of the music it broadcast emanate from indie labels. The station became a magnet for many people who would later play an important role in eighties and nineties punk culture, including Johnson and Pavitt, who both hosted shows on KAOS before they started their labels. Nirvana's second public appearance was a radio broadcast on the station in 1987.

To help promote their releases, K published a newsletter that featured an anthropomorphic version of the label's logo drawn in a cartoon style with the caption "Our hero battles the many armed corporate ogre, breaking the spell of musical repression." Johnson also helped broaden the musical canvas of indie rock culture. Azerrad writes that K was "a major force in widening the idea of a punk rocker from a mohawked guy in a motorcycle jacket to a nerdy girl in a cardigan." As Stella Marrs wrote in the introduction to *Love Rock Revolution*, a history of K Records, "The preening cock-rock god of the dominant music culture had been replaced by a new face of virility that was not afraid to cry." That aspect of the Olympia culture strongly resonated with Kurt.

From the very beginning of his career he was into subverting the image of the macho front man.

Eric Erlandson, who would become the guitar player in Hole and a close friend of Kurt's, says of Olympia, "It was a true underground scene that also had a connection to DC." (Washington, DC, was home to Fugazi as well as Dave Grohl's previous band, Scream.) "It was like a cool little incestuous club but most people in it were warm and welcoming. Kurt made an immediate impact in the Olympia music community." As Krist reminded me, "Kurt had been writing songs for years. He had like three or four years of development of that skill that people in other bands didn't have. Nirvana started playing music in Olympia and Seattle and we're rocking with our contemporaries, but Kurt had years on them as a songwriter."

Slim Moon graduated from high school in Seattle in 1986 and was among a group of obsessed Melvins fans who would go to any show they played within driving distance. Moon remembers, "The Melvins usually showed up in a tiger-striped van owned by their roadie, who was Krist." Moon first noticed Kurt at some of these shows.

Moon moved to Olympia to attend Evergreen. Although he didn't last long in college, he stayed in town because he loved the music scene there. One night Moon and his high school friend Dylan Carlson were at a party in East Olympia at a place called the Dude Ranch, which was the first time either of them actually spoke to Kurt, bonding over their mutual admiration of the punk band Big Black. Kurt's unique aesthetic sense was present even back then. Moon recalls, "Kurt was wearing a very distinctive trench coat."

A couple of months later, Moon went to a party where Kurt and Krist's new band was playing. Dale Crover of the Melvins was sitting in on drums. That evening they called themselves Skid Row. ("They were changing their name every time they played at this point," says Moon.) Kurt was wearing a "fake glam outfit including platform boots," Moon recalls. "It was obviously a parody. What I most remember is that Kurt didn't play a guitar solo. He had a digital delay pedal and it was like he was doing *half* guitar solos, which went along with the spirit of a parody. It was remarkable."

Moon started promoting small shows himself in Olympia and booked Kurt's band for one of their earliest gigs. Moon admits that his friend Dylan Carlson "decided Kurt was a genius quicker than I did." (Kurt remained friends with Dylan for the rest of his life, and it's likely that Dylan was the last person to see Kurt alive.) Kurt was twenty years old at the time and Moon didn't perceive the range of his brilliance until the day Kurt played him a song "and it was super catchy, catchier than almost everything that eventually went on the *Bleach* record." He says, "That really struck me. He is messing around with all these different forms. He was wearing a denim jacket covered with the names of his favorite bands on Touch and Go and other indie labels, but he could actually write a killer pop song."

Even at this stage of his life, Kurt was sometimes attracted to drugs that weren't good for him. Moon recalls, "I was moving and asked Kurt to help. He said he didn't feel well but when I said he was the only person I know with a car, he helped me pack up, opened the door and puked, and then helped me finish the move. It was so nice of him even though he was feeling like crap. I hadn't figured out he was doing dope."

Olympia, Moon acknowledges, "was a tough place to be seen as cool. It had a rep for being elitist. There was talk of cliques. Kurt saw what was cool about Olympia and wanted to be accepted by the cool people, and of course he was. The band was too good not to be accepted." Moon adds, "And he was really funny at parties. He'd be really quiet and then suddenly capture the room."

Olympia was also the center of the Riot Grrrl movement, which was starting to blossom while Kurt lived there. NPR music critic Ann Powers, who used to write for the Seattle music monthly the *Rocket* and has authored several books about feminism and rock, explains, "Riot Grrrl was punk rock with consciousness raised." One of the most influential Riot Grrrl bands was Bikini Kill, who released their album on the Kill Rock Stars label, which Moon founded and which was distributed by K Records. Kurt had a passionate affair with Bikini Kill drummer Tobi Vail when he lived in Olympia. Courtney acknowledges, "Tobi was the first woman Kurt was really in love with."

Powers notes, "That experience made him different from Mudhoney or Pearl Jam. He lived it. He was involved with someone making feminist music, reading those classic books, thinking about the world through that lens." Kurt also influenced Vail. She told Everett True that she learned a lot from Kurt about singing, including the use of screaming as if the voice was a musical instrument.

Every version of Kurt's life story includes the fact that one night Bikini Kill's lead singer, Kathleen Hanna, graffitied over his bed, "Kurt smells like teen spirit." It was a reference to a brand of deodorant Vail used but Kurt, with his artist's alchemy, reappropriated the phrase for an entirely different purpose in his most famous song. Courtney, whose mutual hostility with the members of Bikini Kill has been widely chronicled, spoke to me about them in 2018 in a reflective tone: "I was never a fan of the music, but I loved their culture."

Riot Grrrl and Courtney Love represent two strains of thought in punk rock that Everett True describes thusly: "There were bands like the Sex Pistols and the Clash who believed that you infiltrate and subvert society from within, mess with the system, and have fun with it, and then there were people like Ian MacKaye and Fugazi who had a mind-set that believed that any involvement with the system was corrupting and that you should create completely alternative structures outside. Kurt obviously chose the path of working inside the system. He ended up with Courtney Love, not with Tobi Vail. That says it all, doesn't it?"

The distinction Everett makes between the divergent schools of thought in the indie world was echoed in Kurt's journals from the period after *Nevermind* was recorded, in which he comes down clearly on the side of subverting from within: "Since my freshly found relationship with employees of the corporate ogre, I've learned that there are a handful of very honorable and sincere music lovers who are posing as the enemy to infiltrate the mechanics of the empire to help destroy what we have all known as shit."

Although some biographers ascribe Kurt's decision to leave Olympia to convulsions in his love life, Krist gives a different reason: "He was way more talented than most of the people there. Okay? A lot of people in the art world are poseurs. But they're not really doing anything. He *was* an artist."

Kurt often told me that he had gotten sick of the inverse snobbery of the scene and the way it discouraged his ambitions. Erlandson says, "I saw what Kurt liked in Olympia and I saw what he didn't like in it—that some part of it is so conservative and judgmental and cliquey." Kurt complained to Azerrad, "I just wish people wouldn't take it so fucking seriously. Everyone seems to be fighting for utopia in the underground scene. There are so many different factions. If you can't get an underground movement to band together and people are just bickering about unnecessary little things that they don't agree on, then how the fuck do you expect to have an effect on a mass level?" Of course, the Olympia punk scene had no interest in having an effect on the masses. They loved Kurt's talent and sensitivity but were in denial about his ambition.

Courtney Love spent time in Olympia before she and Kurt got to know each other and she had an even more jaundiced view of the culture around K Records, some of which was expressed in her lyrics to "Rock Star" on Hole's *Live Through This*, in which she savagely mocked the smugness of the scene, "When I went to school in Olympia, everyone's the same / we look the same we talk the same." On the acoustic version of the song she recorded for the BBC's John Peel she added the line "I went to school with Calvin," delivered in a tone dripping in sarcasm.

"Calvin" was Calvin Johnson of K Records who turned Kurt on to artists such as the Vaselines and Jad Fair, whose music was more nuanced than some of the intense loud punk bands whose audiences were overwhelmingly male. Nirvana never recorded for K but in September 1990 Kurt played several songs acoustically on Johnson's KAOS radio show and did a duet with him of the Wipers song "D-7." (Kurt also announced the addition of Dave Grohl to Nirvana during that broadcast.) In 1991, after he'd left Olympia and not long before Nirvana signed with Geffen Records, Kurt got a tattoo of the K Records logo on his forearm, which he said was "to try to remind me to remain a child." Kurt was still corresponding with Johnson long after *Nevermind* became a phenomenon.

The week after "Smells Like Teen Spirit" got its first radio airplay, K hosted the International Pop Underground Convention (IPUC) in Olympia. The manifesto for the conference read in part, "As the corporate ogre expands its creeping influence on the minds of industrialized youth, the time has come for the International Rockers of the World to convene in celebration of our grand independence.—Because the corporate ogre has infected the creative community with the black plague of indentured servitude. Because we are grave diggers who have buried the grey spectre of the rock-star myth. We won't go away . . . Revolution is the end. Revolution is the beginning. No lackeys to the corporate ogre allowed." However, elsewhere in Washington State, other indie forces had emerged.

THREE

SUB POP

In Seattle, an hour's drive away from Olympia, Sub Pop Records would initially emulate K but would eventually prove to be more flexible when it came to dealing with the music business. Evergreen alumnus Bruce Pavitt had originally called his KAOS radio show and related fanzine *Subterranean Pop* before shortening the name. Once he moved to Seattle, Pavitt and his partner Jonathan Poneman became entrepreneurs who had as much in common with Ben and Jerry as they did with K.

The Sub Pop label was created in 1988 and adopted as its slogan "World Domination." Poneman's business card read "Corporate Lackey" and Pavitt's "Corporate Magnate." They presented themselves as both businessmen and rebels who made fun of themselves, and the pose worked.

Kurt pursued Sub Pop relentlessly. Courtney told me, "He wanted them because at the beginning he wanted to be

Soundgarden and they got to Sub Pop first." Kurt soon wore Poneman and Pavitt down and they let Nirvana record some singles
for the label. The band immediately stood out, in part because
of Kurt's voice, and also due to his fearless physicality onstage,
jumping from any available scaffolding onto the stage or into the
audience with unrestrained abandon.

Kurt charmed everyone at the label. Jennie Boddy, who did
publicity for Sub Pop, shared an apartment with Susie Tennant,
the local radio promotion person for Geffen Records. (One of the
singular aspects of the Seattle rock community at that time was
that people there felt more connected to one another than to any
institution they worked for.) During the *Bleach* period, when the
members of Nirvana were on the road so much that they didn't
have places of their own, they often slept on Boddy's floor when
they played Seattle. Like many I spoke to, Boddy exploded with
joy at the memory of Kurt in those days: "He would come over
and put on the ABBA *Greatest Hits* album followed by a Partridge
Family album, and then play the Vaselines and the Beat Happening, and to us, that was a party!" Kurt stood out from more
boisterous grunge rockers. "He was always sweet. Always hypersensitive." Tennant says, "Kurt was really sweet and kind and
really funny. His humor was a crazy mixture of goofy, sarcastic,
with a sharp wit." Recalling Kurt twenty-five years later, Tennant
earnestly adds, "He was exceedingly compassionate and a loyal
friend. He was well read and a true artist, both in the music and
art disciplines. I will miss him for the rest of my days."

Nirvana's initial Sub Pop release was a cover of "Love Buzz"
by the Dutch band Shocking Blue. "Love Buzz" became the first
single in the Sub Pop Singles Club, a brilliant scheme to help
the label's cash flow. Members initially paid $35 a year and were
mailed one single per month. The price was raised to $40 a year
in 1990, by which time they had two thousand subscribers. The

early Nirvana singles got enough attention that an album was soon scheduled.

Thurston Moore met Bruce Pavitt just before Sub Pop started putting out records and he loved one of their first singles, Mudhoney's "Touch Me I'm Sick," so he was predisposed to give Sub Pop artists the benefit of the doubt. Susanne Sasic, who designed the sleeve for "Love Buzz," had previously sold merch for Sonic Youth on the road. In the summer of 1989, she was working at Pier Platters Records in Hoboken and suggested that Kim and Thurston catch Nirvana's debut show at Maxwell's. "She told me that Nirvana were not as good as Mudhoney," Thurston remembers, "but they're kind of interesting. So it was me and Susanne and Kim and J. Mascis [of Dinosaur Jr.]. It was a Tuesday night, and other than us, there were only around twenty people there."

From the first notes Nirvana played Thurston immediately felt "they were amazing," and he went and stood in front of the stage. "They end the set with Chad kicking his drums over"—Grohl would not become the drummer for another year—"and Krist Novoselic throwing his bass across the stage. Kurt just starts slamming his guitar onto the stage and everything is in shambles. J. and I are looking at each other going like, 'Whoa, I hope these guys don't have a gig tomorrow, because this is ridiculous.' They smashed everything but they were just great."

After the show Thurston, Kim, and J. hung out with Nirvana. "J. was talking about going to Seattle and starting a band with Donna Dresch and some people from Screaming Trees. Kurt said, 'Don't do that. Join our band instead.' I thought it was a pretty audacious thing to say." (At this point Dinosaur Jr. had already released three albums and Mascis was a much more established artist in the indie world than Kurt was.)

Sub Pop rarely spent more than $1,000 recording an album and Nirvana's *Bleach* would cost a mere $600. The Sub Pop singles and album were produced by Jack Endino at Reciprocal Recording in Seattle. Most songs on *Bleach* had a hard-rock intensity evocative of the Melvins or Mudhoney, but the album also included "About a Girl," Kurt's first Nirvana song with a pop melody and chorus.

Thurston usually speaks in a measured, cerebral tone, but he choked up as he recalled hearing *Bleach* for the first time. "I thought it was a fantastic-sounding record. It hit certain things that I was really wanting to hear in ways that not too many bands were doing. There were not too many experiences in my life where a record would hit all these points that I was waiting for. I thought it was primal. The songwriting was completely melodious, and it was punk. It had a beauty to it. I really love that record."

When Sonic Youth was mastering their debut Geffen album, *Goo*, Thurston played *Bleach* for Masterdisk engineer Howie Weinberg and said, "If our record can sound like this, I'd be really happy." The engineer gave him a look of incredulity for wanting to emulate such a primitive recording. Thurston realized "it was all a vibe thing. It didn't really matter what the technology was. It was the magic in that group coming off that record; primarily that magic is in Kurt's voice. If anybody else was singing in that band with those songs it would not have flown the way it flew. His voice transcends everything."

Sonic Youth selected Nirvana as their support act on several West Coast dates. Thurston recalls, "They did Las Vegas, Portland, and Seattle. The interim drummer was Dale Crover from the Melvins. They were good, and the audience knew they were good, but it wasn't Nirvana fever yet."

One of Sub Pop's most effective ideas was to fly Everett True from London to Seattle in early 1989 to cover the punk scene in the Northwest. At this point, Nirvana had released only one single, but Everett recognized their uniqueness and featured them heavily in a piece for the influential British weekly *Melody Maker*, which put Northwestern indie rock on an international media stage for the first time.

Soon after *Bleach* was released, Poneman realized that Nirvana needed some help on the road with their sound and he introduced them to Seattle engineer Craig Montgomery, who had worked with several of the label's other bands. Montgomery remembers, "The first thing I noticed was how catchy the music was. They had good songs and a guy who could really sing, which a lot of the so-called grunge bands didn't. Even before I'd seen the band, people in Seattle told me he could sing like [Creedence singer] John Fogerty. I saw my job as connecting Kurt's voice to the audience."

Almost immediately Kurt became attached to having the sound man on the road with them, and for the next several years Montgomery worked at every Nirvana show. "At the start it was the four of us in Krist's Dodge van going to punk rock clubs across the country," he says. And from those early days of Nirvana's career, even when their only fans were those immersed in the punk subculture and their early singles were loud and aggressive, the seeds of Kurt's impending vision of a hybrid punk/pop sound were evident. Krist says that in addition to listening to music from punk rockers they "would play cassettes of Roy Orbison and the Smithereens or the Beatles." Montgomery concurs that "a lot of the time they would listen to cheesy pop music."

Montgomery soon realized that besides the music, the members of Nirvana were connected by humor. "At the concerts, a lot of what they were doing was taking the piss out of rock and roll. They would blow up rock clichés, sometimes just by the way they would look at each other or move onstage. It was like they were letting the audience in on the joke." (Smashing their equipment—at once homage and critique—fit into this attitude.)

The sound man remembers Kurt affectionately: "He was a funny, smart, witty, sarcastic guy, usually fun to be around for sure. He was sometimes quiet and needing alone time but he lived for playing shows."

At the time, Sub Pop was distributed by Caroline Records, which was based in New York City. Janet Billig (now Janet Billig Rich) was a punk aficionado who started working for Caroline as a publicist and A & R person while still a student at NYU. Since Sub Pop had no East Coast staff, she would represent the label when their bands played New York. The bands could never afford hotel rooms, so many of them stayed at Janet's apartment in the East Village at the corner of Seventh Street and Avenue C. "It was four hundred fifty square feet, but it had a loft bed and with futons I could squeeze eight people in there." Thus, there was no problem in putting up the three members of Nirvana and Montgomery on their initial New York visits beginning in 1989.

Janet immediately recognized that Kurt was first among equals. Bands had to load their gear into her apartment because the van was likely to be broken into in that neighborhood. The first time Nirvana stayed there, Janet also needed help moving some mattresses. Kurt looked at her with an amused expression and said that Krist and Chad Channing, Nirvana's drummer at the time, would do that. "Kurt lay down on *my* bed and ate a box of cookies. Krist and Chad knew the drill. Kurt wasn't gonna get his hands dirty." (When I told Krist this story he rushed to Kurt's defense. "When he had to do it, he would haul his own gear. The grim procession, we'd call it.")

Similar to the experience I would have a couple of years later, Janet's realization of Kurt's magic kicked in when she saw Nirvana onstage. She was blown away by how hard the band drove themselves. "I went with them to a Philly show and to an Amherst College show. Afterward they would always say it was the shittiest show. They would be dissecting the show and talking about how crappy they were even when people would be coming backstage saying they were amazing. To me, every show was so emotional, so raw, but they always wanted them to be better."

She saw why Kurt was so beloved by the punk community: "He came from nowhere and had nothing. That's where his connection to the punk ethos came from." But from the time she met him she saw that "Kurt was also ambitious. He straddled both worlds." College radio stations played Nirvana from the beginning, and the coterie of critics who focused on punk rock singled out the band to the point that they were soon able to develop a small cult following outside of the Pacific Northwest.

Because indies like SST and Sub Pop were risking much less money and because they could rarely afford to pay lawyers, they usually didn't ask for long-term contracts. However, at the beginning of 1989, midway through recording *Bleach*, Kurt and Krist had decided that *they* wanted to have a contract with their label. Evidently it signified legitimacy to Kurt at a moment before he had learned much about the business. Poneman didn't even have a template for a contract because none of their artists had ever asked for one before, so he cobbled one together. At the time Kurt felt having a contract represented more of a commitment from Sub Pop, but the way things turned out it was the label that would benefit from it. Without that contract Sub Pop would not have been in a position to make millions of dollars from Nirvana when they moved to Geffen.

I regret that the role I was destined to play in the band's career precluded my getting to know Poneman and Pavitt more than superficially. Kurt never begrudged them the money they ultimately made from Nirvana after they changed labels. (Not only did *Bleach* sell hundreds of thousands of albums in the wake of Nirvana's commercial breakthrough, Sub Pop got an "override" royalty on *Nevermind* that was worth millions of dollars, and the profits from Nirvana's recordings allowed them to sell half of the company to Warner Music for a reported $20 million in 1995.) Sub Pop put out Nirvana's original singles and first album. They bought Kurt new guitars after he smashed his onstage. They introduced him to Craig Montgomery, Janet Billig, and Everett True, among others, and there are many stories of Poneman telling journalists and musicians that Nirvana was going to be their biggest band.

However, the Sub Pop partners were also proponents of indie exceptionalism. In the first issue of his fanzine, Sub Pop's Pavitt had written, "When people buy a record, they are not only plugging into the music, but into the values and lifestyle that are implied by that artist. By supporting huge Hollywood music corporations, you (yes you), are not only allowing middle aged capitalists to dictate what goes over the airwaves, but you are giving them the go ahead to promote macho pig-fuck bands whose entire lifestyle revolves around cocaine, sexism, money, and more money. The 80s need new sounds and just as much they need new heroes." This sort of rhetoric didn't ultimately affect what Kurt did with his career, but it did resonate with many artists. In her memoir, *Hunger Makes Me a Modern Girl*, Carrie Brownstein (whose band Sleater-Kinney recorded for Kill Rock Stars) noted that "abundant treatises about selling out could be found in zines like *Punk Planet* or *Maximum Rocknroll.*"

Upon returning to America after their first European tour, Nirvana recorded demos of "Lithium," "In Bloom," and "Polly," which would end up being three of the most memorable songs on *Nevermind*. Later on, after *Nevermind* became successful, some writers observed that earlier indie bands like the Pixies or the Replacements or Hüsker Dü had combined some elements of punk attitude with more traditional choruses and melodies, but

I always felt these comparisons missed the point. Those bands never wrote songs that actually became big radio hits like Kurt did, songs that worked on Top 40 radio stations as well as on rock radio. And Kurt's biggest hits also had complicated lyrics and raw emotion that rarely were found on pop radio. How and when did he figure out how to do this?

Musical mythology notwithstanding, there is nothing in the lyrics of Robert Johnson's classic blues song "Crossroads" to indicate that he sold his soul to the devil in return for his talent. The persistence of the myth and its invocation to describe transformations of later giants such as Jimi Hendrix and Bob Dylan has, I think, more to do with the mysteries of genius than any sinister occult arrangements.

There are not that many rock-and-roll chords. Every lyricist has access to the same dictionary. Everyone can listen to the same canon. Some elements of the craftsmanship of pop songwriting can be taught, but not the art of getting listeners in touch with their deepest feelings in an instantly memorable way.

Some maintain that mass success in rock and roll is mostly a matter of luck, timing, marketing, and intensity of ambition. However, when it comes to Kurt, I think it has more to do with the way Sonny Rollins described the music of John Coltrane in the documentary *Chasing Trane:* "To play at that level you have to be touched by—whatever." For my generation the great rock savant was Bob Dylan. Bob Johnston, the producer of the albums *Highway 61 Revisited* and *Blonde on Blonde,* said of Dylan, "God didn't touch him on the shoulder, he kicked him in the ass. There was nothing he could do about it. He's got the holy spirit on him. You can look at him and tell that."

I believe that Kurt too was touched by "whatever" at an early age and was kicked in the ass by the spirit, and he knew it. I suspect that Krist knew this from the outset of their relationship as well. Of course, feeling that success was inside him and having it play out on a mass scale virtually overnight were two very different things.

The demos of the new songs were produced by Butch Vig, who lived in Madison, Wisconsin, where he was known for making inexpensive but excellent-sounding records for punk bands in his studio, Smart Studios. Vig had recently produced the Smashing Pumpkins' debut album, *Gish*, which went on to sell a couple of hundred thousand copies, and he was basking in the afterglow of their breakout.

Record producers play different roles for different artists. For many pop, country, R & B, commercial pop, and rock records, producers pick the material and the arrangements, often making an artistic contribution that is almost equal to that of the artist. However, on recordings by rock auteurs who write their own material, such as R.E.M., U2, and Nirvana, producers play a more limited role but they are nonetheless crucial supporting characters in the creation of an album. They are responsible for the sound, and the best producers also help artists make creative choices. Some, like Vig, are also audio engineers and physically control the console in the studio during recording.

He had found most of *Bleach* to be "one dimensional" but Vig was blown away by the evolution in Kurt's songwriting. "He had this innate pop sensibility for melody and phrasing. At some times he felt hindered by what you're supposed to be in a punk rock band, but he had an amazing affinity for melodies and hooks."

These sessions were also where Vig first observed Kurt's mood swings. "The first day Kurt was funny and engaged and chatty, in good spirits. Then, after we got some sounds on drums, Kurt sat down in a corner and put his head down. I asked if he needed anything and he didn't even answer. Krist pulled me aside and said, 'He gets that way sometimes. He needs to chill and then he'll snap out of it.' After another twenty minutes Kurt got up, picked up his guitar, and said, 'Let's go,' and was fully engaged."

At first the band anticipated that these songs would go on a second Sub Pop album, but once they were back on the road, they reevaluated their situation and decided to hold off. Kurt later told me that touring gave them a wider perspective on future possibilities. Montgomery remembers "them talking in the van about what to do next. They were really unhappy that despite the interest *Bleach* was generating Sub Pop didn't seem to be able to get their records into the stores." Slim Moon remembers Kurt "complaining that Mudhoney was getting all the love and marketing from Sub Pop." Kurt was also irritated by an article in the *Los Angeles Times* where Poneman was quoted as describing all the Sub Pop bands as "lumberjacks." Kurt told the *Rocket*, "I feel like we've been tagged as illiterate redneck cousin-fucking kids who have no idea what's going on. That's completely untrue." Moreover, Krist says that in Seattle there were rumors that Sub Pop was going to affiliate with a major and recalls that the band decided, "If we were going to be part of that system anyway, we'd rather have a direct relationship."

In my opinion, none of these reasons really crystallized Nirvana's resolve to leave Sub Pop. I think Kurt had long been interested in the stronger reach and marketing power of the major record companies and he developed a greater comfort level with the idea after touring with Sonic Youth, whose credibility hadn't been hurt in the slightest by their decision to sign with Geffen. With the increased visibility of the Seattle scene in general and *Bleach* in particular, majors who would have ignored Nirvana a year earlier were buying them dinner, and Kurt was intrigued.

There were some in the indie/punk world who intensely resented Nirvana's emigration to a major label. It reminded me of the sense of betrayal felt by some Southern Christians decades earlier when Sam Cooke and Ray Charles had abandoned gospel music for rhythm and blues, or the way that some folk fans in the sixties freaked out when Bob Dylan "went electric."

However, Kurt was not going to be deterred from pursuing the destiny he had long envisioned for himself and he had no patience for indie-purist guilt trips. He later explained to Azerrad, "A band was in a situation where it was expected to fight in a revolutionary sense against the major corporate machine and I just thought—how dare you put that kind of pressure on me? It's really stupid." He was on a different mission.

FOUR

NEVERMIND

Despite the fact that the side effects of fame would disorient and sometimes torment Kurt, it's clear to me in retrospect that success on his own terms was something he meticulously planned for years. The arc and intensity of his career was no accident. It was something he did on purpose.

In the summer of 1990, a few months before we got involved with the band, Nirvana retained Los Angeles lawyer Allen Mintz to help them explore other label options. In September Sub Pop released the single of a new song called "Sliver," which would wind up being one of the label's last Nirvana releases. Like *Bleach*'s "About a Girl," "Sliver" had a catchy chorus, another indication that Kurt wanted to expand Nirvana's sound beyond the confines of grunge.

Shortly thereafter, Nirvana further shifted gears. Creatively, they replaced drummer Chad Channing with Dave Grohl.

Professionally, they decided to get management, which led them to our office in early November 1990, less than a month after Grohl had played his first Nirvana gig.

I didn't see any downside to Kurt's determination to leave Sub Pop. I respected the idea of being loyal to those who had been early supporters, but for how long and at what cost? Stripped of indie rationalizations, this was the same conflict that people in the old-school music business had with artists. Through my forty-year-old eyes this was no different from the argument Peter Grant had with concert promoters who put on early Zeppelin shows and vainly claimed, therefore, that they had a moral right to future ones for lower fees than their competitors. Kurt would maintain a friendship with Poneman and others at Sub Pop for the rest of his life, but he never second-guessed his decision to move on.

Of course, there were still plenty of dicks at the majors. Nirvana had a few big-label meetings before we got involved. Kurt was appalled by a macho promo executive at Capitol Records who joked about identifying with the rapist in his song "Polly" instead of with the victim. The same guy seemed a lot more excited about having obtained floor seats for an upcoming Lakers game than he was about music. However, by 1990 several majors had young executives who were on the same cultural planet as Nirvana and the band found themselves with a number of good choices.

Some books about Nirvana make it sound as if we took the decision of which label to go with out of the band's hands. Executives at a division of Virgin Records called Charisma thought the band had chosen them before Nirvana met with us. Several A & R people from other labels also thought they'd had good meetings with the band and were disappointed that we didn't follow up with them.

However, Nirvana could have easily signed with a label and then picked management afterward. I think that given Sonic Youth's good experience there, Kurt had for some time wanted to be on the DGC imprint of Geffen Records, and our relationship with the company was probably one of the reasons Nirvana chose us. Silva and I would have cheerfully gone elsewhere if the band wanted to, but within days of our first meeting them the band told us to make a deal with DGC.

David Geffen had founded Geffen Records in 1980, by which time he was already a legendary figure in the music business. He had managed Laura Nyro; Crosby, Stills and Nash; and Joni Mitchell, and then created and later sold Asylum Records after it had spawned huge albums by Jackson Browne, the Eagles, and Linda Ronstadt.

It was not lost on Kurt that Geffen Records had released John Lennon and Yoko Ono's final recording, *Double Fantasy*. Later in the eighties David Geffen had expanded his footprint into Broadway theater (*Dreamgirls* and *Cats*) and films (*Risky Business*). He was also increasingly sophisticated about the Wall Street perspective on how to maximize economic value in the entertainment business.

Part of David Geffen's mystique was an aura of accessibility. He typically wore jeans to the office and had a reputation for quickly returning phone calls, even from people far below his level in the business world, such as me. The company's offices were in the middle of the Sunset Strip. Visitors entered through a door that was on the street. Regardless of how engaged he was in non-music activities, Geffen made sure that the record company met its financial targets and he stayed in close touch with select label executives who were intensely loyal to him and who invariably referred to him simply as "David."

By the end of 1990 David had created a structure at the

company that did not require his involvement in every decision, and it was easy to understand why he was preoccupied. That was the year in which he switched distribution of Geffen from his original partner, Warner Bros., to MCA as part of a transaction in which he exchanged his ownership of the label for MCA stock. In 1991, just around the time we were talking to the company about Nirvana, MCA was bought by the Japanese electronics giant Matsushita, a transaction that made David the first billionaire the music business ever produced. Thus, while I had dealt with him from time to time in the past, and would in the future, David was not involved when we signed Nirvana to his label. He only came into Kurt's life later.

Soon after forming Geffen Records, David had hired Eddie Rosenblatt away from Warner Bros. Records to be president of Geffen. Rosenblatt quickly assembled a promotion and marketing team that was competitive with his alma mater. (Other than Rosenblatt's there were no job titles at Geffen.) Rosenblatt's background had been in the music retail business, which was usually more focused on moving units than art, but he had a poetic soul that allowed him to bond with creative types as well. He told one of the young promo guys, "Movies at their best are larger than life. Music at its best is life itself." David once told me, "When people come out of Eddie's office they feel like they've had a warm bath," adding with a fierce gleam in his eye, "I am *not* a warm bath."

When Geffen Records first started, David personally lured Lennon, Donna Summer, and Elton John to the label. However, he soon concluded that his old seventies network of musicians and friends was not sufficient to identify and sign subsequent generations of commercial talent, and so he invested in several of the best and the brightest young rock A & R people in the business.

Sonic Youth had been signed to DGC by Gary Gersh, who was then thirty-five years old and, like me, was a music business shape-shifter intent on rebranding himself for a new era. Gersh was frustrated that, for the moment, he was in the shadow of other Geffen A & R guys, like Tom Zutaut, who had gotten credit for signing Guns N' Roses (at the time Geffen's bestselling artist), and John Kalodner, who had engineered the spectacular commercial comeback of Aerosmith. Before Sonic Youth, the only Gersh artist whom I managed was Rickie Lee Jones at a time when she was going through a commercial lull. The highest-profile artist Gersh worked with at Geffen before Nirvana broke was Robbie Robertson, who had a great artistic pedigree as a member of the Band but whose solo album sold only a fraction of what Guns N' Roses and Aerosmith did.

In 1990 Rosenblatt hired Robert Smith, an old friend of mine from the New York rock critic and PR worlds, and Robert emerged as the overall head of marketing at Geffen, perhaps the most literate figure to ever have such a record industry job. Yet despite the intelligence and taste of these guys, it was not irrational for artists from the indie rock world to have concerns about switching to a major.

Because they had much lower overhead than corporate record companies, indie labels could justify a sustained effort to sell a few thousand records, while majors were usually only interested in big hits. As a manager, my greatest fear for any new artist on a major was that while the A & R people could become intoxicated by the thrill of beating their competitors in signing a "buzz band"— which usually meant an artist that music journalists liked—the ultimate success or failure of an album was dependent on their marketing colleagues, most of whom had little interest in what was hip in the eyes of rock critics.

Major-label promo bosses were much more preoccupied with the cookie-cutter confines of commercial radio stations, whose audience was far bigger and more influential on sales than journalists were. Programmers made their living from ratings and tended to resist the kind of avant-garde music that excited young A & R people. Artists who got caught in the corporate crossfire between those who signed them and their less enthusiastic marketing colleagues felt as if they'd been seduced and abandoned—one of the primary reasons that a lot of artists hated major labels.

The major label that had been the most successful in transitioning indie rock groups into the mainstream record business was Warner Bros., Geffen's biggest West Coast rival. In the late eighties Warner had hired several marketing people with an indie background, and by 1991 they had a big advantage with a roster that included R.E.M., Depeche Mode, Faith No More, and Jane's Addiction, who had all started on indie labels.

To effectively compete, Geffen had created the DGC imprint in 1990 with a small team of promotion and sales people hired with the sole mission of getting new artists off the ground. Critical to these efforts was Mark Kates, an alternative radio promotion maven who had previously helped Australian indie label Big Time Records and Britain's Beggars Banquet navigate American radio. Kates knew Sonic Youth before Gersh signed them, and a couple of years later, after Gersh left the label, Kates became their A & R person, as well as Nirvana's and Hole's.

Kates recalls, "Gersh was the A & R guy I connected most with musically because he'd signed John Doe. We knew that signing Sonic Youth could be really important to broaden the image of our company and they told us we should hire Ray Farrell because he had worked with punk bands like Mission of Burma and Flipper at SST Records." Farrell's primary role was to use his credibility with buyers at indie stores to get them to order and display DGC records.

It was no problem for Gersh to give Sonic Youth a contractual guarantee of creative control, an acceptable concession in Geffen culture. (Robbie Robertson was just as much of a control freak as any punk artist.) However, for the signing to pay off and make his company attractive to the artists he coveted, he had to keep the marketing execs at the label focused on Sonic Youth's album for a decent period of time even if they didn't have radio hits. One reason that we and the members of Nirvana felt comfortable with Gersh was that DGC had not abandoned Sonic Youth even though *Goo* had only sold around 150,000 copies, which, while double the sales of their previous album, was not enough to impact anyone's Christmas bonus in an industry where the signifier of success, a gold record, required sales of more than triple that amount. Gersh knew that Sonic Youth had another value to him: their jeweler's eye for new indie talent. The band seemed to know every new alternative artist's music long before A & R people heard of them. Kates recalls, "Right after Sonic Youth delivered *Goo*, Kim Gordon told me, 'The next band you need to sign is Nirvana.'" Gordon later told me, "We all had a crush on Kurt."

Allen Mintz was an up-and-coming associate at one of the big L.A. law firms, and he knew how to get a state-of-the-art deal for a new artist from a major label. The overall budget for the album that became *Nevermind* was $280,000. After legal fees and management commissions, this left around a quarter of a million dollars. The album would cost $160,000 to record (a lot of that was for three months of lodging in L.A. and rehearsal time), so this left around $30,000 for each member of the band over the next six months, enough to pay some old bills and to eat, but without much left over.

To help provide some extra cash we made a music publishing deal for the band. In the music business "publishing" refers to the copyright for the songs as distinguished from the recordings. Responding to the same cultural drumbeats that had drawn record company A & R people to Seattle, several young representatives from music publishers had made the journey there in the wake of Sub Pop's emergence. One of these scouts was Susan Collins, who worked for Virgin Music. She fell in love with Nirvana and subsequently played *Bleach* for the company's president, Kaz Utsunomiya, the son of a Japanese diplomat who'd spent much of his childhood in England, where he first got into the music business.

By the late eighties Kaz was in his midthirties and living in Los Angeles. He was aware that many Seattle bands were developing careers but was not a fan of most grunge songwriting. Music publishers make most of their income from radio airplay; film, TV, and commercial licenses; and when a band's song is covered by another artist. There were plenty of hip new bands that could sell out clubs and small theaters who were of no interest to him because they didn't write the kinds of songs that would have a life beyond their immediate fanbase. However, when Kaz heard "About a Girl" from *Bleach* he agreed to meet Nirvana, and once Kurt played him acoustic versions of several of the songs that would be on *Nevermind*, Kaz was smitten: "Kurt was one of the most brilliant songwriters I ever met."

Kurt was taken with the fact that Kaz had worked with two of his favorite bands, the Clash and Queen. He also liked Kaz's earnest, soft-spoken style, which was unusual among executives who could write a big check, plus he was fascinated by Japanese culture and liked the idea of having an ally who was a native.

Kurt's attitude toward rock and roll reminded Kaz a lot of the Clash's Joe Strummer. "They looked like punks but liked melodies. They were both geniuses and also the nicest human beings. They wouldn't have been able to write those songs if they didn't have that heart." As was the case with record companies, there was enough competition for the publishing contract that we were able to negotiate a good deal. The band got a much-appreciated $200,000 advance, and just as important, the copyrights reverted back to them after seven years.

As soon as *Nevermind* came out there was speculation about the transformation in Kurt's songwriting that Vig had noticed when Nirvana recorded demos with him. When had he stopped competing with Soundgarden in the Seattle grunge world and become the writer of the most popular rock songs of the era?

Long before *Nevermind* was recorded, Kurt worried about a backlash. He didn't want it to seem like he was suddenly trying to be more commercial but instead wanted it to be clear that he was unfolding a personal vision that he'd held for some time. Nirvana's sound man Craig Montgomery remembers Kurt repeatedly reminding him that "About a Girl" and "Sliver" already indicated his interest in melodic songs. Similarly Kurt told Kim and Thurston, "Our next record is gonna sound more like you guys and like 'About a Girl.'"

He was giving his close allies the spin: the *Nevermind* songs had been written not because of what anyone else wanted but because that was the music he was hearing inside his head. Thurston had mixed feelings when Kurt first told him the next Nirvana album was going to be poppier: "Kurt really was attracted to marginalized music, that being experimental music. He liked the Butthole Surfers, he liked Sonic Youth, he liked Swans." Generally speaking Thurston preferred the "weird shit" too. But then Kurt gave Thurston a cassette of the *Nevermind* demos. At that point he was still planning on calling the album *Sheep*. Once he heard the new material Thurston got excited about where Kurt was going. Thurston played the cassette for J. Mascis, who agreed that Kurt had a sense of melody that was very rare in any part of the rock world.

Apart from the songwriting, Kurt, like many rock stars before him, was intent on creating a mythology about himself. The first time Everett True interviewed the band just before *Bleach* was released, Everett says, "they made a lot of stuff up." Kurt and Krist pretended that they had lived in the woods and created a goofy narrative that made them seem like ignorant rednecks. "It was clear what they were doing," Everett told me, "but it was funny." Everett used the shtick in his early articles about Nirvana, which gave the Northwestern scene an aura of American primitive exoticism for the consumption of *NME*'s British readership.

When Nirvana toured the UK the following year, Kurt feigned indignation at the caricature the band had created and presented himself to journalists as an unpackaged but intellectually sophisticated punk singer who was outraged by their misrepresentation in the press. Privately, he knew they had bullshitted Everett, who was always welcome backstage and became a real friend.

After signing with DGC, Nirvana met with Gersh about how to record their first major-label album. Some A & R people would get into the weeds of recording, arrangements, and material, occasionally making the grandiose claim that they personally "made records," but with rock bands who wrote their own material the A & R role in recording was much more limited. Nevertheless, Gersh and Kurt developed a meaningful personal relationship. In one of Kurt's journals there is a yearbook photo of his father, Don Cobain, under which Kurt wrote, "old Dad," and a photo of Gersh next to it where Kurt wrote, "new Dad."

They went through a list of possible producers with more commercial track records than those the band had worked with in the past, but given the quality of the demos I was not surprised that Nirvana ultimately chose to stick with Butch Vig. In the subsequent decade Vig would develop a brilliant career both as a producer and as a member of the band Garbage, but he is the first to admit that his career is divided into "before *Nevermind* and after *Nevermind*," an album for which he also acknowledges the band came into the studio with a fully developed vision.

Using some of the money from the record deal, we got Kurt, Krist, and Dave short-term rentals at the Oakwood apartments in Toluca Hills, a five-minute drive from our office. The band Europe and pop hip-hop duo Kid 'n Play were staying there at the same time, but the main attraction for Nirvana was the free breakfast buffet. After eating they would practice for hours in a rehearsal studio nearby, and they did this every day for three months.

Kurt described the process to Andy Bollen, the drummer for Captain America, a Scottish band that opened for Nirvana on the UK tour for *Nevermind*: "Everyone just learns their little bit as well as possible, then we rehearse for hours, concentrating on our parts. When we started out we'd rehearse all day. Period. Before we went in to record *Nevermind* we locked ourselves away and rehearsed till we could do the parts in our sleep. Just relentless shit, man, working our parts."

Krist reiterates, "We just rehearsed all the time. We were really happy doing that and we could always come back to that feeling later on. Things got so miserable there for a while, but we had so much fun playing together. We checked things at the door and we just had a lot of fun and remembered, 'Oh yeah! *That's* why we do this!'"

Although Kurt was the undisputed captain of the ship, Nirvana would not have been what it was without his two partners. Krist was not merely Kurt's friend; he was also deeply tuned in to Kurt's aesthetic. Dave was the youngest member of Nirvana, only twenty-two years old when *Nevermind* was recorded, but his talent as a drummer was in full flower and he also become personally close to Kurt at that time, as the two shared an apartment for many months. In an interview recorded for promotional use by DGC, Kurt called Dave "the most well-adjusted boy I've ever met, and he plays better than any drummer I've ever heard. If I had a choice of bringing John Bonham back to life I would chose Dave." And unlike previous Nirvana drummers, Dave also sang harmonies.

The tracks for the album were recorded in sixteen days at Sound City in Van Nuys, a legendary studio where framed gold records by artists such as Neil Young, Tom Petty and the Heartbreakers, and Fleetwood Mac lined the walls. (Years later Dave would purchase the Neve Electronics 8028 console from Studio A where *Nevermind* was recorded and produce a documentary about the studio.)

At first it was disorienting for the guys in Nirvana to work at Sound City. They'd never been in a place where such mainstream music had been made. They found it surreal to see Lenny Kravitz eating at a nearby diner. Later in the process, when they were doing the first mixes, they learned that Ozzy Osbourne was in an adjoining studio. Black Sabbath was a guilty pleasure for a lot of punk kids, and Kurt and Dave wrote "Ozzy" on their fingers in a goofy homage to the famous "love" and "hate" tattoos Ozzy had on his hands, but they never worked up the nerve to actually talk to the metal legend.

Such distractions only intermittently interrupted the intensity of making the right record. Although there would be a handful of overdubs, the vast majority of *Nevermind* was recorded "live" in the studio. Vig soon learned to keep the tape running. During most recording sessions, the lead singer holds back vocally while the rest of the band is laying down the rhythm track, saving a fully intense performance for subsequent overdubs. However, Kurt would never back off on these "scratch" vocals, and as a result his voice could get blown out quickly and the vocal on first takes would sometimes be his best.

Kurt continued to occasionally retreat into his own world during the sessions. A few years after Kurt died Dave told a reporter, "He could be incredibly warm and funny and the next moment he could just become totally absorbed in thought. I don't think any of us truly understood what was going on in his head."

Vig says that during the recording of *Nevermind* it was "unpredictable when that black cloud would hit him. Some days it didn't; some days it would be two or three times that he'd be in a dark funk. A few times he left the studio and walked around for half an hour or an hour or so and never explained himself. We all knew he was gonna come back."

Such interludes involved grappling with waves of depression, but my feeling is that they weren't all filled with despair, that there was a creative process going on as well. Kurt was pushing the band to do something new, combining elements of metal, punk, and pop in a unique way while maintaining intimacy. As close as he was personally to Krist and Dave, and as much as he liked Vig, Kurt was the only one who knew how he wanted the record to sound.

For instance, on the first few takes of "Lithium" Kurt felt that Dave was playing too fast. He became so frustrated that he smashed his guitar and Vig had to find him another one, no simple feat since it had to be left-handed. To dissipate the tension afterward, the band played an improvised jam that became "Endless, Nameless," the bonus track on the album.

The next day, when they came back to "Lithium," Vig, with Kurt's encouragement, insisted on a "click track," in which a metronome set the rhythm. In an interview commemorating the twentieth anniversary of the album's release, Dave said it "was like being stabbed in the heart," but he acknowledged that the end result was worth it.

Echoing Thurston's thoughts about *Bleach*, Vig believes that

Kurt's singing added enormously to the power of *Nevermind.* "His voice was so fragile and vulnerable. If you took fifty other singers doing those songs the records wouldn't have that emotion. His voice had a totally unique character—rage and vulnerability and fear and anger and confusion, sometimes all in one line of a song."

By early 1992, when *Nevermind* was one of the biggest albums in the world, some punk aficionados claimed that the production was polished in a way that changed the essence of what the band had previously been, and even Kurt sometimes paid lip service to the notion that the production of the record had somehow changed Nirvana. At one fraught moment in an interview Kurt compared it to a record by the hair metal group Poison, which was as bad an insult as a punk rocker could give. I always took such remarks with several grains of salt because I knew that *Kurt* knew that he had made exactly the record he wanted. On the other hand, the massive reaction to *Nevermind* turned it into something that actually felt different to him than it had when the band first recorded it.

Vig says, "It was hard for me to read that it was way too slick. Compared to anything else that was on the radio? It was a raw fresh breath! The record is really simple. Sometimes Kurt doubled the guitar or Dave would sing a harmony but that's it. There are no electronic tricks on it. I didn't use more than sixteen of the twenty-four tracks we had available. If anything, it's underproduced." Still, Vig understands why the band needed to feign some distance from it in certain situations. "How can you retain punk credibility when you've sold ten million?"

Over the next several years Kurt usually downplayed his lyrics. He would say that he saved fragments of poetry that were thrown together at the last minute and sometimes claimed that he didn't even know what they meant. That always seemed like bullshit to me. Any time I visited Kurt he was surrounded by notebooks. He reworked lyrics with the same intensity that he brought to recording the music. I think he was just irritated by what he saw as simplistic attempts to "explain" a poetic art form. Occasionally he spelled things out to a writer he had a soft spot for. In the book *Classic Rock Albums: Nevermind* Kurt is quoted as saying, "I like lyrics that are different and kind of weird and paint a nice picture. It's just the way I like art." He was an impressionist who knew that the sound of words in a song was as important as their literal meaning in a dictionary, and he used lyrics to convey feelings as often as he did to make a linear point.

To many Nirvana fans, "Smells Like Teen Spirit" played the same role that Allen Ginsberg's "Howl" did for the beat generation or Bob Dylan's "Like a Rolling Stone" did for mine. Kurt enjoyed the Weird Al Yankovic parody of his most famous song, but I felt that some old-school rock fans missed the point of Weird Al's flippant opening in the voice of a philistine, "What is this song all about? Can't figure any lyrics out." To me, Weird Al is affecting the attitude of someone who doesn't get Nirvana, but actual Nirvana fans had no problem understanding the meaning of lines like "With the lights out it's less dangerous / Here we are now, entertain us." Part of the joy and liberation that the song provides is the ability to separate yourself from those who are overly controlled by mainstream culture, and to know that in rejecting that path you are not alone. People of my generation may have had trouble hearing the words, but young Nirvana fans soon knew them by heart. Those lyrics are why that song became an anthem.

Gersh was determined to make sure the band didn't feel any sense of interference from the label and stayed away from the studio for most of the recording. *Nevermind* was Vig's first gig with a major and at one point he and Dave asked Silva, "Should we be worried that no one is coming down from the label?" to which my partner responded with a laugh, "You should feel blessed."

After a record is fully recorded the process of mixing is the crucial next phase. This involves balancing the volume levels of the various tracks, and the difference between a good mix and a bad mix can make an enormous difference in the sound of a record. There is an aesthetic perspective required in mixing that is distinct from that of recording. As he had on other records, Vig initially mixed the record himself.

Having kept his powder dry during the recording, Gersh asked the band, Silva, and me to meet with him in his office. With a deferential tone that made it clear he was comfortable with the fact that the band made the final decisions, Gersh told us he felt the mixes were too muddy and didn't convey the power that he knew the band had. All eyes were on Kurt, who must have been thinking the same thing, because he calmly mumbled his agreement to try someone else while reserving the right to stick with Vig if he didn't like the remix. Gersh knew that Kurt hated the sound of commercial mainstream rock albums, so he suggested Andy Wallace, who was best known for working with the heavy metal band Slayer. Wallace's remixes gave more clarity to the vocals and at the same time more power to the drums, and Kurt promptly okayed them.

Most artists would agonize about sequencing songs on an album and drag the process out. By contrast, Krist recalls that one afternoon at Geffen shortly after the remix was done, "Kurt did the sequence in five minutes and that was it." I only had one opinion when it came to sequencing any album, and that was to put the best song first, since at the time there were people who would listen to a record in stores before buying and would judge an album by opening track. Over the years I'd encountered artists who overthought the process and failed to follow this simple rule. I was relieved that Kurt opened the album with "Smells Like Teen Spirit," but I wasn't surprised. Kurt had self-destructive tendencies but never when it came to his art.

As the album neared completion, Kurt, Krist, and Dave began interaction with a wider array of executives at their new label. The Geffen staff was used to dealing with temperamental artists. Inger Lorre of the Nymphs had recently urinated on Tom Zutaut's desk in response to some real or imagined slight. By contrast, the guys in Nirvana were relatively low-maintenance and unpretentious. Nirvana was also relieved. The Geffen people were much more laid-back and supportive than they had expected.

Former SST exec Ray Farrell was the label person Kurt could most relax with because he was a record collector and the two of them would talk for hours about obscure titles. Once, while looking through Kurt's albums on a floor of Kurt's apartment (he had not gotten around to getting shelves), Ray noticed *four* sealed copies of *The Chipmunks Sing the Beatles Hits*, a novelty record from 1964 in which early Beatles songs were recorded in the sped-up voices of the cartoon characters. When Farrell confided that he had also loved the record as a kid, Kurt gave him one.

Robin Sloane (now Robin Seibert), who oversaw the making of videos and artwork, recalls, "Kurt was always a nice person and would ask how I was and say thank you, which in my experience was unique for someone with his talent and level of success."

One day during the recording of *Nevermind*, Silva told me that Kurt had asked him to find eye charts that doctors used to determine prescriptions because Kurt was interested in playing around with their graphics for a possible album cover. I was unenthusiastic, having seen reproductions of eye charts in poster shops. It seemed passé and a far cry from the cutting-edge aesthetic I was expecting from Nirvana.

Silva must have mentioned my reservation to Kurt, because

soon thereafter the singer stopped me in the corridor outside my office and asked me about it. I explained my concerns about the idea. Kurt didn't appear offended, just curious. While he was known onstage for his howling vocals, offstage Kurt spoke softly. Could I give him names of specific stores where I had recently seen such posters? (I couldn't.) He flashed a bemused smile as if he was considering whether or not it was worth dumbing down whatever he had in his mind for a mere mortal such as myself but instead he warmly thanked me. He was so nice about it that I was worried he might be putting me on. As I got to know him better, I realized that although Kurt was attuned to an aesthetic wavelength that others could rarely fathom until they saw how it manifested in his work, he was genuinely curious to get perspectives he hadn't thought of yet.

For his own reasons, Kurt jettisoned the eye-chart idea, and for a while contemplated calling the album *Sheep* and using a field full of RVs for the cover illustration before finally settling on *Nevermind* and the now-iconic image of a swimming baby reaching for a dollar bill on a fishhook after he and Dave saw a documentary about water births.

Robert Fisher was the art director at Geffen who executed the design of *Nevermind* and the singles. "Kurt was a sweetheart. He'd come by the office with his notebook and was mellow and thoughtful," he recalls. Fisher found an image in a photo book that could have worked, but the copyright owner asked Silva for an exorbitant sum, so Fisher hired Kirk Weddle to photograph a different baby. The dollar bill and fishhook were added through the magic of Photoshop.

When the Geffen publicity department asked the band to do a bio, they decided to invent a fantastical past, much in the same way they had when Everett had first interviewed them. Krist and Kurt pretended that they'd met at the (nonexistent) Aberdeen

Institute of Arts and Crafts. The PR people knew it was a joke, but they went along with it. Cheekily upending record company orthodoxy was good for the image of a punk band. It went along with the "subvert the establishment" ethos in an amusing and harmless way.

In both the culture and business of rock and roll at the time, the most important way for an artist to connect to their fans was through a music video. MTV was at the peak of its influence and once again, Kurt had a clear vision for what he wanted. He unveiled his idea for the "Smells Like Teen Spirit" video at a meeting of the entire Geffen art department. Robin Sloane recalls, "He was so shy and so soft-spoken. It was clear that he'd never had a meeting like that with a big group of people who had accomplished a lot, but in a quiet but firm voice he said, 'Pep rally gone wrong,' and everyone in the room was immediately captivated." Sloane says, "Even though I was so much older, I felt exactly the same way in high school—being a misfit and feeling out of place around a football team, cheerleaders, and marching bands." A few days later Kurt drew a storyboard for her. Sloane had worked for several other major labels and she had no hesitation about confronting artists, but she was dazzled by Kurt's creative clarity. In her twenty years in the business, Sloane had found that most artists either had no idea how they wanted to be presented visually or they spoke in vague generalities. She says, "What distinguished Kurt from every other artist I worked with was that he always had one central idea." He knew exactly what he wanted.

Because Nirvana was a new band, the video budget was modest by 1991 standards, less than $50,000. Sloane suggested a relative unknown, Sam Bayer, who had never directed a video himself but who had impressed her with his visual aesthetic when he shot secondary footage for one of the big music video directors. To her relief, Kurt agreed.

I visited the set halfway through the shoot with our one-year-old daughter, Katie, and the band was relaxed and in a good mood. However, the teens who had volunteered to play high school students in the video had been hanging around the set for hours. Many of them had been getting high and they were more boisterous with each take. Bayer was concerned they might damage some of the set, but the band loved the sense of chaos.

Sloane recalls, "Kids went crazy at the shoot. Sam, to his credit, just kept filming. None of that was really orchestrated. The way he had it lit gave the film a beautiful quality that was the antithesis of the angry feeling of the music and that tension between those two forces was amazing. Of course, the band's energy was incredible."

There was a brief setback when Kurt couldn't stand the first edit that Bayer did. The director tried to create a story around a janitor at the school instead of the kids, minimizing the pep rally, which Kurt wanted as the central motif. Sloane remembers "being in a restaurant and calling Kurt from a pay phone. He was so unhappy and was so upset he couldn't speak to Sam. I had to find an editor Kurt could work with. The actual video is Kurt's edit."

Being reminded of this all these years later I am taken with the fact that Sloane was willing to trust Kurt so absolutely. It's a testament to the power of his aura even prior to his success. She gushes, "Kurt knew what he was doing visually—in my experience he was unique."

Sub Pop's owners had shrewdly marketed Northwestern punk rock and encouraged the media to describe it as "grunge," which came to mean a hybrid of punk and metal. In June, three months before *Nevermind* came out, Sub Pop released a compilation called *The Grunge Years*, an album that opened with "Dive" by Nirvana and included songs by Screaming Trees, L7, Tad, the Afghan Whigs, and Mudhoney.

Kurt was friends with many of his fellow Seattle musicians but he was not okay with the idea that Nirvana was merely part of a trend. Around the same time Cameron Crowe approached us about getting a song from Nirvana for the soundtrack of a film he was making called *Singles*, which centered on the Seattle rock scene. Crowe had been a wunderkind rock writer before achieving success as a screenwriter and director. When I did PR for Zeppelin, the teenage Crowe interviewed them for the *Los Angeles Times* and *Rolling Stone*. In his twenties he wrote the screenplay for *Fast Times at Ridgemont High* and later wrote and directed *Jerry Maguire* and *Almost Famous*. I figured that if anyone could do justice to the scene it would be Crowe, but Kurt rejected the request immediately because he didn't want Nirvana to be lumped in with all the other Seattle bands, even those he liked. No more *Grunge Years*. This was before "Smells Like Teen Spirit" took the world by storm, but Kurt already had a clear sense of where Nirvana fit in the rock-and-roll cosmos.

Meanwhile, the band was evolving after the recording of *Nevermind*. In Sonic Youth all four members were roughly equal, but Thurston realized that the dynamic in Nirvana was different: "They're at that age, in the very early twenties, and so there's still this immaturity that goes on, you know, with boys talking to each other, or not talking to each other. I think they all felt very empowered." However, Thurston also sensed that Krist and Dave were starting to feel a little distant from Kurt. "'This guy's doing all the creative work, we're playing. We're just playing.'"

Regardless of the division of labor, Kurt got a lot of emotional sustenance from the band's camaraderie on the road. As Thurston notes, "I remember him when we were on tour with Neil Young and playing at the arena in Seattle and those guys were in the dressing room. Kurt had a horrible green dye job on his hair that was streaking down his forehead. Krist was getting completely inebriated and creating so much trouble backstage and Kurt had this really kind of Mona Lisa smile on his face while his bandmate was creating all this chaos."

In August 1991, in between the completion of the recording of *Nevermind* and its release, Nirvana accepted an offer from Sonic Youth to open on a ten-date tour of Europe. Dinosaur Jr., Babes in Toyland, and Gumball were also on the bill. Nirvana also got an afternoon slot at the legendary Reading Festival in the UK. Kurt would later tell me that these few weeks were among the happiest of his life.

Sonic Youth recognized that a cultural inflection point was at hand and they enlisted filmmaker Dave Markey to document the tour for what eventually became *1991: The Year Punk Broke*. Thurston says, "We had a sense there was a quantifiable increase in numbers of people responding to the kind of music that bands like us were making. We were also playfully saying, 'Punk is broke.' It was a double entendre. MTV Europe was playing punk more. Punk was in the clothing stores. Mötley Crüe covered a Sex Pistols song."

Cork, Ireland, was the first show on the tour and Thurston, who up until that point had not seen Dave play with the band, remembers, "The first song was spectacular. Grohl bangs the drums, he's singing backup vocals with Kurt, beautifully. It was just ferocious; they galvanized the audience. They were consistently incredible on all those dates. In retrospect I realize that we really did get to experience that band at their very best, at their apex, on that tour."

In an interview for *Spin* in 2011 Markey said, "The moment that stands out for me is that Reading performance. Nirvana played at 2:00 in the afternoon and they ended the set with 'Endless, Nameless' in its entirety. And that's when Kurt jumped into the pit, and Thurston came out and grabbed him. Thurston getting Kurt out of the pit was kind of perfect. He and Kim were like parental figures for Kurt in a way. At one festival, Nirvana were delayed getting into Germany, at the border. They missed their time slot. But Thurston took it upon himself to ask all the bands to remove ten minutes from their set so they could get Nirvana to play."

Thurston told me, "Kurt had a sense of being kind of morose and kind of quiet, but he also had a typically perverse humor that we all had. We would go to a record store, or a charity shop, and he would laugh at the same stuff." Thurston recalls that backstage "Kurt would just sit in a chair, or just sort of skulk around a little bit. But he certainly was happy. He got into the fun of everything that was happening, and we were having fun. We had enough catering! There's this thing of being in a band that you get to this point if you're lucky enough where you have food waiting for you in a dressing room. You're not worrying about who's paying for these things. You're playing your music and people are responding, because it's new and exciting. Those are glory years and they're fantastic. Nirvana didn't seem anxious about it at all. They came out as if they were playing in a basement even though they were on a stage in front of five thousand people."

A few months later, as the editing of the "Smells Like Teen Spirit" video was being completed, Silva told me that Bayer, by then exiled from completing it, had vainly lobbied for the exclusion of a shot in which Kurt looks right into the camera, breaking the fourth wall between the rock-singer character in the video and the viewer. The director evidently thought that it wasn't cool to so directly engage the audience. Kurt had already decided to use the shot in its entirety near the end of the video. Silva and I shared a ripple of excitement about where Kurt was taking this.

FIVE

GET OUT OF THE WAY AND DUCK

There were some in the Seattle music world who had a sense of what was coming. Jennie Boddy remembers when she and Susie Tennant first saw Nirvana play the songs that would be on *Nevermind* at a Seattle club called the OK Hotel. "They played 'Teen Spirit' and 'Lithium' and all of our mouths were open. Susie was hyperventilating at how good they were. Even the guys who jumped into the mosh pit knew how good they were."

A few months later she saw them again at the Off Ramp. "Grohl had recently become their drummer and it was even more amazing hearing him play the new songs. The band played a full set. Then they shut down the club at two A.M. and cleaned it out and then we all went back in and the band played for another couple of hours. Kurt was so happy."

In January, when *Nevermind* would go to number one on the *Billboard* album chart, Geffen president Eddie Rosenblatt was asked by the *New York Times* to describe the label's marketing strategy and he modestly answered, "Get out of the way and duck." It was indisputably true that "Smells Like Teen Spirit" had so much magic that it made everyone's job a lot easier, and there is no question that the song would have been huge no matter who was or wasn't involved with it. Nevertheless, the band and DGC did spend a lot of time and energy launching Nirvana's major-label career in a particular way.

In marketing terms, the band wanted to keep its credibility with their early fans while also pulling in lots of new ones. A lot of the angst that artists went through with record companies and with the media was really related to the tribal differences within the rock audience. It was one experience to love an artist that only you and a few of your friends were into, and a very different one if they became popular and the kids at school whom you hated were suddenly humming their songs. On a personal level, Kurt wanted a success that was acceptable to all the facets of his inner teenager. He identified deeply with outcasts whose sense of self was wrapped up in being part of a small subculture, but he also embraced the joy of being part of a large audience who could come together around an anthemic chorus or a powerful riff.

At the time radio was the primary marketing tool for music, since hearing music is always more powerful than reading about it. Many of the college stations that reported to *CMJ* had been early supporters of Nirvana and played "Sliver" and tracks from *Bleach*. Connectivity to these young college DJs was a critical element in staying in touch with Nirvana's punk rock fans. The DGC promo people knew without the band's having to tell them that the marketing for *Nevermind* had to start at college radio.

For instance, the kids who appeared in the pep rally in the "Smells Like Teen Spirit" video were recruited through one such station, KXLU, a tiny commercial-free, listener-supported radio station affiliated with Loyola Marymount University near the airport in Los Angeles. KXLU was to the far left of the dial, and whenever I listened to it I felt as if I were being let in on a secret. They played indie rock you couldn't hear anywhere else on the radio in Southern California in those days. In keeping with Nirvana's desire to show they hadn't forgotten where they came from, the band chose to visit the KXLU studio and premiere "Smells Like Teen Spirit" the day before other radio stations received the track.

Kurt was driven out to the station by the young promo man John Rosenfelder, a.k.a. Rosie. Krist and Dave rode with Sharona White, an assistant in the promotion department. Rosie recalls the band "joking around and throwing food at each other in between cars on the 405 freeway." They did their first on-air interview for *Nevermind* that day and invited listeners to come to the video set for "Smells Like Teen Spirit" the next day and be part of the filming.

But while staying connected with their indie fan base was important to them, one of the main reasons Nirvana wanted to be on a major label was to get exposure on commercial radio.

These stations were divided by format, designed to attract particular demographic groups that the station then offered to advertisers. Pop (or "Top 40") radio stations focused mostly on preteens and young teens and much more on women than men. The various "rock" formats generally appealed more to older teenagers and college-age kids, mostly male. There was a cottage industry of programmers and consultants who claimed to have figured out what combination of records at any given time would result in the best ratings for the target demo in the geographical market covered by the signal of the station.

A lot of the limitations of the major labels derived from their dependence on corporate radio stations. No matter how much swagger some record company promo people had, they were supplicants when they dealt with broadcasters, who in turn were at the mercy of their listeners. Even those radio programmers who were also music freaks had to keep their eyes on audience research. Two or three bad quarterly ratings in a row and they were likely to be looking for another job. Advertisers paid rates based on those ratings, and the music stations that usually got the best results tended to avoid songs that might make some listeners change the channel. People who had the radio on in the background and didn't even know the names of the artists they were listening to were just as valuable to advertisers as passionate fans who bought concert tickets. To artists and those of us who represented them, it often seemed as if the most apathetic music listeners had veto power.

The influence of audience research was the major reason that the top-rated rock stations in the majority of the country focused on bands with melodic pop songs, so-called hair bands like Poison and Skid Row whose popularity was further enhanced by MTV. Most MTV programmers got their start in commercial radio and were influenced by the same kind of research, although some of them realized that they could afford to have a broader and more diverse playlist because unlike radio stations, MTV had virtually no competition.

In several larger markets there were two or even three rock stations whose primary business agenda was to compete for male listeners between the ages of eighteen and thirty-five. A handful of the stations were focused mostly on heavy metal, like Ozzy Osbourne or Pantera. Guns N' Roses had become America's biggest rock band by dominating both commercial rock and metal stations, while also having a hit on pop stations with "Sweet Child O' Mine."

Although he emphasized the band's punk credibility to college stations, Rosie was intent on convincing commercial programmers that Nirvana was in the rarefied category of "alternative metal," which included bands like Jane's Addiction and Faith No More, whose recent records were played on both formats. In their quest to gain a larger audience, the band didn't mind if people at the label pitched them this way. But Kurt was also wary of doing too many interviews on these stations. There was a difference between metal media embracing his music and the appearance that he was sucking up to them.

A couple of months before *Nevermind* came out, Kates had gone to a Dodgers game with Silva, after which my partner played him a cassette of the Andy Wallace mixes of *Nevermind* in his car. "It sounded really big and I realized we probably could get it played on KNAC [an LA station that focused on heavy metal], and if we did, maybe it could be a gold album," which in the nineties meant sales of five hundred thousand copies in the U.S. Rosie recalls, "I remember when Gersh played *Nevermind* for the DGC staff, he played it *loud*," reinforcing his wish that the promo people work the record at metal radio as well as the college and indie rock stations.

These were the first hints at the record company that Nirvana might be a lot bigger than Sonic Youth. In addition to the commercial ramifications of this observation, it indicated that Nirvana's album might create a very rare convergence of cultures. For the most part metal fans and punk fans were adversarial tribes.

The commercial category that was initially most relevant to Nirvana was "alternative rock" (sometimes called "modern rock"). Stations like KROQ in Los Angeles avoided metal and hair bands like the plague and played the most commercial of the songs that emerged from college radio. KROQ developed a substantial audience in Southern California for bands such as Depeche Mode, the Smiths, and the Cure, who weren't being played on mainstream rock stations.

It was no surprise that the day after the KXLU premiere, "Smells Like Teen Spirit" was played on most CMJ stations across the country, but it was exciting that the track was immediately added at several of the most widely listened-to commercial alternative rock stations as well, starting with WFNX in Kates's hometown of Boston and immediately followed by KROQ in L.A. and 91X in San Diego. As much as Kurt, Krist, and Dave affected an ironic distance from music business hype, they were privately excited to have their music played on the big alt-rock stations that they and their friends often listened to.

The next week Silva and I sat in on a marketing meeting at DGC and Kates was vibrating with excitement. Typically, when a commercial radio station added a record they played it once or twice a night, waited for a reaction, and only considered increasing the rotation after several weeks. However, "Smells Like Teen Spirit" was getting, in the parlance of radio promo, "heavy phones," which meant a lot of people were calling to request the song. The feedback was so substantial that rotation had been increased to "heavy" on several important stations after just a few days. Farrell was getting reports that there were lists at many indie stores of fans who had preordered the album, which wouldn't be available for a few more weeks. In those days such preorders were an extremely rare occurrence, especially for an artist with only one indie album behind them. Since he'd started at DGC, Kates had been wondering if he'd ever be able to work a record as big as those by the Cure or Depeche Mode and suddenly he had one that felt bigger.

Krist reflects with pride that there was very little advertising or other high-pressure marketing for *Nevermind*: "Later, when the internet became so popular, people would talk about the difference between culture that was 'pushed' by marketing and that was 'pulled' by people discovering it for themselves. We were pulled."

The week after the single was released to radio stations, Silva got a call from Sonic Youth's booking agent Bob Lawton, who had been at a Guns N' Roses concert in New York City the night before. "Smells Like Teen Spirit" had been played on the PA system before the show and the crowd cheered as soon as they heard the intro. We were psyched. New York didn't even have a commercial alternative radio station but some of the fans must have heard the song on WDRE, a Long Island radio station with an alternative rock format. That was a very short time for a song to become familiar enough to get cheered in a situation like that. In any case we hadn't thought that *anyone* who was a fan of Guns N' Roses would be into Nirvana.

Despite these promising signals, most of the Geffen staff still saw Nirvana as another arty signing that would get a lot of press but was unlikely to be a breakout in terms of sales. To remedy this, the DGC team asked us to schedule a show at the Roxy, a venerable rock club on the Sunset Strip that was right across from the record company's offices. They wanted the non-alternative execs at Geffen to see Nirvana perform so they could see for themselves the band's unique power. This was in mid-August, right after Nirvana shot the video, and virtually everyone from the label came.

The Geffen people I spoke with decades later remember that concert as a peak moment in their careers. The Roxy holds five hundred people and it was packed, mostly with music business types, although there were some fans and musicians there as well. (Rosie remembers the singer from the metal band Warrior Soul moshing during "Breed.") Nirvana was in their prime, tight and powerful. Afterward Kurt characteristically claimed he was worried that the show was a disappointment, lamenting that he had broken a guitar string. I gave the requisite, and in this case sincere, managerial assurance that it had been great.

I walked across Sunset Boulevard with some of the label execs. "I feel like I just saw the Who in London in 1964," gushed Robin Sloane. Robert Smith looked at me pensively and said, "I'm thinking they might actually have a gold record."

It was important to the band to be in Seattle on the day that *Nevermind* was released. Rosie was blown away by the way Nirvana rose to the occasion. "The week of release I was in Seattle and Susie Tennant and I went to KCMU and KISW. The band was very businesslike doing interviews. They were on time, they were funny." On release day there was an appearance at Seattle's Peaches record store and a record release party. Beforehand, wanting a break from promo mode, Nirvana went to Tennant's house, which also served as her office. "I had a long living room. There were tons of Geffen CDs and they took them out and stacked them up like dominos. Dave and Kurt each put on one of my dresses. Then they'd run toward the stacked CDs and dive into them." The first hit album that DGC had had was by the pop teen brother duo Nelson. Kurt grabbed one of Tennant's lipsticks and defaced the Nelson gold record with it.

At the in-store, where fans overflowed onto the street, Nirvana played live. "It was a super-fun show," Tennant remembers, "the first time most of the fans there heard the new songs." Kurt had an additional agenda that day: "He was insistent on getting a Riot Grrrl fanzine into Peaches for them to sell there," Tennant recalls admiringly. "It was supposed to be a day for Nirvana, about celebrating Kurt and the band, and he was taking care of his old friends."

Jennie Boddy remembers that afterward Kurt looked out

the window of the store and saw Sub Pop partner Bruce Pavitt sitting on the curb, his head in his hands, waiting for a cab. Kurt shouted down at him with bittersweet affection, "There is the daddy bird! We need to fly from the nest now!"

In the wake of the album release, it seemed like everything worked for the band even when they were being boisterous. They set fire to a sofa in the dressing room of a club in Pittsburgh but somehow avoided any adverse consequences. At the same time, Rosie recalls, "It seemed to me that Kurt had a critical view of everything that was going on, as if he had been thinking for years of what a poster should look like. The three of them seemed to enjoy each other's company but when it came time to decide something, such as whether the mood of an interview should be jovial or serious, Kurt set the tone. If there was a food fight *he* threw the first slice of pizza." (Several people I spoke to mentioned food fights. They never had one in front of me. This was the good news/bad news of being seventeen years older than Kurt was.)

Considering the bitter feelings that Kurt and Axl Rose would soon develop for each other, it is ironic that in the weeks before *Nevermind* was released, Rose was talking up Nirvana even though he had never met them. He can be seen with a promotional Nirvana hat in the "Don't Cry" video. Another incongruous but useful endorsement came from the legendary former Vanilla Fudge drummer Carmine Appice, an icon in the metal world. His new band, Blue Murder, was signed to Geffen, and Appice was so impressed with his advance copy of *Nevermind* that he praised Dave Grohl in a column about drumming he wrote for *Circus* magazine.

By the end of the fall, KNAC, the metal station in Los Angeles, had seven tracks in rotation. Rosie recalls that "the program director of Z-Rock, a nationally syndicated metal station based in Dallas, initially worried that fans in pickup trucks who liked Van Halen wouldn't relate to Nirvana. 'Smells Like Teen Spirit' ended up being the most played track in Z-Rock's history."

Rosie, though only in his early twenties at the time, was in old-school promo mode, not always tuned into the sensitive line that Nirvana was walking. Part of Kurt loved that headbangers were playing *his* riffs on air guitar. He was proud of being able to *rock*. But another part of him knew that metal fans were over-whelmingly male and that few of them shared his feminist and gay-rights leanings, which left him with mixed feelings about the label's metal push. One day when Nirvana was at the Geffen of-fices, Rosie surprised Kurt by putting him on the phone with the editor of the *CMJ* metal section and "Kurt clammed up and Silva said I'd steamrollered him." Rosie was kept at a distance from Kurt for a while after that.

Every year there were a handful of rock bands that got a song played on both rock and pop radio, usually catchy rock ballads like Poison's "Every Rose Has Its Thorn." When Gersh and Silva and I had speculated about whether or not *Nevermind* had a song that would work on pop stations we had assumed that the best contender was "Come as You Are" because it wasn't too loud and had melodic hooks. However, the reaction to "Smells Like Teen Spirit" quickly exceeded our wildest expectations. It's an axiom of the record business to double down on something that you know people like.

I asked the Geffen pop promotion guy if he thought it was worth promoting the song at some adventurous pop stations. He condescendingly reminded me that pop radio at that time was playing danceable records like those of Paula Abdul and eschewed anything with loud guitars. I couldn't even convince him to try to work the Top 40 stations in Seattle. The problem was solved shortly thereafter by Leslie Fram, who was the music director of

Power 99, a pop station in Atlanta. She had noticed that alternative rock records were increasing in sales at local record stores and was looking for a record to play to see if the Top 40 audience in Atlanta was up for going in a new direction. Fram remembers, "I was dumbfounded when I heard 'Smells Like Teen Spirit.'" The track did so well that she and her colleagues decided to change the format of the entire station to be more alternative leaning and started calling themselves 99X. Once a *programmer* said it was a pop song, the old-school promo guy became a convert. It didn't hurt that many other pop stations copied 99X's format. "Smells Like Teen Spirit" became a pop hit, going to number 6 on the Billboard Hot 100 chart.

The breakthrough into pop radio put Nirvana into a category all their own. Their music worked for fans of punk, commercial alternative, metal, mainstream rock, and pop. This had been Kurt's vision all along. In his journals, those favorite-album lists regularly included ABBA and Black Sabbath as well as R.E.M. and Black Flag.

MTV was at its peak of influence on American musical culture. In late 1992 Kurt would tell an Argentine writer, "In the United States, MTV is like God; it's very powerful. Everybody watches and listens to that channel." Scott Litt, who produced R.E.M.'s biggest albums and who would work with Nirvana as an engineer on various projects, including *MTV Unplugged*, says, "MTV was so powerful, you didn't say no to them. It was like pop radio in the fifties. If you didn't play ball, good luck."

Amy Finnerty had gotten an entry-level job at MTV in late 1989 and soon thereafter became friends with Janet Billig, who had taken her to the Pyramid Club in the East Village to see Nirvana when *Bleach* came out. "It was such an incredible show. It didn't start till long after midnight and there couldn't have been more than twenty or thirty people there, but Kurt still broke his guitar at the end." Afterward she went back to Janet's apartment with the band, which is where she first met Kurt.

A few months later, when Nirvana had been flown to New York to meet with Columbia Records, she saw Kurt backstage at a concert and reintroduced herself. He said, "I can't believe you know who I am; I'm just in a dumb little band." Kurt and Krist teased Finnerty about working for "corporate" MTV and pretended that they were going to throw their beers at her, but they were just kidding.

In the summer of 1991, Finnerty was twenty-two years old and was still immersed in the same eighties punk culture that had inspired Kurt. The people programming MTV were all at least a decade older and were blind to it. With the zealous assurance of youth, she persuaded the higher-ups at MTV that she should attend the all-important "music meeting" that took place every Monday, where decisions were made about which music videos would be played and how often. "I was still low on the totem pole, but they realized that I was the only one in the demographic they were going for. The other people there had all been there for ten years and thought that artists like Phil Collins were what kids wanted to hear."

The people at record companies who were championing "alternative" rock soon realized they had a new ally at MTV. In late summer Mark Kates told Finnerty to meet him at a listening party Geffen was having for the forthcoming Guns N' Roses album at the Electric Lady studios in New York and promised that he would give her an advance cassette of *Nevermind* afterward. "I had nothing against Guns N' Roses, but it was a double album and the party went on for a long time and all I kept thinking was I wanted it to be over so I could get that Nirvana cassette. I listened to it on my Walkman while I walked home afterward, and I knew it was gonna be huge."

Music video submissions usually occurred on Friday to give the programmers the weekend to think about it. On the Friday that the "Smells Like Teen Spirit" video came in, the Smashing Pumpkins were in Finnerty's office, having crashed at her apartment the night before. She remembers, "We saw how incredible it was," and as she walked Billy Corgan and the other Pumpkins around to meet various MTV execs, in each of their offices they were playing the video from "this other cool band." By the end of the day, Finnerty recalls, "there was palpable excitement" in the hallways, and "people that I didn't know were coming into my office to see the video."

Prior to the Monday music meeting Finnerty met privately with her boss Abbey Konowitch and made the case for putting the Nirvana video into heavy rotation right away. "I said that if I was wrong and the record wasn't a hit, they could kick me out of the music meeting. I put my job on the line." Konowitch loved the passion but pointed out that there was only room to add one new video into "heavy" that week and MTV had also gotten a new Guns N' Roses video that had to go first because the band was an established favorite with MTV viewers, but he promised that the Nirvana video would be moved up to heavy the following week.

On September 29, a few days after *Nevermind* was released, the video premiered on MTV on their alternative show *120 Minutes*, after which it then went into "medium" rotation, which was exactly what they had done with Sonic Youth's "Kool Thing" a year earlier before dropping it after a few weeks. Fearing a rerun of that pattern, I harangued people at Geffen about how we all had to pressure MTV to play the video in heavy rotation. I had no idea that thanks to Finnerty an increase in rotation the following week was already a fait accompli.

"Within a few weeks my life changed," Finnerty recalls. Her status at the network skyrocketed and she was the liaison to

Nirvana for the rest of their career. MTV was crucial to making Nirvana a mass-appeal artist, but once they became famous the band was among the small group of stars that attracted viewers to the channel, so the relationship became one of mutual exploitation. Kurt resented it when MTV pressured him, but he hated it when they ignored him. He regularly watched the channel himself and wanted Nirvana to be a big deal there, and he hated the part of himself that cared that much.

Kurt would insist on making three other videos for the *Nevermind* album and rarely turned down MTV when they wanted the band on one of their shows. A month after the album was released, for an appearance on the MTV heavy metal show, *Headbangers Ball*, Kurt wore a vintage canary-yellow ball gown. When the host Riki Rachtman asked him why, Kurt answered coyly, "It's a ball, isn't it?" Twenty years later the MTV website ran an interview with Rachtman in which he complained that getting answers from Kurt for his show was "like pulling teeth" and that Kurt acted like "he didn't want to be there." Displaying that sullen punk attitude on a heavy metal show was Kurt's way of having his heavy metal cake and eating it too. He was determined to let old and new fans know that he detested macho attitudes but he still liked the idea that a metal show played his video. Finnerty and her bosses at MTV didn't share Rachtman's ire and understood what Kurt was doing.

When Kates and Smith had dreamed of having a gold record, they had envisioned that it would come after a year of methodical effort. The enthusiasm that the Roxy show generated at Geffen notwithstanding, the initial pressing was only around fifty thousand units, which was more than *Bleach* had sold but hardly an indicator that a runaway success was on the horizon. That initial shipment sold out of stores almost immediately, followed by massive reorders. *Nevermind* was certified gold (500,000 copies shipped) on October 12, a mere eighteen days after it was released. Boddy remembers, "Everyone in Seattle was so excited. Everything good that happened to *Nevermind* was happening to *us*. It was like, '*Our team won!*'" Kurt, Krist, and Dave were excited too but things were moving so quickly that there was an air of unreality to the accomplishment, and it seemed to me that the band was doing their best to ignore as much of the "success" as they could during these days.

I had no such inner constraint. I made up a song I sang to myself in the car: "I've got the biggest band, the biggest band in the land." Jimmy Iovine, who had cofounded Interscope Records the previous year, was someone I was always trying to impress. "I really think this is going to be bigger than anything I've ever been involved with," I said to him on the phone one day. Iovine supportively answered, "It reminds me of the Police." I don't know where I got the balls to respond, "I think it's gonna be *bigger* than the Police." I was out of control, but no matter how optimistic I got about the success of *Nevermind*, it kept exceeding my expectations.

Commercial radio and MTV were for the masses; the print medium was for the cult fans. On the last of the band's trips to New York before *Nevermind* came out, Janet Billig took Kurt to Madison Square Garden, where Metallica was premiering their new album at a giant listening party. Kurt liked Metallica and had a good time, yet he was also brooding about how to stave off a possible press backlash to Nirvana's forthcoming album. Echoing the spin he'd given Montgomery and Thurston, Kurt once again brought up "About a Girl," reminding Billig that he'd always written melodic songs. He wanted people to know he hadn't changed just because he'd signed to a major label, and he knew that Janet was a publicist who was regularly in touch with most of the journalists who covered the indie subculture and that she would give his spin to them. She remembers, "Kurt read everything. He was always into straddling between the indie and the mainstream rock worlds, and he pulled it off."

Kurt needn't have worried. Most writers who identified with punk rock recognized that Nirvana had made an album that retained and expanded their personal version of rock and roll and saw it as the triumph of the eighties punk culture they had long championed. It was also a huge validation of the Seattle rock community. Boddy remembers, "Critics all over rejoiced, even at *Maximum Rocknroll* and *Flipside*. They did not feel that the band sold out. Nobody felt that. Being a press person for Sub Pop, I'm telling you, *nobody*."

Meanwhile I did what I could on a more mainstream flank. I had been friends with Bob Guccione Jr. since he had started *Spin* in 1985. Like me, he was a businessperson who was an emotional step removed from the punk culture he'd identified as an underserved audience his magazine could appeal to. When we had lunch at the end of the summer, he told me that he was going to put Soundgarden on the cover of their year-end issue. (At that moment, Soundgarden was still Seattle's most popular new rock band.) I brashly told Bob that by the end of the year the biggest Seattle band was going to be Nirvana, not Soundgarden. Guccione's young staff must have concurred, because he assigned Lauren Spencer to write what would be the band's first cover story in a national magazine.

By the end of September Kurt knew how fast things were moving and wanted a different look for *Spin* than the PR shots that had been taken for the label a few weeks before. The day before the photo session the band visited WOZQ in Northampton and he asked a young woman who worked there to dye his hair blue, which is how he appeared on Nirvana's first national magazine cover.

Many older rock critics saw *Nevermind* as a revival of American rock and roll that was *about* something. R.E.M. had been the last band that both commanded a mass audience and touched on deeper themes, but since they'd been around for almost a decade, their core audience was now mostly college age or older. Guns N' Roses had added adrenaline to the teenage rock-and-roll world, but they lacked cultural depth. It seemed to many middle-aged critics that rock and roll had morphed into a louder version of shallow pop, but in late 1991 most of them saw the breakthrough of *Nevermind* as rock's return to a level of cultural centrality that they feared had become irretrievably out of reach. Critics usually looked down on very popular artists and only a small fraction of the mass musical audience read reviews. *Nevermind* became one of the very few albums that had massive chart success and also placed first in the *Village Voice*'s highly respected Pazz & Jop poll, which tabulated the top ten lists of hundreds of American rock critics at the end of the year.

Kurt kept telling everybody that he had only wanted Nirvana to be as big as the Pixies. I'm almost certain that he was being disingenuous and that he had been thinking about how to react to success with the same intensity that he had brought to musical rehearsals. Notwithstanding whatever personal struggles he had with lurking demons, and as unprepared and sometimes repelled as he was by the personal experience of fame, as an *artist* Kurt was preternaturally well prepared and he always seemed to be thinking several steps ahead.

Just as he had figured out a way to uniquely transcend divisions in radio formats, Kurt endeavored to go beyond the pigeonholes that rock journalism had created. "People think I'm a moody person, and I think it's lame that there are only two kinds of male lead singers," he complained. "You can either be a moody visionary like Michael Stipe, or a mindless heavy metal party guy like

Sammy Hagar." Once he knew he was becoming famous, Kurt was determined to play both roles.

Silva and the band thought it was important that the first time Nirvana played each major market they return to a small club where they had appeared before. In the parlance of the business these were "underplays" and helped them remain connected to their core audience. Because "Smells Like Teen Spirit" had gotten such a quick reaction, the shows sold out immediately, even though the tour actually started in mid-September, a week before *Nevermind* came out. Montgomery recalls, "It was insanity. At every show there were more people outside who couldn't get in than there were inside." For those who had tickets, the trajectory of the record gave all the early shows a sense of instant rock-and-roll history, and the audience often worked themselves into a frenzy.

In St. Louis, security guards were getting rough with some kids who were rushing the stage. After trying to cool down the guards, always difficult in the middle of loud music, Kurt stopped the show and invited a bunch of the kids to stand on the stage while Krist earnestly explained to the audience that "anarchy only works if we all accept responsibility."

In Los Angeles, where Geffen was headquartered and much of the media was based, we wanted to make room for more people to see them so an underplay didn't make sense. October 27, a month after *Nevermind* had been released, Nirvana headlined at the Palace Theatre, which had 2,200 seats, the biggest place Nirvana had headlined up until that moment, and the show quickly sold out. The band had been consistently playing great shows and this was no exception. Backstage afterward, Eddie Rosenblatt told me that he had come with Axl Rose and asked if he could bring him into the dressing room to say hi to Kurt. When I conveyed this request, Kurt grimaced and said he really didn't want to meet the Guns N' Roses singer. I didn't want to put Geffen's president in an untenable situation, so I suggested to Kurt that he and I leave the dressing room and then I'd give Rosenblatt a couple of passes. That way it wouldn't be like we were excluding them, just that Kurt couldn't be found. Kurt nodded and I walked outside, delivered the passes to Rosenblatt, and asked if he and Rose could wait five minutes for Nirvana to "change clothes." Then I went back in and grabbed Kurt and we ducked out a back door. Rosenblatt never gave me shit about it afterward so the charade worked on some level, but I doubt it left Rose with a great taste in his mouth.

Kurt and I stood in the corner of a corridor backstage where music business hangers-on walked by, not realizing that the slight guy in the shadows was the singer who had just given a classic and powerful performance, his sweat still drying. Kurt took this moment to tell me that he'd been concerned that a lot of the recent articles about Nirvana had emphasized his anti-misogynistic lyrics to such a degree that he was worried about coming across as being too serious and without a sense of humor. While he admired overtly political punk bands like Fugazi and the Dead Kennedys, he didn't want Nirvana to be perceived that narrowly.

I always dreaded conversations with artists who were unhappy with how they were described in the media because it was extremely difficult to do anything about it other than be more selective about who they talked to in the future. I launched into a generic rap about the limited ability we all had to influence nuances like this.

Kurt's response has always stayed with me because it was a moment when I had a glimpse of a level of calculation in his head I hadn't previously known was there. He looked at me with that same patient look I'd seen in the office and gently interrupted, "I know, and I've been trying to think of why this is, and I think it's because there is some political stuff in the press kit the label is giving to writers."

He was a step ahead of me even in my supposed area of expertise. Since the official "bio" was the mostly fictitious parody, Geffen had added some earlier articles about the band, some of which focused on the anti-rape song "Polly." I felt like an idiot for not thinking of this. "So, you want me to ask the label to remove those pieces?" I asked. He nodded appreciatively. "Yeah, that would be great."

Those kinds of adjustments were easy. More complicated was the fact that, as of a couple of weeks earlier, a new person had entered Kurt's life whose presence would be felt by everyone who knew him for the rest of his days.

SIX

COURTNEY LOVE

The early nineties have become so fundamental to the way I think about my career that it is easy to forget that for the first forty-one years of my life I did not know the name Courtney Love. I first heard about Courtney from Rosemary Carroll, then my wife and the mother of my children, who was also the lawyer for Courtney and her band Hole. By the fall of 1991, Janet Billig had signed Hole to Caroline Records and Kim Gordon of Sonic Youth had produced the band's low-budget debut album, *Pretty on the Inside*.

Hole fans, including some in the rock press, were transfixed by Courtney's uninhibited rock power at a time when only a handful of female artists had emerged in the punk scene, and she was the only one who also had the burning ambition and talent to transcend punk in the same way Nirvana had. Courtney was twenty-seven years old at the time, three years older than Kurt, and a force to be reckoned with.

Shortly after *Nevermind* was released I got a call from Peg Yorkin, who ran the Feminist Majority Foundation and who was also on the Southern California ACLU board I chaired. There was a Rock for Choice benefit coming up with the bands L7 and Sister Double Happiness, and she wanted Nirvana to headline it to ensure a sellout. Silva told me the band was up for it. They supported feminism and Dave Grohl had recently dated Jennifer Finch of L7, so it was an easy sell. Shortly after Nirvana signed on, Yorkin added Hole to the bill, and soon thereafter Rosemary told me that Courtney (I think this was the first time I heard her name) wanted to make sure they were able to play a long enough set, a presumptuous demand for an opening act.

Hole's guitarist Eric Erlandson was also Courtney's boyfriend when their band first started. "Courtney and I saw a Nirvana gig in Long Beach after *Bleach* was released and we weren't that into them. To me it seemed like Melvinesque sludge and I wasn't interested in that." However, in May 1991, while Nirvana was rehearsing the songs that wound up on *Nevermind*, Eric and Courtney saw them play at a Los Angeles club called Jabberjaw and the lightbulb went on. "That was the night that everyone realized Kurt was mixing Pixies and poppy elements into the band and it was the perfect timing for it," Eric recalls. "There was already a mystique around Kurt. He was lovable, but also erratic and drug fueled, but he had something about him that everyone was drawn to." A few months later Eric remembers, "early cassettes of *Nevermind* were being passed around and when Hole was touring we listened to it in the van over and over again." Not long after the Jabberjaw show Eric and Courtney ended their romance while remaining friends and bandmates, and Courtney got involved with Billy Corgan from the Smashing Pumpkins.

On October 12, three weeks after *Nevermind* was released,

I saw Nirvana at the Metro, a club in Chicago that held around five hundred people. It was one of the underplays that sold out quickly. This was an exciting time for the band. They knew that *Nevermind* was exceeding all their expectations, but they weren't overwhelmed or burned out yet. Decades later, Chicago rock writers still described it as one of the best shows they'd ever seen. The set ended with the ritual instrument destruction, the first time I'd seen them do it. Both Kurt's guitar and Dave's drums were trashed.

Nirvana's dressing room after the show was crowded with musicians and other friends of the band from the local punk scene. Courtney immediately introduced herself to me. She was with Lori Barbero of Babes in Toyland, a band Courtney had briefly been a member of before forming Hole. Courtney had been able to get to Chicago in part because Kaz Utsunomiya also was exploring a professional relationship with her. Without money for a plane ticket from Los Angeles to Chicago or for a hotel room, Courtney asked Jane's Addiction's manager, Tom Atencio, who was also courting Hole at the time, for help, and he in turn called the music publisher. Kaz remembers Tom saying "it was important for her to see Nirvana so she could be exposed to great songwriting in the punk world." It seemed like a contrived rationale but Kaz had a soft spot for Courtney, so he came up with $1,000. (Courtney talked Rosemary into loaning her an additional $1,000 for the trip.)

I was charmed by Courtney's wit and warmth. "Are you going to be my friend?" she asked, and I nodded, knowing exactly what she meant. She had a characteristic many stars did, a way of making anyone she was intent on winning over feel that they were somehow more interesting and fabulous under the spotlight of her attention. Not only were we connected through Rosemary, she knew that I was not at all concerned about her rumored feuds in the Northwest indie scene. Those people weren't crazy about me either given my association with Nirvana's transition to the corporate music world. In the newly formed cosmos that was rapidly developing around the band, we were soon to become allies.

Courtney told me that Lori had a crush on Dave Grohl and she was merely tagging along for moral support, which I assumed was bullshit even at the time. What I didn't know was that her real reason for coming to Chicago had been to see Corgan, but that when she showed up at his place he was with another woman. Courtney acknowledges, "Billy threw me out and it was just serendipity that Nirvana was playing that night. I had a crush on Kurt so I went for it. It seemed so natural and organic. We'd been flirting for two years from a distance."

Immediately after schmoozing me, Courtney made a beeline for the back of the dressing room, where Kurt was sitting. Although she was several inches taller than he was, Courtney was soon perched on Kurt's lap. They each had grins on their faces like the proverbial cat that swallowed the canary. It was the first night that Kurt and Courtney slept together. By the time of the Rock for Choice benefit two weeks later, Kurt and Courtney were a couple, and it would stay that way for the rest of Kurt's life.

Courtney took and gave offense very easily, but I loved her sense of humor and her intelligence. Although others around Nirvana seemed to think that the liaison would last no longer than a typically evanescent rock-and-roll fling, it was soon obvious to me that Kurt was deeply in love with Courtney and that the feeling was mutual.

Thurston also figured out quickly that the relationship was the real thing: "I remember a gig where I was sitting next to Courtney on the side of the stage and Kurt pointed up at us and said something about Courtney, and then I'm realizing, like, 'Oh, these two guys are in love. This is really happening.' And that was really cute."

Kurt and Courtney could communicate with each other on numerous levels that no one else around them could understand, and they carried many of the same chips on their shoulders. Although Kurt was uniquely talented and much more successful, Courtney had more street smarts and a broader awareness of culture. She was a remarkable lyricist and compelling performer with a media sophistication that rivaled Kurt's. She was also intensely ambitious. She recalls, "Kurt liked that about me. I was gonna take Madonna down. He was ambitious too but he hid it really well."

Because they both had been emotionally abandoned by their parents at a young age, they learned to be grown-ups only after they had some success in the music business. They created their own world together and anyone who wanted to be around Nirvana had to accept it, and some didn't. Some of Kurt's old acquaintances were possessive and had a hard time grasping the velocity at which his life was changing.

Some men were threatened by a strong, outspoken woman, and the Riot Grrrls in Olympia didn't care much for Courtney either. In addition to the inherent tension caused by the clash of Courtney's ambition and the Olympia community's contempt for commerciality, Courtney wasn't crazy about the fact that Kathleen Hanna and Tobi Vail knew Kurt before she did and that they stayed in touch with him. Courtney's abrasive territoriality infuriated many of his old friends. I never paid much attention to any of this. The only opinion that mattered to me was Kurt's.

He was deeply offended by anyone who didn't approve of his new relationship. He displayed a sentimental side, cherishing the romance that had been absent in his own family. One day he looked at me with a pained expression and earnestly asked,

"Wouldn't any man be upset if people disrespected the woman he loved?"

Courtney wanted Hole to follow Nirvana's path from indie to major and had been looking for a manager for her band. Uppermost in my mind at that moment was being supportive of Kurt. I asked if he thought it would be a good idea for me to manage Hole and he gave me a look of relief, saying, "That would be awesome." Courtney thought so as well and it was a done deal.

Silva must have had a bad experience with Courtney in some previous era, because when I told him that Gold Mountain was going to manage Hole he brusquely told me, "You deal with her." Fine with me. The unexpected velocity of Nirvana's success had already drawn me into a more prominent role than we had originally contemplated when it came to certain business and media issues. Prior to then, I had mainly been limited to dealing with the record company on some key issues, while Silva was much more involved in the day-to-day reality of managing the band. My embrace of Courtney was a turning point in my relationship with Kurt, and I soon became the businessperson who dealt with him directly on most sensitive issues from then on.

Nonetheless, Silva and I shared a lot of this part of the journey. On Halloween, a month after *Nevermind* came out, we went to Seattle to see Nirvana's first headlining show in the city that had spawned them since the release of the big album. Geffen made up gold record plaques to give to the band and we had arranged to have the show filmed, realizing that it was a moment worth documenting. Although they'd agreed to this plan the band was a little weirded out by the cameras, worried that it signaled the kind grandiosity they were intent on avoiding.

Over the last month, Nirvana had been on an intense roller-coaster ride, and it was disorienting for them to be back in Seattle as "rock stars." Always looking for ways to deconstruct rock clichés, Kurt asked a few of their friends to dance onstage as a punk parody of go-go dancers and he made sure that Bikini Kill and Mudhoney were booked to perform at the concert before Nirvana did.

It was at this show that I first met Kurt's mother, Wendy, who made the drive from Aberdeen. Kurt often talked about how devastated he had been by his parents' divorce when he was nine years old. He hadn't spoken to his father for almost a decade, and although he had felt abandoned by his mother as well during certain periods in his childhood, he told me that he appreciated the fact that she always complimented his paintings when he was a kid and he never lost touch with her. Wendy was blond, pretty, sweet, and, by this time in her life, deferential to Kurt. Krist introduced me to several members of his family, including his mother, Maria. "She got her hair done!" he recalls. "Everybody was really happy and really proud. Some people wanted to borrow money!"

The concert was at the Paramount Theatre, which held 2,800 people, the biggest place, by far, that Nirvana had played in Seattle. Silva and I got to the venue after the sound check and Kurt, Krist, and Dave were not in their designated dressing room. As we walked up a staircase in the theater looking for them, Mark Arm of Mudhoney was walking down. Silva asked him, "Have you seen my band?" to which Arm sneeringly replied, "They're not *your* band." I thought to myself, "Well they're not *your* band either." The evening was an emotional moment for the Seattle rock scene, and the show that night was a triumphant homecoming, but the notion at this point that Kurt Cobain belonged to any city or subculture was delusional.

Robert Smith recalls, "Kurt was in his pajamas and went to

sleep in the corner of a room backstage. I really felt sorry for him at that moment." My memory is somewhat different. Kurt often dressed in pajamas, and I recall his being a bit uncomfortable having to deal with family and old acquaintances but also amused by it. Maybe Smith saw something that I missed. As must be obvious by now, I was predisposed to see all things Nirvana through rose-colored glasses, but the excellence of the show comes through in the film, which is one of my favorite documents of the band from that time.

That said, I was aware that any artist new to the intensity of overnight success is disoriented by it. Part of Kurt was happy to have accomplished this huge goal, and there was that camaraderie among the three band members in the shared success. At the same time Kurt made no effort to hide from me the reality that he was also a little freaked out by his abrupt transition to being a public figure. I had some experience in walking artists through the early stages of fame but nothing to match the meteoric rise of Nirvana. I often felt helpless when I'd see the anguished expressions that sometimes crossed his face for no apparent reason. I think it was dawning on Kurt that the success he had worked so hard for would not erase a lot of the emotional scars that he had lived with since childhood. I was reminded of Peggy Lee's mournful song "Is That All There Is?"

Having agreed to manage Hole, I was immediately confronted with work to do, and I knew I needed help. Fortunately, Janet Billig agreed to leave Caroline and come to work for Gold Mountain. I had seen her several times outside of CBGB after shows giving her take on various artists to denizens of the punk scene, and I was impressed by the weight her observations were given, especially by journalists. Initially, Janet was hired to do the day-to-day work for Hole, but she soon became integral to

Nirvana, as well, becoming the primary media contact for both bands.

My initial task was to figure out which record company should release Hole's next album. The success of *Nevermind* had exponentially increased the value of artists in the punk world overnight. Eddie Rosenblatt joked that it took weeks to get a plane ticket to Seattle because so many flights were sold out thanks to all the A & R people going there to find "the next Nirvana."

By the time I got involved, several labels were already interested but I couldn't resist the notion of signing Hole to DGC/Geffen. They knew how to market a punk artist to a mass audience without compromising their identity, and I knew we would always be treated with respect there. Courtney and Eric figured if they were good enough for Nirvana, they were good enough for Hole.

I told Rosenblatt that if they wanted the band we needed to make a deal quickly because others were being aggressive. Although Courtney would later imply to the press that the deal was "a million dollars," the actual commitment was almost identical to what Nirvana had signed even though some of the other labels offered more.

A few months earlier, the trade magazine *Billboard* had changed the way they compiled their sales charts. Previously based on a hodgepodge of anecdotal data and various kinds of hype, the charts were now compiled by SoundScan, a new technology that tracked bar codes as albums were sold over the counter. This meant that for the most part the chart positions were, at long last, a mathematically accurate description of the reality of the marketplace. On November 2, *Nevermind* took a huge jump on the *Billboard* album sales chart, from number 63 to 35, eliminating any question that the album was on a trajectory much more intense than any previous punk or alternative album.

On a brief European trip, Courtney did some promo of her own. I went with her to a BBC Radio session where she played an acoustic version of a song I hadn't heard yet called "Doll Parts," and I was mesmerized. Once again, I realized I was fortunate to be working with an artist who was more talented than I initially realized.

On a personal level Courtney, like Kurt, contained many contradictions, including a personality that alternated between that of a little girl and that of a jaded adult. She was the ultimate cynic but had streaks of the same kind of idealism that often animated Kurt. When she was on, she could light up any room but when she was unhappy it was no fun to be around her. Courtney's arrival in Kurt's life coincided with Nirvana's explosion of success. Any woman in her position would have been the subject of public scrutiny and would have gone through the kinds of adjustments that sudden visibility demands. Amid a group of people who were having their own issues dealing with the unanticipatedly bright glare of the spotlight, Courtney added an incendiary personality; her own artistic aspirations and talent; a new group of friends, many of them in the rock press; and enemies, many from the punk world. She was more interested in the music business than Kurt was and asked questions that he was hesitant to pose (especially those regarding the band's compensation). Kurt loved how outspoken Courtney was. She would often loudly articulate things that he was quietly thinking, and he got off on that. Not everyone else was charmed.

Rosemary remembers, "Courtney would call a lot and would start by saying, 'Kurt is here,' before expressing a new idea or demand." She liked spending money more than Kurt did and insisted that the band start staying in nicer hotels commensurate with their new commercial status. ("I liked Four Seasons, instead of Omnis," she texted me recently, still annoyed that it was ever an issue.)

Almost immediately there were people who referred to her as "Yoko." To some people around the band and in the extended rock world it was meant as an insult. To me the comparison was a compliment. I am a fan of Yoko Ono and think that a lot of the political and philosophical elements in John Lennon's solo career were positively influenced by her. Kurt and Courtney agreed. "They were always calling themselves John and Yoko," Everett True recalls.

There were those in the rock press who implied that Courtney was manipulating Kurt, but I always felt such claims were absurd. Kurt was one of the strongest-willed people I ever met. He did get enraged when people disrespected Courtney. While on a European tour, he insisted that his old Sub Pop bandmate and friend Tad be replaced as a supporting act to Nirvana after Tad called Courtney a bitch in an interview. Some in the Seattle community took umbrage at this but Kurt was unapologetic, and he was scarcely the only man who would react that way if the woman he loved was publicly insulted.

However, Kurt had no problem saying no to Courtney when it suited him. One day he called to tell me that Courtney had bought a Lexus, the same kind of car I drove at the time. "Is that a car I should have?" he asked with a stressed-out edge in his voice. I told him that if he was asking whether or not he could *afford* it, the answer was yes, but if he was asking whether he *needed* any particular kind of car just because he had a hit record, the answer was no. "That's what I thought," he answered. "I'm going to have her return it," which she promptly did.

When Kurt fell in love with Courtney, he and Eric Erlandson also quickly became close friends. "It was a weird dynamic because I became like a caretaker and friend to both of them. It was a very strange threesome and I still haven't wrapped my head around it," Eric said with a laugh when we spoke twenty-five years later.

Kurt and Courtney rented an apartment on Spaulding Avenue in Hollywood. Silva's assistant Peter Rauh helped them move in. Courtney found an ornate wrought iron bed at a store in the neighborhood, but the owner didn't want to take a check from people who looked, to him, like they lived on the street. Rauh couldn't convince him that they were actually rock stars, but he did get the owner to promise not to sell it to anyone else for twenty-four hours, during which time Nirvana's business manager Lee Johnson overnighted a certified check so that the bed could be delivered the next day. The landlord of the apartment frequently complained about loud music, and it soon became obvious that they would want to find another place as soon as Nirvana's schedule permitted.

Erlandson recalls visiting Kurt: "He was always working on something. He wasn't out partying. He was a stay-at-home person who was constantly working on something at all hours. He was always being creative. I'd hear him playing in the closet over and over making noise on the guitar that seemed like useless rambling nonsense, but then he'd come up with a gem and work it to death like the Beatles, and keep working on it over and over again until it was perfect. Courtney and I did that with Hole's music to an extent, but Kurt's focus was super intense, and he had that talent, so he was able to go past where other people would normally stop."

Kurt hung around with Hole when they were rehearsing and frequently jammed with them. Eric says, "If he wasn't working on music he'd be painting. It was a little unnerving to be around, realizing this person has created a character and is living it twenty-four/seven."

For better or worse, the art form Kurt cared about most could not be entirely executed from seclusion and he was committed to all aspects of his chosen path, which included touring on a global scale.

SEVEN

INTERNATIONALE

Ever since the seventies, rock journalism had much more influence in England than it did in America. British fans were avid enough readers to support several national music weeklies, including *New Musical Express* (*NME*), *Melody Maker*, and *Sounds*. There was nothing like them in the States. (*Rolling Stone* only came out every two weeks, and while it still mattered, its clout in America was nowhere near that of the British weeklies in the UK.)

England had a radio-driven pop business like America's, but the parallel power of the British music press and the wider diversity of the musical culture it covered, as well as the existence of several edgy national radio shows that played non-pop music, enabled many American punk artists to build bigger audiences in England than they had at home.

In the late eighties, Anton Brookes, the indie publicist who represented Sub Pop in the UK, brought the Seattle indie to the attention of John Peel, a legendary tastemaker at BBC Radio. Peel promptly played several of the label's singles, including Nirvana's. It was also Brookes who had arranged for Everett's fateful first trip to Seattle.

Six months after *Bleach* was released, Nirvana appeared as the opening act at a Sub Pop showcase called Lame Fest in London and Everett recalls lovingly that Kurt was "in turn full of terror and gentleness and threw himself around like nothing existed outside of each moment he played and sang." Eric Erlandson recalls with both admiration and envy that "Kurt was a darling of the British press."

On that first UK tour, the only journalists who paid attention to the band were a handful of younger writers. As had been the case in America, initially Nirvana was covered as part of a Sub Pop "sound" that included bands like Tad and Mudhoney. However, Jonathan Poneman of Sub Pop told Brookes to pay particular attention to Nirvana because they were already drawing bigger crowds than Mudhoney did in Seattle and, unlike the audiences for most grunge artists, a large percentage of Nirvana's fans were female. As Brookes got to know Kurt he soon agreed that there was a greater potential for Nirvana than their labelmates.

He recalls, "At the beginning some media people would dismiss Nirvana as a Seattle noisy band whose members looked like they just got out of bed. They'd get their name wrong and call them Nevada." However, it was clear to Brookes that Nirvana had a wider vision than most punk bands. He admired Kurt's "opposition to patriarchal rock. Nirvana always cut through misogynist bullshit." At first the publicist had no inkling of the coming magnitude of the band's audience. "I thought that their peers would be the Butthole Surfers and Jane's Addiction." However he acknowledges that as early as their first UK tour, "Kurt was always confident. He told me that they had songs that were gonna go to number one. He actually said, 'We're gonna go to number one.'"

Brookes went on the 1991 European tour that Nirvana did with Sonic Youth and says, "It was already like Kurt was royalty, the chosen one. Kurt was very humble and approachable, a really nice guy who would have a good laugh, but everybody, even Sonic Youth, knew they were in the throngs of greatness." At the Reading Festival, "they came on midafternoon on a Friday. The weather was wet and cold and miserable but afterward everybody was talking about them. All the media absolutely loved them."

Later in 1991, five weeks after *Nevermind* was released, just as it was exploding on the American charts, Nirvana did a six-week headline tour of the UK and continental Europe, and I met Brookes for the first time in London. He was tall and wild-eyed and wanted my help. Geffen didn't have a separate British staff, so the Nirvana album was marketed in the UK by their distributor, MCA, an old-school major with mainstream artists like Elton John. Brookes asked if I could go with him to MCA's offices. "*You've* got to explain the band's philosophy to them," he said with a look of panic at the prospect of encountering major-label executives face-to-face.

I wasn't sure I was up to that particular task, and "philosophy" seemed like a pretty formal word to describe the way the band felt about their relationship with the punk and indie worlds, but I was the only old-school rock guy on the Nirvana team, so I agreed.

Nevermind came out on the same day in the UK and the rest of Europe as it did in North America. Brookes remembers in the weeks leading up to the album's release, "Everywhere I went over the summer everybody wanted a cassette of *Nevermind*. It captured the zeitgeist. People were connecting with it on a different level." As in the U.S., the initial shipment of albums to stores (around forty thousand units in the UK) sold out right away and it was a week or two until the supply was replenished.

As it turned out, there was no stress at all between Nirvana and MCA in England. Once an artist is hot, executives, who in other situations can be indifferent or arrogant, are transformed into enthusiastic helpers. There was no pushback when I explained that in order to protect their image the band would only talk to writers whom Brookes picked, people who had a history of respecting the artists that Nirvana admired, many of whom had already written about *Bleach*. Brookes now acknowledges that his fears about MCA were unfounded and that they did an effective job that did not conflict with Nirvana's integrity.

One of MCA's roles was to secure TV appearances, the first of which was for the Channel 4 show *The Word*, at which Kurt proudly told the studio audience, "I'd like you all to know that Courtney Love is the best fuck in the world." Nirvana then played a spirited version of "Smells Like Teen Spirit," after which Kurt stage-dove into the crowd.

Later that month, Nirvana performed "Smells Like Teen Spirit" on *Top of the Pops*, Britain's most famous music show, on which the Beatles and Stones and every other British rock star had performed in the days of yore. When it came to media, "Kurt was very savvy," says Brookes, and part of Kurt's strategy was to avoid repetition. Having performed the single straightforwardly on *The Word*, Kurt cooked up a different approach to the hit. Instead of singing the song in the famous rock rasp that was on the record, Kurt *crooned* the song. It blew my mind that Kurt could deconstruct his own hit a mere two months after it had been released. To my ears his vocal sounded like Jim Morrison of the Doors, but when I made the comparison to him Kurt gave me one of his bemused looks and said he had actually been thinking of Morrissey, the legendary moody lead singer of the Smiths, an homage that the young British music writers all recognized.

Jonathan Ross's TV show was the closest British equivalent to David Letterman's, witty and irreverent. Ross introduced the band as doing "Lithium" but at the last minute (literally) they switched to "Territorial Pissings," beginning with Krist's tormented rendition of the chorus from "Get Together" and ending with Dave toppling his cymbals onto the TV soundstage. A nonplussed Ross smirked at the camera afterward and said, "I hope we didn't wake the neighbors up. That was Nirvana doing a tune we didn't really expect but they wanted us to tell you they're available for children's birthday parties and bar mitzvahs." The producers gave us a hard time for surprising them, but the band understood their own persona so much better than anyone else did. They had figured out a way to be shocking without being vulgar.

While in London, Nirvana also did a live session for BBC Radio. Focusing on his punk fans, Kurt refused to do "Smells Like Teen Spirit," which had already become a pop hit in England. Instead, the band performed "Polly," "Aneurysm" (which was the B-side of the hit single), and an older song called "Been a Son," which would show up on the *Incesticide* compilation the following year.

Brookes says, "Kurt was just this kid who had the biggest band in the world. It was such a journey and such a privilege to be part of that journey, to be there and look in Kurt's eyes and see his reaction to things," adding, "Dave and Krist were also a huge part of the equation. They provided that chemistry. When they were on form together they were as funny as fuck and so great to be around."

As in the States, *Nevermind* introduced the punk and mainstream rock audiences to each other. The band names on most of the T-shirts at the British gigs—the Ramones, Mudhoney, and Sonic Youth—reflected the punk subculture, but there were also kids wearing Beatles and AC/DC shirts.

Kurt was determined to use his newfound fame to support the kind of indie rock he loved. Nirvana offered Captain America, later known as Eugenius, the slot to play before them for all of the UK dates starting in Bristol on November 4. A few days later Nirvana did a photo session for several British publications and Kurt wore a Captain America T-shirt. One of the pictures wound up on the cover of *NME* at the end of November, which raised the fortunes of the Scottish band overnight. (In 2018, after it was announced that *NME* was ceasing print publication after sixty-six years, the *New York Times* chose to run a picture of that cover, accompanied by an article by Mary Ann Hobbs, the author of the story, in which she recalled, "They were staying in a shabby hotel in the Bayswater district of London. Kurt Cobain was in real pain with stomach ulcers, and only interested in talking about women's rights.")

Captain America's drummer, Andy Bollen, kept a journal, much of which he later published as *Nirvana: A Tour Diary*. Kurt, who kept journals himself, took a liking to Bollen and answered a lot of his questions even while teasing him for being a journalist in disguise. Bollen writes of meeting Nirvana's front man, "The first thing you notice about Kurt is his piercing blue eyes. He has peroxide hair in two styles and two colors, blond with darker roots. He preferred roll ups rather than filtered cigarettes. I was expecting a few signs of debauchery and hedonism and was met with calm erudition."

The British shows I saw were at the same level as the ones in America. There were no groupies in evidence, but there were a lot of punk fanzines in the dressing rooms. The band would seem exhausted beforehand and then explode with energy onstage.

Bollen was surprised by Kurt's lack of superstar affectation. "He slept a lot and had a persona that made people wary of him. When meeting the real fans, though, he was generous, responsive and always aware of their nervousness and made them feel at ease. He never forgot that he was, despite the band's success, just like them: a fan of independent, underground music."

Sometimes Eugene Kelly sat in and sang harmony when Nirvana covered his song "Molly's Lips." Nirvana let Captain America use any of their equipment, including Dave's drum kit, a display of generosity rare for a headliner. Just as important, they shared the beer that promoters provided.

Bollen recalls having the paradoxical feeling that he was seeing Nirvana at a peak moment, when they had a momentum comparable to what he imagined the Beatles had thirty years earlier, yet at the same time having a desire to *protect* Kurt.

Reading Bollen's memoir twenty years after the fact, I learned that the band, or Dave Grohl at least, had more complicated feelings about their business team than I had realized. In one dressing room there was a Magic 8 Ball and Dave asked, "Does David Geffen have our best interests at heart?" Answer: "Ask Again Later." New question: "Shall we stay with Danny Goldberg at Gold Mountain Management?" Answer: "It Is Certain." Dave laughed. "That can't be right, let's do it again." Answer: "Decidedly So." I have no idea if Kurt was paying attention to any of this, but I can't help but feel retrospective gratitude to that 8 Ball.

This tour was the inflection point at which Nirvana's day-to-day life changed in the wake of their success. As friends from home reported how often they were seeing the video, with every passing day the members of the band were feeling the magnitude of *Nevermind* and the weight on their shoulders of new fame that seemed to grow continually. They started smashing guitars, drums, and amplifiers onstage more frequently. They were also in constant talks with the press, in which Kurt was painting and repainting the image of the band. The website LiveNirvana.com has an archive of forty-three interviews for the single month of November 1991 in which the band spoke, usually at considerable length, to members of the British and German media.

As had been the case on the recent American tour, the shows were all sold out, with hundreds of people outside unable to get in, and the fans who made it inside were manic. Kurt always stopped the show if a bouncer was pushing a fan around, but the overall stress caused by the *Nevermind* phenomenon reached a peak in Ghent, Belgium, where Kurt dove into the audience. After re-turning to the stage he uncharacteristically spit at people in the front row.

As I reread the interviews Kurt did during this time, I was reminded of how thoughtful he was with each one, even when he was physically exhausted. Most artists develop a collection of an-swers and repeat them in interviews almost like a piece of theater (as do book authors), but Kurt usually came up with something fresh each time.

When speaking to European writers Kurt was often more forthcoming than he was at home. On the rare occasions when American writers asked him about the band's name, he was in-tentionally vague, but he genially told Italian journalist Luca Collepiccolo, "Nirvana is a name belonging to the Indian religion and refers to a sort of divine consciousness." He told a German writer that he had taken LSD but didn't do it often "because [he] laughed too much." Kurt befriended French journalist Youri Lenquette, who had flown to Australia to interview him, after which "Kurt couldn't sleep and [he and Lenquette] listened to cassettes of sixties garage rock." Because Nirvana spent limited time in these countries, any contact with him was a big deal. Years after Kurt died, another Italian writer, Luccio Spiccia, wrote, "Young people ask me about Kurt, as if I were a member of Nirvana."

After their set at a regional festival was delayed so that locals could watch Denmark win the European Championship soccer final, Søren Rud, the photographer the local record company hired, remembers, "Kurt came straight up to me, shook my hand, and congratulated me on Denmark's victory. He even made some comments about the game, which the band obviously had watched."

Swedish TV journalist Lars Aldman reflects on an interview with Kurt that he filmed by a canal in Djurgården, a park in Stockholm: "Kurt was hiding his face under a hood attached to a jacket with a sort of map pattern. Kurt revealed a sincere and thoughtful side that day but there was a bit of sadness and pain in his voice too. Afterward I had this great feeling of having been part of something unique and spectacular."

Kurt and Courtney were married on February 24, 1992, in Waikiki, Hawaii. Only a handful of people attended, and Silva and I were not among them. Neither was Krist or his wife, Shelli, whom Courtney was feuding with for reasons I never could figure out. Although by normal standards the wedding was a major event in Kurt's life, at the time it seemed almost perfunctory and neither Kurt nor Courtney ever said a word to me about it in the years to come.

Soon afterward Nirvana made what would be their only trip to Australia, beginning with an underplay at the Phoenician Club in Sydney, a performance that instantly became legendary in that country. (In 2004, the Australian edition of *Kerrang!* magazine would name this show as number one of all time on a list of "gigs that shook the world.") The next day Nirvana played to a much larger audience at the Big Day Out festival, which they co-headlined with the Violent Femmes.

In conjunction with the band's first tour of Australia and Japan, Kurt compiled an EP called *Hormoaning* that was only released in those two countries. It consisted of six tracks, including covers of songs by the Vaselines, Wipers, and Devo, which were originally broadcast on BBC Radio Peel Sessions, as well as "Aneurysm" and "Even in His Youth," which had been produced by Montgomery and had originally been released on the B-side of "Smells Like Teen Spirit" in the UK. *Hormoaning* went to number 2 on the Australian charts and also charted in Japan.

Mandy Barron was a publicist who had represented a number of Sub Pop bands as well as Fugazi and Sonic Youth in Australia, and she was asked by MCA and the promoters to publicize both the EP and the tour. Like other publicists, she connected with Kurt by talking to him for hours about punk artists they both liked. Nirvana gave the support slots to local indie bands, including the Meanies, Tumbleweed, Guttersnipe, the Village Idiots, and the Cosmic Psychos.

Barron, like Brookes, remembers Nirvana shows of that period rhapsodically: "The sound was brilliant. Everything was amazing. We all felt that they were possibly the best band anyone had ever seen. They were so tight. I watched some of the Australian guitarists watching Kurt play left-handed, sitting in the room trying to work those chords and thinking, 'It will never happen unless you tune your guitar upside down.'"

The same cultural impact that Nirvana had made over a period of a couple of years in Europe happened within weeks in Australia. "Nirvana changed the mind-set of mainstream radio and even the way people dressed. Guys started wearing cardigans," Barron remembers with a laugh, "and Kurt had a real impact in the way he talked about women and the way he stood up for Courtney."

Courtney arrived halfway through the brief tour, and after that Barron traveled with her and Kurt while Dave and Krist traveled separately. Barron remembers, "It seemed like there were some bad feelings about that but Kurt and Courtney were in love and wanted to be with each other." They stayed mostly to themselves and Kurt used days off to finish editing the music video for "Come as You Are."

Nirvana did one show in New Zealand, and then they went to Japan for several shows. They were met there by Kaz, who observes, "In those days most American or European bands would wait till they were huge before they came to Japan because there was no internet and it would take months for stories about them to get into Japanese magazines. Nirvana went at a very early stage of their career and they had fans right away, in part because 'Smells Like Teen Spirit' was a hit even in Japan." Nirvana was also known to many Japanese punk fans because Shonen Knife, an all-female Japanese trio who had opened the shows that Captain America did with Nirvana in Europe, raved about Nirvana to the local press when they got back home.

Kaz fondly remembers being with Kurt in Osaka: "He was really interested in Japanese pop culture, especially the games and animation. We would go into department stores to buy stuff. He was interested in Japanese high school student uniforms and Japanese pajamas, which he wore onstage for the Japanese shows."

Courtney had some Hole media to do in Australia so she stayed there a few days longer than Kurt did. Kaz recalls, "Back at the hotel he kept trying to get ahold of Courtney to find out when she was arriving in Japan. We traveled to Tokyo on a bullet train arriving just in time for me to get to the airport to pick her up while Kurt went to the sound check. I drove her to the venue, which held around a thousand people and was sold out. Once Courtney arrived they were inseparable. They would stay in the room or go to a restaurant together. In between sound checks and the show, they would go to a video arcade. Kurt was fascinated by the games, which were different than the ones in America." Kaz glowingly recalls that as a result of the band's concerts "they gained the hearts of Japanese kids."

For years, France had been the hardest international market for American rock bands to crack, so I was relieved to see Nirvana go over so well at the Trans Musicales festival in Rennes. Kurt and Courtney kept to themselves during the day, and Krist and Dave handled media requests. Doudou, the young promoter, was ecstatic. For much of the concert I stood next to Gérard Drouot, a mainstream French concert promoter of my generation who was skeptical about most punk artists. He recalls watching the show from the front of the stage near the barricade and being impressed that such a loud, powerful band played songs with such memorable melodies ("like Lennon and McCartney"). Drouot would promote all subsequent French Nirvana concerts.

Some people now say that there were already whispers that Kurt was shooting heroin when the band was in France, possibly fueled by the fact that he'd missed a couple of sound checks. Smack was easy enough to get in the country at the time so in retrospect I suspect the rumors that Kurt was using were true, but the problem would not show up on my radar screen for several more weeks.

EIGHT

HEROIN

In early January 1992, while I was on a brief vacation in the Caribbean with Rosemary and our eighteen-month-old daughter, Katie, Silva called to say that *Nevermind* had gone to number 1 on the *Billboard* album chart. Even more astonishing was the surreal fact that it had knocked Michael Jackson's *Dangerous* from the top slot. Moreover, Nirvana was booked to appear on *Saturday Night Live* on January 11, another remarkable milestone for a punk band. (The Clash had performed on the show in 1982, but none of the American punk bands that Nirvana looked up to ever got such a shot.) Sadly, the sense of euphoria I felt over these accomplishments was fleeting.

My family and I arrived back in New York prior to the *SNL* broadcast and I was greeted by faxes of two recently published pieces that strongly suggested Kurt and Courtney were shooting heroin. Jerry McCulley's article for *Bay Area Music* (*BAM*) centered on an interview he'd done with Kurt a few weeks earlier after Nirvana had played at the Los Angeles Memorial Sports Arena on a bill that was headlined by the Red Hot Chili Peppers. (Pearl Jam, who would not break through commercially for several more months, was the opening act.)

Before *Nevermind* came out we had arranged for Nirvana to be the special guest star on half a dozen such shows. At the time the $10,000-a-night fee was financially meaningful to the band, and in the normal scheme of things one of the primary ways to build the career of an artist was to have them play in front of the audiences of their more successful peers. Because Nirvana had exploded in popularity so quickly we all came to regret the decision but the band had to fulfill the commitment.

I had been at that L.A. show but I had Katie with me, so I left shortly after Nirvana's set and a quick post-show hello. Kurt didn't seem stoned to me, just a little spent, as he usually was after a performance. As I was leaving, I ran into Bob Merlis, the head of publicity for Warner Bros. Records, who was backstage with his thirteen-year-old son, Ben, a fanatic punk fan.

Now in his late thirties, Ben vividly remembers being introduced to his hero outside of Nirvana's dressing room. "Kurt had dyed magenta hair and a black-and-white Alice in Wonderland dress on. At some point I said, 'It's up to you to bring back punk.' He looked me dead in the face with those cold blue eyes, and he said, 'No. It's up to *you* to bring back punk.' He left and came back with a black, long-sleeve Nirvana shirt. He said, 'I want you to have this shirt. This isn't for sale. Only the band and crew have these.' I was stoked! I was thirteen years old and the singer of the biggest band in the world gave me a shirt no one can buy."

Kurt evidently got high sometime after that. Although he didn't tell me so at the time, Thurston saw Kurt backstage later that evening and was worried. "The whole backstage thing felt druggy with Eddie Van Halen coming back and Courtney yelling at some girl who was snipping a lock of Kurt's hair off about being a witch. I was like, 'God, I haven't really seen *that* before.'"

McCulley, the writer for *BAM*, arrived shortly thereafter, and the way he described Kurt was an unmistakable alarm bell to everyone connected to Nirvana. "He nods off occasionally. He's had but an hour's sleep, he says, but the pinned pupils, sunken cheeks, and scabbed sallow skin suggest something more serious than mere fatigue." The other damning clipping was a column in *Hits* magazine that included the line "Kurt slam dancing with Mr. Brownstone," which was slang for heroin.

Euphoria was replaced by fear. Suddenly a deadly beast was in our midst. We knew we had to do something about this quickly, but we had to get through the next few days.

Backstage at *SNL*, Kim and Thurston were hanging out in the greenroom that was set aside for guests of the performers. Thurston recalls, "Courtney really wanted to talk, talk, talk, talk and Kurt wasn't hanging out. I felt a little bummed. Like, 'Where's Kurt? How come he's not hanging out with us?' Then Kurt stuck his head in the door and anxiously said to Courtney, 'I need you.' She jumped up and I was thinking, 'I know that kind of communication. They're going to get high.' I felt a little depressed."

However, Kurt displayed a baffling resiliency. He could be out of it one minute and deeply engaged the next. A little later Janet Billig ushered Kim and Thurston into Nirvana's dressing room along with Amy Finnerty from MTV. Thurston said to Kurt, "You should thank Amy," and Kurt asked what he was talking about. Thurston told him how the young exec had put her job on the line pushing to get "Smells Like Teen Spirit" on the air. As if there were nothing else on his mind, Kurt asked everyone but Finnerty to leave for a minute so he could talk to her privately. He had not understood that his young friend actually had influence over the programming. "He jokingly said he thought I'd been in charge of putting Post-its on the bulletin board, and he thanked me. He was so sweet."

SNL was being hosted by Rob Morrow that week. Janet was "so fucking excited" about Nirvana's being on SNL and she says the band was too, but they played it cool with me. After rehearsal, there was a spirited discussion about what T-shirts they should wear for the broadcast. They remained determined to use their newfound visibility to promote far more obscure bands. Kurt wore a handmade Flipper T-shirt, Krist's featured L7, and Dave's the Melvins.

While I was wandering around the sprawling group of rooms at NBC given over to SNL, cast member Victoria Jackson asked me if I worked with the band and explained that she was friends with Weird Al Yankovic, who wanted to know if he could talk to Kurt about doing a parody of "Smells Like Teen Spirit." (Since Weird Al changes the lyrics for his parodies, he asked for the original writer's permission.) Kurt told me he was up for it. Jackson dialed Weird Al and I put Kurt on the phone with him. Kurt listened, nodded his head, and said, "That sounds great, Al."

A few months later we got advance copies of the video for "Smells Like Nirvana" and when I didn't hear from Kurt for a couple of days I was worried that he was pissed at me for facilitating it. I had initially felt it was an honor of sorts to be on a list of superstars that Weird Al had made fun of, but I didn't know how Kurt would react to actually seeing a caricature of himself on MTV, and I was a little unnerved by the comic premise that also made fun of Nirvana's fans. Finally I asked Kurt what he thought of the video and to my relief he answered, "I laughed my ass off," adding that it was a sign that the band had really made it. However, a few months later when the Weird Al album came out with a promotional image of himself naked in the water chasing a donut on a fishhook, Kurt told a writer for *Flipside* that he thought Weird Al had taken advantage of Nirvana to market himself beyond what Kurt had expected. Characteristically, though, he never gave me any shit about it.

The band, tight after months of touring, nailed "Smells Like Teen Spirit" and "Territorial Pissings." The image of Kurt on that first *SNL* appearance with his long hair dyed red, wearing a blue cardigan over that homemade Flipper T-shirt and torn jeans, is one of the most iconic of his career. Over the end credits the band made an additional cultural statement. Kurt and Krist kissed each other on the mouth, which they gleefully told everybody afterward was a fuck-you to the Aberdeen homophobes they'd had to put up with as teenagers.

My excitement over their successful appearance soon dissipated. Kurt's mother, Wendy, had flown out for the occasion and was jazzed up after the broadcast, having never been around that kind of show-business glamour. Kurt must have gotten stoned after the broadcast because he was struggling to keep his eyes open and he and Courtney couldn't wait to get back to the hotel. Any lingering doubts I had about the severity of his heroin problem vanished. "Don't you want to come to the party, Kurt?" his mother asked plaintively. (*SNL*'s after-show parties were famously star-studded.) Kurt responded in a mournful tone, "No, you just go, Mom."

The next day I called Aerosmith's manager Tim Collins for advice. Collins was sober himself and had successfully shepherded a couple of band members into twelve-step programs and subsequently presided over an extraordinary rebirth of Aerosmith's career. He connected me with a counselor named Bob Timmins, who had helped some members of the band get clean, and we made plans for an intervention in L.A. when Kurt and Courtney got home.

Two days after *SNL*, the band was at MTV's studios in New York to tape live versions of several songs. In the four months since MTV had first played the "Smells Like Teen Spirit" video, Nirvana had become one of the channel's biggest stars. MTV had pushed hard to get the band into their studio to give them more content, and Kurt didn't want to say no to them.

Right after they performed nine songs from *Nevermind*, one of the MTV editors was showing Kurt various camera angles. He was clearly high again and I cringed inwardly, counting the days till we'd all get back to the West Coast. Kurt sat on a couch in front of a TV monitor, literally nodding off, but whenever appropriate he lifted up his head and gave clear direction on when to cut to a shot of the drums, when to use a close-up of his singing, when to go to a long shot, and so forth, and the editor accepted every one of his suggestions. As scared and depressed as I was by the shape Kurt was in, I was equally dazzled by the intelligent precision of his decisions and the performance he had just given. Janet remembers it the same way: "He was so locked in."

One of the many blessings of my life is that the few times I shot heroin as a teenager, I didn't particularly enjoy the effect. If I had liked it, I'm sure I would have become a junkie, since at that time in my life I viewed doing drugs as some sort of a statement. The drug that gave me an intoxicating rush and drove all my worries away was crystal meth, but when I found myself spending five nights in Alameda County Juvenile Hall shortly before my eighteenth birthday, I was "scared straight," as the saying goes. I never wanted to put myself in that position again. I didn't drink or do any kind of drugs for years afterward.

In the early eighties the famed Hollywood club the Whisky a Go Go was known to name drinks after various rock-and-roll figures, including the "Danny Goldberg": "Club soda and lime—the executive look for teetotalers." I never attributed my sobriety to any kind of virtue on my part. I knew it was something akin to luck that I didn't have the brain chemistry of an addict or an alcoholic.

Over the years I'd had plenty of exposure to people who were not so fortunate, many of them artists, who went into a downward spiral of self-destruction, some with heroin, others with cocaine or booze or a combination of them. Many of them, including some of my closest friends, transformed their lives for the better in twelve-step programs such as Alcoholics Anonymous or Narcotics Anonymous. Unfortunately, despite numerous attempts by many friends and people who worked with him to encourage him to go down that path, Kurt would never feel that a twelve-step program was for him.

As this book is being written, the news media is filled with reports of a new "opioid crisis," but in the realm of the arts, and especially among musicians, there has been a heroin crisis for as long as anyone alive can remember. There are various theories about why the rate of drug abuse is so high among artists and performers. One factor is that much of a performer's professional life revolves around late nights in clubs and concert halls, at which there is no "boss" like a conventional employer. An artist who is on the road endures long, boring drives and an uneven sleep schedule, and there are emotionally disruptive contrasts between the euphoria of performing a good show and the self-hatred that comes with a bad one, and between soaking up the adoration of an applauding crowd and the loneliness of a hotel room. There is also a theory that the sensitivity that foments creativity is somehow aligned with the aspects of the brain that are prone to an excessive desire for painkillers.

Whatever the causes, the history is clear. Billie Holiday, Chet Baker, Hank Williams, John Coltrane, Charlie Parker, Jimi Hendrix, Janis Joplin, Gregg Allman, Jerry Garcia, Eric Clapton, and Keith Richards are just a small fraction of the great musical artists who were heroin users. In the Velvet Underground song "Heroin," Lou Reed tried to describe the attitude of an addict in search of a fix: "I have made / big decision / I'm gonna try to nullify my life . . ." Neil Young contemplating the death of a friend in "The Needle and the Damage Done" lamented, "Every junkie's like a setting sun."

Some say it's the weather and the shorter sunlight hours, but for some reason Seattle has long had a particularly severe heroin problem. In March 1990, as Nirvana's career was starting to blossom in the wake of *Bleach*, Andrew Wood, the singer of the local band Mother Love Bone, which also included future Pearl Jam members Stone Gossard and Jeff Ament, died of an OD.

Kurt also had another reason/excuse, chronic, excruciating stomach pain that doctors were unable to help or diagnose. From the first days when we managed Nirvana, Kurt would periodically complain about it. Janet remembers, "We got so many doctors to examine him and no one could come up with a diagnosis. It definitely wasn't an ulcer." It was tempting to think that it was psychosomatic, but the pain was real to Kurt and heroin did make it temporarily go away.

Krist recalls Kurt having episodes long before the band was successful and he always felt Kurt's diet, which primarily consisted of comfort food like cheap burritos and macaroni and cheese, had something to do with it. "One day he was having horrible stomach pain. He was puking air. I was hanging out with him because I didn't wanna leave him alone. And then he feels better and we go to 7-Eleven to eat, which is a bad place to eat. He gets an ice-cream cone. And I go, 'What the fuck are you eating this ice-cream cone for? No wonder you're sick.'" Krist still shakes his head indignantly with the recollection. "I was mad at *him* but he got mad at *me* for telling him that."

Silva's assistant Peter Rauh has a similar story. In mid-1991 he drove Kurt to Cedars-Sinai hospital to get a tracheal exploration in an attempt to identify what was generating the pain. The procedure was invasive enough that it required going under general anesthetic, which meant Kurt hadn't eaten that day. Afterward, as they were leaving the hospital Kurt asked Rauh to stop at an IHOP. Rauh says, "I couldn't believe how much syrup he poured on his pancakes."

Although both Kurt and Courtney had done heroin earlier in their lives, their level of engagement with the drug was dramatically impacted by the success of *Nevermind*. Once an artist has even a fraction of that kind of fame and commercial success, they feel more empowered, knowing they can always get ahold of cash. As a result, there's never a shortage of dealers worming their way into a star's orbit. I had seen many of these lowlifes hanging around Led Zeppelin when I worked with them in the mid-seventies and their presence nauseated me. I have long felt that one of the worst aspects of heroin is the deadening effect it has on a user's spirit. The specter of death is always close at hand.

A few days after the MTV taping, when Kurt and Courtney were back in Los Angeles, we staged an intervention at Cedars-Sinai. Courtney had just found out that she was pregnant and the pretext to our getting them there was for her and Kurt to meet with an obstetrician. Among those who greeted them instead were me and Rosemary, Janet, Silva, Gersh, and Eric, as well as Bob Timmins and Dr. Michael Horowitz, who specialized in chemical dependency.

Timmins had long hair and wore a cut-off jacket that allowed him to display several tattoos. We chatted while waiting for Kurt and Courtney to arrive, and the counselor immediately name-dropped famous rock musicians he had "helped," an indiscretion that gave me a sinking feeling.

When Kurt and Courtney got there, we all implored them to get off drugs. The conversation quickly turned to Courtney's pregnancy and Horowitz said he felt that in order to deal with the drug problems it was not a good idea to have the baby. "You're not telling me to have an abortion, are you?" Courtney asked incredulously.

Before Horowitz could answer, Timmins pulled Gersh and me aside, walked toward an elevator, and said in a panicky voice, "I have never dealt with a situation like this with a husband and a wife and a pregnancy. I have to get out of here." The elevator arrived, Timmins entered it, and the doors closed. So much for our "counselor." Timmins later had the nerve to send us a bill for $600 for "professional services rendered." We ignored his follow-up requests for settlement of this "debt" but a year and a half later, in October 1993, finally paid him rather than risk a drama in the press.

Gersh and I exchanged a look of shock and returned to the group, where Courtney was still railing at Horowitz and trying to determine whether he was giving an opinion as a therapist or based on medical factors. "Show me in a medical book where it says I can't have a healthy baby!" she screamed. Even as I was desperately hoping that Kurt and Courtney would be serious about getting clean, I was proud of her for questioning the "expert," who, after all, was an addiction specialist, not an obstetrician.

Rosemary suggested that Courtney meet with Dr. Paul Crane, who had delivered our daughter at that very hospital. Besides being an excellent doctor, Crane had a nurturing personality and Kurt and Courtney immediately trusted him. Crane said that since it was so early in the pregnancy, if Courtney would stop heroin immediately and substitute methadone or buprenorphine on a strictly controlled basis, the baby could be weaned off of it right after birth and would be fine. Crane agreed to be her doctor under those conditions, which included regular drug tests in his office. After that, Kurt and Courtney went into rehab.

With Timmins out of the picture, I called Buddy Arnold, whom I had met socially and whom many of my twelve-step friends swore by. Arnold, who looked and spoke like one of my Jewish uncles, was then sixty-six years old. In his mid-twenties, as a jazz saxophonist with the Glenn Miller Orchestra, he said he had "made a conscious decision to be a junkie," and was addicted for decades. Before Buddy got sober in the 1980s, he had accumulated thirty-four narcotics arrests on his rap sheet.

After several years of sobriety Buddy decided to devote the rest of his life to helping other musicians get straight. His colorful past helped give him credibility with artists. In 1991 he started the Musicians' Assistance Program (MAP), which gave Buddy a small infrastructure that increased the number of people he could help. Even though he was several generations older than Kurt, Buddy was palpably different from conventional authority figures. He never name-dropped and had exactly the kind of unpretentious sweetness that got through to Kurt.

In a 1999 *Los Angeles Times* article about Buddy, he said that when Kurt first met him and explained that Courtney was pregnant he asked in a childlike tone, "Fathers shouldn't be junkies, should they?"

Kurt got a kick out of Arnold's stories about jazz legends and his old-fashioned Jewish humor. One day Kurt told me, "You know, you're very *hamish*" (a Yiddish word for "down-to-earth"), and then cracked up, explaining that Buddy had told him to say that to me.

After Kurt told him about his stomach pain, Arnold recommended a doctor named Robert Fremont who had a lot of experience dealing with people coming off addictive drugs. Fremont was a tall, barrel-chested guy with short white hair who seemed to be in his late fifties. Kurt immediately took to him as well. "He is a compassionate man," Kurt earnestly enthused to me after his first meeting with Fremont. Just to hear some optimism in Kurt's voice instead of despair meant so much to me. The doctor began a protocol of giving Kurt shots, and for the next several months there was no talk from Kurt about stomach pain.

Fremont wasn't as sentimental as Buddy was about artists like Kurt and Courtney and vented one day to me in an aggravated tone, "They're *meshuganeh*. Thank God they're not Jewish." I initially was under the impression that Fremont was giving Kurt vitamin B_{12} shots, but Fremont insisted that the shots were a "placebo" and that Kurt's stomach felt better because he *thought* the shots were medicinal. In retrospect I suspect that the doctor was bullshitting me. In the extensively researched Cobain biography *Heavier Than Heaven*, author Charles Cross writes that the shots were buprenorphine.

For the rest of the year, while Fremont was treating him, Kurt seemed happy and stable most of the time. Fremont died early in 1993, supposedly of a heart attack, although there were rumors that he had OD'd. Courtney told me that Kurt wept when he heard the news.

After Dr. Fremont died, Kurt started experimenting with various antidepressants that other doctors prescribed for him. One day I told him that when I saw words on street signs I compulsively counted the number of letters and if there was more than one word on the sign I'd multiply those numbers. He said he had similar compulsions and then extolled the virtues of the antianxiety drug Klonopin as a remedy. I never tried it, and over time I saw scant evidence that it or other pharmaceuticals stabilized Kurt the way Dr. Fremont's protocol had.

As soon as he got out of rehab, Kurt played down his drug use in interviews. He would admit that over the years he had done heroin but insisted that he had stopped and that drugs were stupid. Of course, one characteristic many addicts share is lying about using.

Mark Kates reflects, "I think Kurt hated the idea that any kid would think it was cool to shoot heroin because he read that Kurt had done it." Similarly, Rauh reflects on a conversation he had with Kurt en route to the hospital the day he had the stomach scan. Kurt was reading a copy of *NME* in the car and came across an interview with Krist in which the bass player had said that he thought marijuana should be legalized: "Kurt looked over to me and said he didn't think that Krist should be saying things like that in the press because kids read those magazines." Rauh was amused by the apparent contradiction but such compartmentalization was a constant with Kurt. No matter what else was happening in his life, a part of his mind was always thinking about the vision he wanted to project to the world.

NINE

BE CAREFUL WHAT YOU WISH FOR

Kurt publicly insisted that *Nevermind*'s breakthrough was as big a surprise to him as it was to everybody else. However, while some of the by-products of fame were bewildering for him personally (he said he wished that there was a "Rock Star 101" course he could have taken), it often felt to me as if Kurt had planned the next several moves for Nirvana with as much rigor as he had rehearsed the music. While the personal side of Kurt was dealing with the physical and emotional task of getting clean (which was a struggle) and Courtney's pregnancy (which he was genuinely excited about), the artistic side of his brain was thinking incessantly about his role in both the punk rock culture and on the larger canvas that *Nevermind* had so quickly created. He was determined to walk the line between the punk and mainstream cultures in a way that no one else had ever done.

On one level all three guys in the band were overwhelmed.

Dave has said that he got panic attacks, and at six foot seven, Krist was the most publicly noticeable. Krist says of the time soon after the "Smells Like Teen Spirit" video went on MTV, "I was getting recognized everywhere I went. I started having dreams in which I'd be naked, classic anxiety dreams." Krist acknowledges that he was psyched when Tom Hamilton, his counterpart in Aerosmith, praised his bass lines, but in the wake of sudden stardom he told Spanish journalist Rafa Cervera, "We're stressed; it's made us all anxious. We're just working-class guys and we're not suddenly going to start loving the people who ignored us before all this happened. Fuck that. We're not going to become materialistic and screwed up."

Krist now reflects, "We came from counterculture. We got our music not from mainstream press but from fanzines. We felt like outsiders and all of a sudden we're the number one band in the world." Nirvana was, Krist says, determined "to show [they] weren't sellouts but were promoting the revolution."

Kurt's role in the band put an additional focus on him, according to Krist: "He was the head dude, the vocalist and songwriter." Some of the mainstream press propagated the absurd but predictable notion that Kurt was some kind of a spokesman for his generation. Even among fans who shrugged off that kind of cliché, many looked to him for more than music. This pressure was as weird for Kurt as it had been for Dylan or Lennon or Bowie. At certain times, Kurt didn't like being recognized publicly, and he occasionally took to wearing fake glasses and other tricks to change his look.

Montgomery reminded me, "Every artist wants to be free and success interferes with that. Even though Geffen Records and Gold Mountain were committed to giving the band complete control of their career and trying to keep that atmosphere of freedom, they couldn't stop the pressure the band put on themselves when MTV or *Rolling Stone* wanted things from them."

However in many important ways, Kurt was unchanged by fame. He never hung out with movie stars or other celebrities. He didn't change the way he dressed or develop expensive habits (except for drugs when he slid back into them). Even on future tours when the band could afford better catering, Krist recalls, "it was too fancy for Kurt. He liked macaroni and cheese or a bologna sandwich."

Krist also reminded me of how contradictory Kurt could be about success. "When we were shopping record labels, we met with the head of Columbia Records, Donny Ienner." Ienner had had an illustrious career, but his background was pop radio promotion and his intense, hard-charging persona epitomized the mainstream record business.

Nonetheless, Kurt was intrigued and told the executive, "We want to be the biggest band in the world; we want you to buy billboards promoting our band," and he wasn't kidding. Krist laughs and then, with a touch of sarcasm in his voice, adds, "So then we become the biggest band in the world and then he's like, 'Oh, I don't want this.'"

The role that I played in Kurt's career required that I see the side of him that *did* want it. One afternoon Kurt called me anxiously and said, "I've been watching MTV and they played Pearl Jam videos three times and only played ours once. Is someone mad at us?" After *Nevermind* exploded, Kurt often told people that he was not paying attention to chart positions or sales figures. However, near the end of 1991 in a phone interview Australian writer Robyn Doreian asked Kurt "How do you feel about selling six hundred thousand copies of *Nevermind* in the United

States alone?" and Kurt corrected him, "Umm. We've sold one point four million in America."

After the album came out, a decision had to be made about which single would be released after "Smells Like Teen Spirit" had run its course. Silva, Gersh, the band, and I met at Jerry's Deli in Van Nuys to discuss the matter. We had always assumed that "Come as You Are" had the kind of chorus and melody that would work for pop radio, but Kurt was concerned that the guitar riff was too similar to the one in Killing Joke's song "Eighties." After toying with the notion of "In Bloom" as the follow-up (the melody for the chorus really stuck in my head), we decided to stick with the original idea. I told Kurt that I couldn't imagine Killing Joke would actually sue Nirvana for plagiarism, and for-tunately I was right. (In 2003 Dave Grohl played drums on a new Killing Joke album, perhaps as a partial payback.)

The choice for the next single having been made, Kurt spent the rest of the lunch trying to convince Gersh to sign Mudhoney. "They're the best band in Seattle," Kurt insisted. Gersh demurred, "They don't have the songs." It drove Kurt crazy that a band he admired didn't have a major record deal, but not long afterward Warner Bros. signed Mudhoney, so that was one less thing for Kurt to worry about.

Kurt was always thinking about all aspects of the band's pre-sentation. While we were eating that day, he was scribbling on a napkin and then handed it to me saying, "This is the design for the next T-shirt." For the sleeve art for the single of "Come as You Are," Kurt told Geffen's art director Robert Fisher to use "some-thing with microscopic images and the color purple" and then let him run with it. For the video Kurt was much more hands-on. Because of the conflict over the edit of "Smells Like Teen Spirit," he didn't want to use Sam Bayer again, so he chose Kevin Kerslake, who had directed several Sonic Youth videos. (Courtney also recommended him, having had a good experience with Kerslake on the video for "Garbadge Man" on Hole's first album.)

When the "Smells Like Teen Spirit" video was shot, Nirvana was a new band. Now they were superstars, so both the expectations and the available budget were higher. Robin Sloane gave Kurt carte blanche. "All the videos were Kurt's ideas," she says, "and then he worked out the details with the directors." Kurt didn't want another "story" video. He envisioned something much more impressionistic with lots of purples and blues in the frame. The first shot of the video is a pistol floating in space.

For the portions that showed Nirvana performing, Kurt wanted to make a comment on the new reality of superstardom and insisted that their faces be blurred by shooting the band through a stream of water. It seemed to me that the way Kurt's face goes in and out of focus in the video was also a metaphor for his personality. Sometimes I felt as close to him as a brother and other times he seemed a galaxy removed, barely perceptible.

The visuals were not all abstract, though. Kurt made sure that some of the images were clear enough that fans could see the handmade Flipper T-shirt he had first displayed on the SNL broadcast. "Come as You Are" was an aesthetic contrast to the more linear "Smells Like Teen Spirit" video, but it was also commercially savvy. In case any MTV viewer was too stoned or stupid to realize it was Nirvana, there was a brief reenactment of a baby underwater reaching for a dollar bill on a fishhook.

This was around the same time that Kurt and Courtney had moved into the Spaulding Drive apartment. My main memory of the place was the volume of paintings and drawings Kurt had produced the first few weeks they were there. He was always creating something. Eric Erlandson was living in Seattle and flying back every week. He says, "When it would get out of control Courtney would ask me to come. They were living like in a little cave. Kurt was freaked at being recognized when he walked around Hollywood, so he'd want me to go with him when we went shopping."

In the car on these excursions Kurt was always lecturing Eric about fastening his seat belt. "He was conservative in that way," Eric says, "wanting to be physically safe, which I thought was pretty funny considering that at shows he would throw himself off of balconies into the crowd."

His anxiety about safety intensified on April 29, 1992, when the Los Angeles police officers who had been captured on videotape beating up Rodney King were acquitted of criminal charges. Riots started that afternoon and Eric recalls, "Kurt and I drove to several stores because he wanted to get supplies in case the city shut down. A lot of shelves were already getting cleaned out but we found some cigarettes, water, and soup. There was looting on Melrose Ave., very close to Kurt and Courtney's apartment. Kurt was pretty freaked. I stayed with them till the middle of the night watching CNN, watching buildings burn."

Despite such distractions, Kurt always returned his attention to his artistic mission. Even though Kurt had often bitterly complained about how *Rolling Stone* ignored most of the punk culture, he always read it. "He thought it had real gravitas," Janet says. After an initial hesitance to talk to the magazine, it didn't take long for Kurt to reverse course and cooperate for a cover story.

Because of the lead time required to produce a cover, the photo shoot was scheduled ahead of the interview. Nirvana was on tour in Australia and Kurt called me from the road with anguished second thoughts. He rehashed his complaints about how *Rolling Stone* had treated the bands he loved over the last few years. I told him it was fine not to take a photo for them. After a pause he asked, "Will we still be on the cover if we don't take a new photo?" He was vainly hoping *Rolling Stone* would use one of the PR shots the band had taken when the album was being released. I told him there was no chance that *Rolling Stone* would put a record company photo on the cover but that it wasn't a big deal either way. They had a number one album without being on the cover of *Rolling Stone*.

The next day, without telling me, Kurt reversed course again and took the photo standing next to Krist and Dave while wearing a T-shirt on which he'd written, "Corporate Magazines Still Suck." At first I thought it was pretty silly to insult the magazine while at the same time posing for its cover, but as usual Kurt was right. *Rolling Stone* loved it and that photo added to his legend in the same way the *Headbangers Ball* appearance had.

Rolling Stone assigned Michael Azerrad to interview him, correctly assuming that Kurt would respect the writer's track record of covering punk bands. The interview was at Kurt and Courtney's apartment. Azerrad had no idea what kind of a scene he would be walking into: "I'd never met a drug addict, and he was someone who smashed guitars onstage and had badmouthed *Rolling Stone* in the past. What if things got weird?" When Courtney opened the door she smiled and warmly said, "Welcome. Would you like some grapes?" holding out a plate of them.

Azerrad followed her down a hallway in the apartment, which in his mind kept elongating because he was so nervous. Kurt was lying in bed. His feet were sticking out under the bedspread and Azerrad could see that he'd painted his toenails. Kurt looked up and said, "Oh. Hi," and Azerrad says, "In that second I realized—I *know* this guy, and I was also instantly familiar to him." Kurt liked that the writer was wearing a Buzzcocks T-shirt, but more importantly, Azerrad remembers, "We had all sorts of things in common. Our parents had been divorced. We were both physically small and had been bullied. We had loved the same Arlo Guthrie song as kids, the one where he sings, 'I don't want a pickle, I just want to ride on my motorcycle.'"

Kurt told me afterward that he saw Azerrad not as a *Rolling Stone* guy but as a kindred spirit, and he was happy with the article itself. Among other things he used it as a forum to say he was no longer shooting heroin and that he thought drugs were stupid. However, he also exacerbated a feud with the other giant Seattle band of the moment. Azerrad wrote, "His favorite target is Pearl Jam, also from Seattle, which he accused of 'corporate, alternative and cock-rock fusion.'" In response Jeff Ament of Pearl Jam claimed that Kurt hardly said hello to him on the dates the two bands did with the Chili Peppers: "I don't know what I did to him; if he has a personal vendetta against us, he should come to us. To have that sort of pent-up frustration, the guy obviously must have some really deep insecurities about himself. Does he think we're riding his bandwagon? We could turn around and say that Nirvana put out records on money we made for Sub Pop when we were in Green River—if we were that stupid about it."

Given how little money was spent recording *Bleach*, Ament's last remark didn't make much sense, and Jennie Boddy says it was actually Mudhoney's sales that kept Sub Pop going pre-*Bleach*. Kurt's usual impulse was to be supportive of other artists, but he often got competitive with Pearl Jam. Although Nirvana became famous first, Pearl Jam soon became their commercial equal, and they were also politically aware, committed to the same kind of countercultural ethos, and equally well liked in Seattle's indie community. Kurt was jealous that the critics didn't seem to hold them to the same punk rock standard he felt he had to live up to, and that tabloids didn't obsessively cover Eddie Vedder's personal life. I believed, then and now, that Kurt's work had a particular kind of emotional depth that no other rock star equaled, but I cringed when I read Kurt's public diss of Pearl Jam. It rarely looks good when one artist disparages another, and more to the point, the things the two bands had in common were far more significant than any minor differences between them.

While coping with his newfound fame on a personal level, Kurt continued to want to use it to support the indie world. He kept in touch with Corey Rusk, who owned Touch and Go Records. Without telling me, Silva, or anyone at Geffen, he agreed to give the Chicago indie label a new Nirvana recording and release the song "Oh, the Guilt" on one side of a single, the flip side of which was a new track by the Jesus Lizard, a band Kurt loved. Not surprisingly, Touch and Go got resistance from the Geffen business affairs people, who were blindsided by the request to let one of their most successful artists record for another label. When Rusk complained to him, Kurt asked me to fix it and I called Gersh, who convinced Geffen's lawyers to withdraw their objection provided the song was not promoted to commercial radio stations or used on any compilations or other albums.

With Geffen's ground rules for such one-offs now clear, Nirvana also contributed a cover of "Return of the Rat," originally recorded by the influential Portland punk band Wipers. It was for a box set of seven-inch singles put out by Portland indie label Tim Kerr Records featuring various artists (including Hole) doing Wipers songs. The same label recorded a spoken-word track of William Burroughs reading a poetic rant called "The 'Priest' They Called Him." Kurt, who idolized the legendary beatnik, overdubbed guitar music onto the record, which was released as a single, and was thrilled to meet Burroughs briefly in Kansas the following year while Nirvana was on tour.

Kurt also contributed a Nirvana track called "Beeswax" for inclusion in a compilation album for Slim Moon's Olympia label Kill Rock Stars. And while these gestures of support to the indie world didn't completely eliminate a Nirvana backlash among the kinds of writers Jello Biafra referred to as "punk fundamentalists," they kept such recriminations to a minimum. More to the point, Kurt liked being part of these projects.

The success of *Nevermind* had huge reverberations for the Seattle music community. "Smells Like Teen Spirit" was the song that made commercial radio stations and MTV realize there was a much bigger audience for "alternative rock" than programmers had realized, and they started giving exposure to grunge artists they had ignored in previous years. Pearl Jam's debut album, *Ten*, was actually released a month before *Nevermind*, but its commercial explosion came several months afterward, peaking the following year, in late 1992. Soundgarden had their first major-label album, *Louder Than Love*, on A&M Records in 1989, but it never made it into the top hundred. However, the follow-up, *Badmotorfinger*, which came out on the same day as *Nevermind*, went platinum within a year. Similarly, Alice in Chains had released their first album in the summer of 1990, but their breakthrough album, *Dirt*, came out in September 1992, a year after *Nevermind*.

Members of the mainstream media and culture who had previously exhibited little or no interest in the artistic roots of these artists glommed on to the notion of a "Seattle sound" and aesthetic. Soon there were "grunge" fashion lines and the *New York Times* even published a "grunge lexicon," a lot of which was invented on the spot by people at Sub Pop, making the article the source of well-deserved ridicule in the Seattle rock community.

The notion of a "Seattle sound" continued to irritate Kurt, who saw artists as individuals, and he mocked the increasingly prevalent cliché. He told a European journalist, "They say we put Seattle on the map. What map?" Janet Billig Rich says, "I hated it when writers would lump in Nirvana with those other bands. The people *in* those bands all knew how special Kurt was but a lot of the press was in love with the idea of a trend." Jennie Boddy says that even in her circles in Seattle there was a recognition that there was a fundamental distinction between Nirvana and other bands. She says that it was a bit "cheapening" to glibly compare them to Alice in Chains, Soundgarden, or Pearl Jam. In my biased eyes, Kurt was not part of Seattle's narrative; Seattle was part of Kurt's.

However irked Kurt was by the media meme about Seattle, he respected and liked many of the musicians in those other bands as individuals and remained attached to people in Seattle who had befriended him before he was famous. Boddy recalls, "He was very genuine no matter what. Long after *Nevermind*, he would come over to get his hair cut at our home. He wasn't going to a fancy salon."

In February 1992, I accepted a job offer from Doug Morris, who was the cochairman of Atlantic Records and someone I'd worked with on several projects over the prior decade. I would be the senior VP of the label in charge of A & R on the West Coast, and as a sweetener they bought my half of Gold Mountain. There were rumors that Doug might soon be promoted to a higher corporate job, and I thought I could move up; indeed, I would be promoted to president in the fall of the following year.

David Geffen asked why I was walking away from management, saying, "You've just hit the jackpot." But I had a sense of foreboding about the fragility of Nirvana in light of Kurt's struggles with drugs, and I was exhausted by the pressure of running a small business.

A condition of my Atlantic deal was that while I'd be giving up the responsibility of running a management company and compensation from it, I'd still be available to serve as an unpaid comanager for Nirvana. This sort of arrangement with an executive was not unique at record companies. Just a few years earlier when Irving Azoff left management to run MCA Records he had maintained his relationship with the Eagles.

Kurt and I spoke as often as before and there continued to be certain personal matters that he wanted me to handle. Although it sounds weird in retrospect, I was working out of a different office but I played essentially the same role for him I had previously. My boss at Atlantic was fine with it. After all, my affiliation with Nirvana was one of the main reasons they hired me, and on my end my connection to Kurt had long ago evolved into something separate and apart from a conventional business relationship. Around the same time, Kurt retained Rosemary as his lawyer too, a connection that would last until his death. Hole, however, left Gold Mountain when I left and was subsequently managed by Peter Mensch and Cliff Burnstein of Q Prime, the company that also managed Metallica.

Shortly after I started at Atlantic, Kurt called me to say that from now on he wanted all the songwriting royalties on songs he wrote, which comprised the vast majority of the material that Nirvana recorded. Up until that point the songwriting income had been split evenly among the band members, a common arrangement for new groups who typically made little or no artist royalties from album sales because recording costs and some marketing costs were recoupable, while travel and crew expenses often ate up most of the money made on early tours. Songwriting money was paid "from record one," meaning that every album sale generated around a dollar of income, which was divided between the songwriter and the publisher, and there was another stream of money for songwriters from radio airplay. For the average indie band, the songwriting money comprised the lion's share of total income that actually got to the artist.

Now that Nirvana was big enough for members of the band to make a lot of money in other ways, Kurt wanted the royalties on his songs for himself. This sort of thing can drive nonwriters in rock bands crazy. There is a thin line between being a *musician* in a band and being a writer. Bass parts and drum beats are vital to any record, and Krist and Dave "wrote" their own parts. However, the counterargument is that such playing is what a musician does as an *artist*. The traditional definition of "songwriting" is "the authorship of the lyrics and the melody," and Kurt usually did those things by himself.

After talking to me, Kurt also called Rosemary, who would be the one to draft the paperwork, and the next day Kurt came to her office "by himself to make it clear that this was something that really mattered to him."

I had great trepidation about calling Krist and Dave to broach the subject since many rock bands had become paralyzed by or even broken up over this issue, but they both initially seemed cool with the notion although I heard later from others that this change in economics took a toll on the band's camaraderie over time.

While the copyright assignment was being drafted, Kurt asked me to write a memo to the three band members showing that the other guys would still make plenty of money if they agreed to Kurt's proposal. Based on assumptions I made at that point, under the proposed new arrangement Kurt's income before taxes or commissions would be $8,052,000, and Krist's and Dave's $5,050,000 each. As things turned out, *Nevermind* made more money than I'd projected, they toured less, and the follow-up album was delayed until 1993, but the bottom line over the next year was pretty close to this estimate.

Courtney remembers that at the end of the process "Krist and Dave were pissed," and she suggested that Kurt let them retain cowriter credit and ownership on the most valuable copyright, "Smells Like Teen Spirit," a compromise that dissipated a lot of tension. The whole process, which might have been a night-marish experience with a different group of musicians, gener-ated only minor stress. Once the three of them resolved the only intraband negotiation they would ever have, Rosemary became the lawyer for the band as well.

Krist and Dave had dealt with four huge changes in a very short period of time: massive success, the presence of Courtney, Kurt's heroin addiction, and the change in the way songwriting income was divided up. While I was now closer to Kurt and Courtney, I became more distant with Krist, Dave, and Silva. Over the years Krist and I stayed connected through our shared political activism, but other than my repeating a few stories about Led Zeppelin drummer John Bonham, it seemed like Dave and I didn't have much to talk about. In the years since Kurt's death, Dave's post-Nirvana career in the Foo Fighters has been ex-traordinary and he has conducted himself with a decency that is consistent with the ethos that Nirvana embodied. I often joke that if I had known how talented he was, I would have spent more time with him, as Silva did. One person who *did* know that Dave was more than just a great drummer was Kurt, who told me early in the *Nevermind* cycle, "I hear Dave doing harmonies every night and he is a much better singer than you might think." Kurt's tone had a touch of envy to it, as if he were looking over his shoulder in more ways than one.

When I'd written that memo to Nirvana, it was less than six months after *Nevermind* had been released and they hadn't actu-ally *received* much money from "superstardom" yet. Silva and I knew that the band was starting to resent the disparity between their fame and their bank accounts. The way to remedy this in the short term was to make a merchandising deal. Sales of T-shirts and other branded items were an increasingly big share of what artists made on the road, and there were several companies who bid for these rights, anticipating that future tours (the primary place where such merch was sold) would be in front of much bigger audiences than the band played for up until then.

Silva sketched out a deal with a merch company called Giant. It was owned by Irving Azoff, who, after leaving MCA, created both a new label and the merch company. Giant was willing to pay a $2 million advance, and we were expecting to have the band sign the agreement shortly when I got a call from an agitated David Geffen. David and Azoff had a roller-coaster relationship that was going through a down period. He said that if the band wanted cash, he'd have the label advance the same amount of money and then we could make a merch deal with another company. This way Nirvana would come out significantly ahead in terms of short-term cash, receiving both a record advance, which Geffen wasn't legally obligated to give them, *and* a merch advance.

Silva was annoyed at the idea of torpedoing a deal he'd almost closed, but he agreed to hold off till we met with David the next day. It didn't take long to change Silva's mind. In addition to David's charisma, what he was offering was better for the band. Peter Rauh, Silva's right-hand man at the time, remembers, "After you guys got back from the meeting, John said I had to stay late until an envelope came from Geffen, and around eight o'clock a messenger brought an envelope that had a check for $2 million made out to the Nirvana partnership."

MTV wanted more of Nirvana, which was, despite his mixed feelings about fame, the way Kurt liked it. He asked Kerslake to do the third and fourth videos for songs on *Nevermind*. For "In Bloom" he wanted a humorous contrast to the darkness of the first two videos and imagined Nirvana as a mid-sixties rock band performing on a network program like *The Ed Sullivan Show*, where they would be introduced by a corny, old-school emcee. This skewering of rock-and-roll clichés even while enjoying them was a return to form for Nirvana. The band wore matching striped suits. Kerslake found the kinds of cameras that had actually been used for old TV shows, and the result had the feeling of vintage black-and-white footage. It was the easiest video to shoot, taking only a few hours, and that included a couple of run-throughs where the three band members all wore dresses that Courtney had borrowed. The final version cut between the parody and the burlesque.

For "Lithium," the final track released from the album, Kurt wanted a composite of live performances. Most of the footage in that video was from the Halloween show that had been filmed in Seattle. However, Kurt asked me to get him a short clip from *1991: The Year Punk Broke*, which had been completed but not released yet. At roughly ten seconds long, it was comprised of Kurt being carried around the stage on Krist's shoulders.

The film was controlled by Sonic Youth, and to my surprise, Kim Gordon initially resisted. She was in love with the shot and thought its inclusion in a music video would diminish its impact in their movie. She came by my office at Atlantic to make her case and it was terrible to see her in anguish over this. Sonic Youth had meant a lot to both Nirvana and me. However, my loyalty was to Kurt and I knew that he was fixated on getting the footage. I pointedly reminded Kim that Nirvana had agreed to waive any payment for their performances of five songs (including "Smells Like Teen Spirit") in the movie, something that would have cost any other filmmaker hundreds of thousands of dollars at this point. She reluctantly agreed to let Nirvana use the clip Kurt coveted, but she was pissed at feeling pressured, especially by someone who until recently had been one of her managers, and, I suspect, a bit overwhelmed by the speed of the role reversal between the two bands.

In June, Nirvana was in Europe again. Janet joined them,

and it is not one of her best memories. Kurt and Courtney were both "managing" their addiction with pharmaceuticals, and the laws varied from country to country. "I was in Paris and it was the worst. Kurt was so fucked up and depressed and he wouldn't throw away the drugs. I told him that a doctor was meeting him in Stockholm and that he could not get on a plane with drugs. We had an insane fight with Courtney chasing me down the street. He would only throw out the drugs right before they boarded the plane." Courtney went back to Los Angeles shortly thereafter.

There were a few great moments during the tour, such as the Danish Roskilde Festival, where the band put on one of their most memorable performances, and in Belfast, when Kurt dove into the audience and took a punch from a bouncer to protect a fan. However, the following day Kurt collapsed and had to be taken to a hospital. Janet told the press it was due to an ulcer (we never knew how to describe his stomach pain), but Kurt later admitted to Azerrad that it was because he'd forgotten to take one of the methadone pills he'd been using to mitigate his addiction.

On July 3, seven months into her pregnancy, Courtney started having contractions. The last two European dates, which would have been in Spain, were canceled so that Kurt could be with her. Within weeks, a huge new crisis disrupted our world.

TEN

VANITY FAIR

In "Territorial Pissings" Kurt warns, "Just because you're paranoid / Don't mean they're not after you." Courtney probably should have kept this in mind when she decided to talk to Lynn Hirschberg for a feature about her in *Vanity Fair*.

Hirschberg usually wrote about celebrities a cultural universe removed from punk rock, but Courtney had no reason to assume that her entry into mainstream media wouldn't be another triumph. For the previous couple of years, she had been on a roll. She had traveled an extraordinary distance, from living on the margins of society and eking out a living as a stripper to signing to Caroline, securing Kim Gordon as her producer, being warmly embraced by the rock press, falling in love and marrying Kurt, and getting signed to DGC/Geffen. By the alchemy of her intelligence, talent, persistence, Buddhist chanting, and good timing, she seemed to have cracked the code for the life she wanted.

Long magazine profiles are months in the making. Late in the process Hirschberg called me and I gave her a few quotes, but I was careful in choosing my words. Courtney, alas, was not. I had a wave of anxiety one day when I saw her animatedly chatting with Hirschberg, turning the establishment journalist on to a Riot Grrrl fanzine. Rosemary laments, "Lynn seduced her, obviously. Courtney thought that she had charmed her. She thought that Lynn was eating out of her hand and that it was going to be a great article."

The piece was published in mid-August. An advance copy circulated by fax a week before it hit the newsstands and it was devastating. In a few passages, the piece captured Courtney's wit, but overall Hirschberg's polished writing was curdled by condescension and contempt. She barely acknowledged that Kurt and Courtney were both visionary artists but instead depicted them as amoral and decadent people with the depth of cartoon characters. In pursuit of her character assassination, Hirschberg relied predominantly on unattributed "quotes" from "friends" and "people in the business." I didn't doubt that Hirschberg had found some Courtney haters to give her their opinions, but that didn't mean it was intellectually honest to take such gossip at face value.

What made the Hirschberg piece a nightmare rather than a mere PR mistake was a portion that said that several un-named sources claimed that Courtney was doing heroin even after she found out she was pregnant, and contained a quote from Courtney in which she said that she did heroin "for a couple of months" after *Saturday Night Live.*

Courtney denied saying it. She always insisted that she stopped right after the intervention—only a few days after both *SNL* and finding out that she was pregnant—and that she followed Dr. Crane's instructions to protect the fetus. This scenario might not have been all that attractive to some *Vanity Fair* readers, but there was a huge moral difference between shooting dope before she knew she was with child and having continued to do so afterward. I believed Courtney and I was positive that Dr. Crane wouldn't have been involved with a prospective mother who was not mindful of the health of her baby, and indeed Frances Bean Cobain was healthy when she was born.

We knew immediately that the publication of this piece was a crisis that could have legal ramifications for them as parents. When we got the first fax of the article Courtney was already in Cedars-Sinai because she was days away from delivering and Dr. Crane wanted to be extra careful. As a precautionary measure to make sure no one would try to take the baby away from her, she briefly considered giving birth somewhere else. We got a hastily written legal opinion dated August 13 (the day after we first saw the article) from a lawyer named Michael Levanas, who gave two other options. Someone had told Courtney that Swedish authorities would not make an issue of a healthy baby born with methadone in its system, but given how close she was to giving birth it was risky to fly and the ten-and-a-half-hour plane ride from L.A. to Stockholm was out of the question. Another theoretical possibility was to enter a different local hospital under an assumed name. But Levanas cautioned, "I have been told that Martin Luther King Hospital reports everything and that hospitals like Cedars-Sinai are more discreet in their reporting." So Courtney stayed where she was.

Kurt was there too on another floor. My recollection was that Kurt had gone into rehab again, but Eric corrected me: "I only remember him being upstairs from Courtney at Cedars and struggling with his stomach issues." Whatever the case, once Courtney was about to give birth Kurt left his room to be at her side.

Gold Mountain issued a statement from Kurt and Courtney about the accusation that she knowingly risked the health of her baby. "We unequivocally deny this ... As soon as Courtney found out she was pregnant, she immediately contacted an obstetrician and a doctor specializing in chemical dependency and has been under their care since then and has been assured that she can expect to have a healthy baby."

Rosemary wrote a fierce letter to *Vanity Fair*'s parent company, Condé Nast, asking for an apology and a retraction. She pointed out several factual errors regarding the music business to demonstrate the sloppiness of the journalism (for example, it said I was an executive at Polygram, a company I'd never had any involvement with at that point). Hirschberg had asked if it was true that music executive Clive Davis had offered one million dollars for Hole; Rosemary and Davis had both denied this, but Hirschberg still wrote it was "reportedly" true. Rosemary argued, "This evidences her smug disregard for the truth which, unfortunately, characterizes her entire article."

Regarding the main issue, Courtney's alleged quote about doing heroin for "months" after *SNL*, Rosemary's letter continued, "This quotation is inaccurate and deliberately misleading. As Ms. Hirschberg knows, Ms. Love described a binge which lasted a couple of days, not a couple of months. This period occurred in early January 1992, shortly after she conceived and before she or her husband knew she was pregnant. This deliberate distortion of Ms. Love's quote combined with Hirschberg's numerous references to vaguely worded worries and concerns of unnamed 'friends,' 'business associates,' and 'industry insiders' suggests that Ms. Love was using heroin after she became aware of her pregnancy, a suggestion that my client unequivocally denies. This misrepresentation of my client is viscious and irresponsible."

Hirschberg's article also contended that Courtney was responsible for Kurt's drug problem, again using unnamed sources ("many people believe she introduced Cobain to heroin . . . reportedly, Kurt didn't do much more than drink until he met Courtney"). I am still sometimes asked, even by people who knew Kurt pretty well, if I thought that Courtney turned him on to heroin. Definitely not. Kurt always said that he had tried it repeatedly when he was younger, and a number of his old friends concur. "Negative Creep," the opening track on *Bleach*, written long before they met, includes the line "I'm a negative creep and I'm stoned." As Krist notes, "Kurt loved heroin. He loved the way it made him feel." Rosemary's letter to Condé Nast claimed that Hirschberg "had been told by three separate sources, all of whom spoke for attribution, that Mr. Cobain had used heroin before his involvement with Ms. Love. Mr. Cobain himself acknowledged this in an interview in *Rolling Stone* with Michael Azerrad published on April 16, 1992."

Overall, Kurt was mortified by the way he was portrayed. While touring, he had often used Simon Ritchie, Sid Vicious's real name, as a pseudonym in hotels, but he did so as an ironic commentary on his image. He knew he was a million times more talented than the Sex Pistols' bass player and he deeply resented being reduced to a punk-trash stereotype. As Krist says, "Kurt hated to be embarrassed. He *hated* it." As expected, Hirschberg stood by the piece and no apology from *Vanity Fair* was forthcoming. Libel litigation was prohibitively expensive and very hard to win when it involved people as famous as Kurt and Courtney, so the idea of suing Condé Nast was dropped.

Meanwhile we had other media fires to put out. While there was nothing we could do about a couple of ghoulish pieces in supermarket tabloids that inaccurately suggested the baby would be born deformed, when some of the music media reported on the *Vanity Fair* piece uncritically we were able to make them back off quickly.

Janet had called Finnerty asking her to make sure that MTV didn't give the article their seal of approval, but it turned out that her immediate boss didn't have authority over the news department. Before they could get to someone higher in the pecking order who could intervene, Kurt Loder quoted uncritically from the article on *MTV News*. In Kurt's journals there is a rant written at the time about "Emp-TV" but this problem was easy to turn around. MTV had their own reasons for wanting to stay on Nirvana's good side, and going forward they stuck with Kurt and Courtney's version of reality.

A similar reversal was accomplished at KROQ, the biggest rock station in L.A., which regularly played Nirvana and on which a friend of Courtney's claimed he'd heard the article discussed approvingly. Program director Trip Reeb wrote Rosemary a passionate letter claiming that they had found "no evidence" of such heresy, that he was a new father himself, and that the station was available for any messages Kurt and Courtney wanted to convey to their fans.

Kurt and Courtney called many of their friends to dispute the damaging allegations. Among their chief concerns was what David Geffen thought. On August 14, a fax was sent to my office at Atlantic Records for me to forward to the famous boss of Nirvana's label.

> *Dear David Geffen,*
>
> *Hi my name is Kurt Cobain, I'm the lead singer, guitarist and songwriter for the band NIRVANA. Supposedly I've made your company a lot of money.*
>
> *Oh well, it never was a goal of mine to be part of the mainstream corporate world but once I entered it I realized that there are other employees, especially at DGC, who are as honest and sincere about music and have basically the same*

values as I have. I have never met you, I guess cause I never wanted to. Kind of a big boss phobia of mine but something so severely defamatory towards my family has come up in an article in Vanity Fair.

To reassure Geffen that Courtney was responsible, Kurt continued, "She has stopped using and has since been visiting Danny Goldberg's pediatrician on a regular basis." (He meant Dr. Crane.) Kurt didn't make clear exactly what he expected Geffen to do other than to shun Lynn Hirschberg.

Rereading it after a quarter of a century, it seems to me that he sent it so that his label's boss would feel that Kurt was a good human being, not the trash depicted in the article. However, Kurt's feelings about the execs he knew at the label weren't only conjured up in a moment of crisis. Defying the expectations of punk journalists, Kurt had been saying the same things about the label people in interviews for months.

I am struck again by Kurt's complexity. He was feeling extremely hurt and vulnerable to a cascade of negativity and was hoping that a powerful person for whom he had made money would be on his side, at least in the court of industry opinion. (I never thought there was a possibility that Geffen would drop its biggest band because of a sensationalistic story like this, but it didn't hurt for Kurt to be extra careful.) But most of all Courtney was devastated and Kurt wanted his wife to know that he was standing up for her.

I also am reminded of the part of Kurt's brain that was always so sharp, even in the worst of times. He handwrote the letter so Geffen would know it came directly from him and not a handler. He found a way to mention that he and Courtney were supporters of gay rights. He concluded:

*We are capable of displaying a healthy attitude before
our audience and the next record is easily as good as the last
one but I'm so extremely pissed off about the piece of trash
journalism that I'd lay anything on the line for the love of my
wife and daughter.*

Sincerely, Kurt Cobain

David called me, irritated to be drawn into the tawdry problem, and I assured him that we were handling things and that Kurt was just trying to reach out to him, person to person.

Frances Bean Cobain was born on August 18, 1992, six days after the *Vanity Fair* piece became public. Knowing how embattled Courtney was feeling, I asked Eddie Rosenblatt to visit the hospital when he had the chance, and he immediately got up from behind his desk and said, "Let's go right now. I love babies." The hospital was a five-minute drive from the Geffen offices, and it was great that he reacted that quickly, because Courtney was disconsolate and sobbing, with huge tears running down her face. "Don't give me any of your optimistic shit," she yelled at me. "I'll never get over this." But it meant a lot to her that her record company's president was also standing by her.

Meanwhile, someone at Cedars-Sinai sent a copy of the *Vanity Fair* piece to the Los Angeles Department of Public Social Services along with their own note disparaging Courtney. This helped trigger the very thing we'd hoped to avoid. The article was stapled onto the legal letter from the city agency that initiated an investigation into the couple's fitness as parents. Understandably, Kurt and Courtney were both totally freaked by this development. I tried to calm them down with assurances that they had enough resources and friends to avoid the nightmare scenario of losing custody of their daughter, but this was now a legal problem and it was Rosemary who actually had to craft a strategy to get a solution. The first step was to diligently follow the rules of the various city agencies involved.

In such cases parents need to find other family members to take temporary custody until a decision is made. Courtney's mother, Linda Carroll, came to see me in my Atlantic office. Courtney had rarely talked about her, but I gathered that she was a therapist who had been married several times and had other children. She launched into a monologue about how difficult a daughter Courtney had been to raise and suggested that she, the grandmother of Frances, would be able to do a much better job of raising the baby than Kurt and Courtney could and appealed to me to help make that happen. I guess she thought that because I was in my forties and in a conventional office that I would sympathize with her contempt for her daughter.

I was appalled, but I didn't need to tell Courtney about the conversation because by the time I saw them that night, Kurt and Courtney had already ruled out having any grandparents involved. This was, I felt, a remarkable reflection of how fucked up their own childhoods had been. They felt the least risky choice was Courtney's half sister Jaime Manelli (Linda Carroll was also her mother).

Jaime was going to college in Oregon and needed money and Courtney correctly assumed she would be cooperative. Although she and Courtney had never been particularly close, Jaime accepted an offer of five thousand dollars to come to Los Angeles and act as guardian for the time we anticipated it would take to get through the process. We got her a temporary apartment close to Kurt and Courtney and Jaime had official custody, attending the requisite meetings with the authorities but also ensuring that Frances spent much of her time with her parents. Kurt and Courtney didn't get legal custody until the following March and we paid Jaime several thousand dollars more, which was appropriate because of the time she had to take away from her studies.

The hospital sent out a press release on August 25. "Frances Bean Cobain, child of Courtney Love and Kurt Cobain, was born at Cedars-Sinai Medical Center on Tuesday, Aug 18, 1992, at 7:48 A.M. According to her pediatrician, the infant is in stable condition, she is feeding well and is gaining weight at the normal rate expected for a newborn. She now weighs 6 lbs. and measures 20.5 inches." The key word was "normal."

The week after Frances was born Nirvana was scheduled to play the Reading Festival again, this time as the main attraction. Kurt was determined to do it. Nirvana was the headliner and he didn't want to let down the fans and just as important he didn't want to feel defeated by the drama caused by the *Vanity Fair* piece. While Courtney stayed home with the newborn, Eric Erlandson accompanied Kurt. "Courtney said I should go. It was that co-dependent thing, my caretaker role, and I felt protective 'cause he was not in a great place." Eric brought along a video camera to help document the performance.

Nirvana had canceled their most recently scheduled European tour, and Anton Brookes recalls the atmosphere around the band in the wake of the *Vanity Fair* article and other rumors about Kurt's drug use: "Every phone call and everyone I bumped into was feeling Nirvana was not going to play. There were rumors that the band was split up. It was just *assumed* that they weren't going to play. I'd tell people that I had just been eating with them or in their dressing room and the press thought I was making it up. It was so typical of the drama that seemed to follow Nirvana."

The day before Reading an article by Keith Cameron appeared in *NME* based on an interview he had done with Kurt in Bilbao, Spain, earlier in the summer before Frances was born. Unlike Hirschberg, Cameron was a writer that Kurt and Courtney had reason to trust. He had been enthusiastically covering the band almost as long as Everett had. Nevertheless he repeated

Hirschberg's damning accusation that "various credible sources" said that Courtney had shot heroin while pregnant. Cameron also wrote, "The overriding issue here is not that Kurt Cobain is on heroin (or isn't, or was, or is and is trying to get off) but that his wife is a Grade A pain in the arse. She seems almost universally disliked. 'The Wicked Witch Of The West' is one crew member's assessment, while someone else refers to Kurt being a nice guy BC—'before Courtney.'" Cameron also referred to Janet as "a cross between wet nurse and human sponge, indulging whims and soaking up all of Courtney's excess bullshit."

Reflecting on this moment, Kurt later told a British journalist, "A lot of it is simple sexism. Courtney is my wife and people could not accept the fact that I'm in love and that I could be happy, and she is such a powerful and threatening person that every sexist within the industry just joined forces and decided to try to string us up." Once, while complaining to me about the tabloid interest in the couple, Kurt observed with a bewildered tone, "I don't even know the *name* of Bono's wife." The ripple effect of the *Vanity Fair* piece had put Kurt and Courtney in an unenviable category of their own. In much of the media they had become cartoon characters.

Given how much he cared about his wife's reputation and the other stresses he was under, it wouldn't have been a shock if Kurt had indeed canceled Nirvana's performance. Discussing his feelings before the show, Dave Grohl told the *Scotsman*, "I really thought, this will be a disaster, this will be the end of our career for sure. Kurt had been in and out of rehab, communication in the band was beginning to be strained. Kurt was living in L.A., Krist and I were in Seattle. People weren't even sure if we were going to show up. We rehearsed once, the night before, and it wasn't good. It turned out to be a wonderful show, and it healed us for a little while."

Indeed, Kurt led Nirvana to what is widely considered one of their greatest performances, so powerful that a film of it was released many years later. He began with a brilliant improvised piece of theater. To mock the rumors that he was at death's door, Kurt had a wheelchair brought to the stage area and sat in it wearing a long blond wig and hospital robe. Brookes says, "Kurt asked me to push him out in the wheelchair and I said no fucking way am I going onstage in front of seventy to eighty thousand people. Everett overheard us and of course said *he* would do it." Montgomery, sitting at the mixing board, was relieved. "They hadn't played in quite a while and were just coming out of a lot of problems, and Kurt returned to the idea of doing something really funny. The humor was still there."

Sitting in the wheelchair, Kurt began by mournfully singing the first line of "The Rose," a song Bette Midler had recorded for the film of the same name, in which she played a rock singer struggling with the pressures of fame who dies of a drug overdose. He then flopped over onto the stage as if he had passed out and Krist, playing the straight man, told the crowd in a voice of mock concern, "With the help of his friends and family he's gonna make it."

Then with a flair reminiscent of James Brown, Kurt leapt up, strapped on his guitar, created some loud feedback, and, eyes blazing, launched into "Breed," one of the most "punk" songs from *Nevermind*. Listening a quarter of a century later to the recording of Kurt howling the opening words of the song from the Reading performance—"I don't care, I don't care, I don't care"—I am still in awe of how intimate the emotion was. It's as if he was saying to the vast audience "I don't care about *them*; I just care about *us*."

A couple of songs later the blond wig was dispensed with and Kurt continued to perform with full intensity and musical clarity. Just prior to playing "Smells Like Teen Spirit," Nirvana played the opening chords of Boston's classic rock hit "More Than a Feeling," a fuck-you to the critics who had pointed out that Nirvana's biggest hit shared some of the same riffs. They also premiered a new song at the festival, which was introduced as "The Eagle Has Landed" and eventually renamed "Tourette's" when it was recorded and released on *In Utero*.

Brookes says, "I remember looking out at the audience, almost all of whom were there to see Nirvana, and it was almost biblical. Nirvana meant more to them than just a band. When they came onstage and played the synergy was amazing. People were dancing and singing and enjoying themselves. It was spiritual. It was cathartic. Everything you ever wanted. One of the greatest experiences I've ever had in my life. I was standing on the side of the stage with my business partner and we were just laughing and saying how incredible it was. Just grinning and laughing." Azerrad flew there to cover the show for *Rolling Stone* and concurs, "It is the greatest rock concert I've ever seen."

As Dave later said, the chemistry of the band magically reasserted itself. Kurt asked Krist to "tell a joke" and his old friend obliged: "A nurse told a doctor, 'The invisible man is here,' and the doctor replied, 'Tell him I can't see him now.'" At another point Kurt said half-jokingly, "This is our last show," and Krist answered, "No it's not." Kurt said, "Right, we're gonna do a November tour. Do you want to make a record before that?" and Krist replied, "Yeah, make a record." Kurt nodded in assent. It was as if they were actually deciding this while onstage.

Krist later wrote of the Reading performance, "Hearing tens of thousands of people sing along with 'Lithium' was a very cool moment in the history of the band." Near the end of the set, Kurt walked up to the microphone, asked the audience to quiet down for a minute, and said, "This song is dedicated to my twelve-day-old daughter and my wife. There's been some pretty extreme things written about her and she thinks everybody hates her. This is being recorded so could you say, 'Courtney, we love you,' on the count of three?" The crowd happily obliged, and then Nirvana played "All Apologies," which would be recorded for *In Utero* several months later.

The last encore was "Territorial Pissings." After the song was done, Kurt played "The Star-Spangled Banner" in the same psychedelic style Jimi Hendrix had at Woodstock while Dave trashed his drums.

Eric walked away from the back of the stage area with Kurt, who had lit up a cigarette. A boy who looked to be around ten years old asked for his autograph, and Kurt obliged, then earnestly told him, "Don't smoke." Eric laughs ruefully at the memory of the contradiction. "That's Kurt."

MTV's Video Music Awards (VMAs) was broadcast ten days later, on September 9. Nirvana was expected to win several awards and had been asked to perform. We initially declined given everything else that was going on and because Kurt hated the whole idea of awards shows. Judy McGrath, who was president of MTV at the time, prevailed upon me to get Kurt to change his mind. Some written accounts say that MTV threatened not to play videos by artists on Geffen Records or managed by Gold Mountain and that they threatened to fire Amy Finnerty. This is false. The MTV people were under a lot of pressure to get good ratings, but they weren't bullies, just noodges.

Kurt wasn't happy to hear from me about the award show and asked how it would impact the band if they didn't do it. On one hand, he was a new father at a critical crossroads in terms of grappling with drug addiction. He had returned to rehab. On the other hand, he had just aced Reading and he was always concerned about how MTV treated Nirvana. I told him that in the short term I was sure they'd still play Nirvana a lot, but obviously MTV would be much happier if the band showed up for their biggest broadcast of the year.

I had called Kurt about this from home and Rosemary, who was well aware of the situation, overheard me and asked if she could speak to Kurt as well. She had spent a lot of time in the previous couple of weeks dealing with the fallout from the Lynn Hirschberg piece, and she knew the toll it had taken on him. Choking with emotion and on the brink of tears, she told him she worried that turning it down would play into the flaky image of him *Vanity Fair* had presented.

After Rosemary handed the phone back to me Kurt sighed, "I guess this is the kind of thing I have to do. Who knows, maybe in a few years I'll be wearing a tuxedo at one of these things." I was pained to hear the self-loathing in his tone, but I thought it was the right move.

The stress intensified when McGrath called me on the afternoon of the show to complain that during rehearsal the band was playing a new song called "Rape Me." She was worried that the lyrics would make it seem like MTV was normalizing rape. I reminded her of Kurt's commitment to feminism and that "Polly" was an antirape song, and assured her the new one was as well and that no Nirvana fan could be confused about Kurt's values on this subject. I also said it would be cool for the band to debut a brand-new song on the VMAs given that *Nevermind* had been out for almost a year. McGrath wasn't having it. She didn't want to risk having the word "rape" be the focus of media attention around the VMAs and she wanted them to do their most recent single, "Lithium."

"Kurt couldn't believe they didn't get it," says Finnerty. "He felt he was giving MTV a gift." I went back and forth between Kurt and McGrath over the next hour, but she was implacable and eventually Kurt capitulated. After all, the whole point of doing the show was to kiss MTV's ass.

When I got to the Pauley Pavilion at UCLA, where the broadcast was taking place, Jaime Manelli, now Frances's official custodian, was there and was dazzled to see so many celebrities backstage. "I can't believe that I was just rapping with Whitney Houston," she told me breathlessly. I was nervous that Kurt would be pissed because of the "Rape Me" debacle, but he and Courtney were preoccupied playing with the baby and were in a good mood.

For all his mixed feelings about awards shows, there were a couple of other artists there whom Kurt was excited to meet. When he saw Peter Gabriel walking in, Kurt actually went up to him and introduced himself—something I'd never seen him do. Kurt walked back in my direction and told me with boyish enthusiasm, "He said such nice things about our band."

Queen had been one of Kurt's favorite groups while growing up and they were going through a revival thanks to the fact that "Bohemian Rhapsody" was featured in the movie *Wayne's World*. As a result, the rock classic was nominated for best song in a film. Kaz had worked with Queen when he lived in England and he brought band members Roger Taylor and Brian May to meet Kurt in the trailer that served as a dressing room for him. "I still remember his blue eyes shining when they walked in," Kaz recalls. "He was like a kid in a candy store."

Just before the sound check, John Rosenfelder was sitting by himself on the side of the stage. He'd had less contact with Nirvana since the early weeks of *Nevermind*'s release. Kurt had kept his distance after Rosie pressured him to schmooze the heavy-metal radio guys. "Kurt walked by and tapped me on the head as if to say he was cool with me now and then sat next to me and played a perfect version of the Jim Croce song 'Time in a Bottle' on the guitar and smiled and walked away to find Courtney." It was a moment that Rosie would never forget.

A bit later, Kurt, Courtney, and Frances sat with Rosemary and me at a table in the VIP area that had been set up for performers to eat and drink. Axl Rose; his girlfriend, Stephanie

Seymour; and two huge muscle-bound bodyguards sat down at a table right next to ours. (In Kurt's later telling of the incident, he often said that there were "five" or more bodyguards, but my memory is two plus a cameraman who was evidently filming Rose for some possible future documentary.)

In the year since *Nevermind* had been released, the early good feelings that Rose had about Nirvana had completely dissipated. Kurt had not hidden his disdain for the macho posturing of Guns N' Roses. Not long after we had ducked out of Nirvana's dressing room to avoid Rose, Nirvana turned down a request to perform at Rose's birthday party. (As if! Celebrities sometimes played at other celebrities' birthday parties or weddings—but not punk bands. It was an absurd favor to ask.) Then I turned down a very lucrative offer to do a stadium tour with Guns N' Roses and Metallica. A member of Metallica then appealed to Kurt directly, and Kurt reiterated that there was no way he would ever want to be on the same stage as Guns N' Roses, a response that probably got back to Rose.

Rose also might have been feeling jealous that not only had Nirvana eclipsed them in the rock-and-roll world writ large, they had done so at the very same record company. Whatever the reason, at a recent Guns N' Roses show in Florida, Rose had ranted about "Kurt Cobain, who basically is a fucking junkie with a junkie wife. And if the baby's born deformed I think they both ought to go to prison."

Courtney looked at Rose and loudly said in a mocking tone, "Hey, Axl, wanna be the godfather of our daughter?" Stephanie Seymour turned to Courtney and cattily asked, "Are you a model?" to which Courtney, without missing a beat, replied, "Are you a rocket scientist?"

At this point Rose and a huge bodyguard got up from the table and walked toward us. The Guns N' Roses front man leaned over to Kurt and said, "Keep your woman quiet or I'm going to throw you to the pavement." I could scarcely believe I was witnessing such cartoonish behavior and it was hard to keep a straight face. Amy Finnerty was sitting right next to Kurt, who whispered to her with a giggle, "I'm scared," and then he turned to Courtney with a subversive grin and said, "Shut up, bitch," in a tone that made it clear he was ridiculing the demand. We all cracked up and Rose walked away in a huff. Kurt was pissed at the lame attempt at intimidation, but we finished our food.

Krist and Dave were furious at Rose when they heard about the confrontation. To make matters worse, a couple of Guns N' Roses roadies, along with bass player Duff McKagan, rocked Nirvana's dressing room/trailer back and forth until Finnerty screamed at them to stop because Courtney and the baby were inside. McKagan then threatened Krist, although no blows were exchanged. There were two stages to facilitate changeovers from one artist to the next. As Nirvana was about to perform they passed a stage that was set up for Guns N' Roses and Kurt spit on Axl's keyboard.

Kurt started Nirvana's performance with a couple of chords from "Rape Me" just to fuck with the MTV staff. "I was standing next to Judy McGrath and she was holding my hand," remembers Finnerty. A director looked at McGrath and gestured to find out if she wanted them to cut away. McGrath shook her head but she breathed a sigh of relief when the band segued to "Lithium." Dave Grohl taunted Rose as the song ended, calling out, "Hi, Axl. Hi, Axl. Where's Axl?" In a weird moment of an already weird day, Krist threw his bass up into the air after the song was done and it landed on his head, nearly knocking him out.

Just before the award for Best Video was presented, Kurt saw Eddie Vedder on the side of the stage and, in the aftermath of the ugly confrontation with Rose, recognized the Pearl Jam singer as a kindred spirit. While Eric Clapton played "Tears in Heaven" on the broadcast, the two singers did a slow dance that signaled an easing of the public discord between the two biggest Seattle bands.

Nirvana got the Best Alternative Video award for "Smells Like Teen Spirit," and Kurt, always looking for ways to undermine rock clichés, had arranged for a Michael Jackson impersonator to accept it for them. When they won a second award for Best New Artist the band accepted it themselves. Kurt began, "I'd like to thank my family and our record label and our true fans," and then he paused for a moment. Krist, knowing that Kurt wanted to tell a mass audience how he felt about the *Vanity Fair* piece, interjected, "You can't believe everything you see and hear, can ya?" and Kurt reiterated, "You know, it's really hard to believe everything you read," and smiled at the camera, but it was a forced smile that turned into a grimace. After the broadcast, award winners were escorted to a press tent and Kurt, with his impeccable sense of how to use the media, indignantly told the story of Rose threatening him and his wife.

In the weeks that followed, despite the stress caused by the aftermath of the *Vanity Fair* article, Kurt was besotted with his daughter, Frances. He and Courtney treated her with the goofy abandon typical of new parents. However, without relatives he had confidence in, Kurt often called Rosemary for advice on parenting, including what, if anything, should be done if a baby didn't poop for a couple of days.

Courtney was doing everything required of her to convince city officials that she should have custody of her child. Dr. Fremont sent a letter on her behalf on September 22 stating, "Starting September 9, Courtney has been given random urine tests which have all been entirely clean. She is seeing a drug counselor, a clinical psychologist, attending aftercare meetings at CPC Westwood and is examined in my office weekly. She seems determined to succeed and her prognosis is very good with the above safeguards in place."

Since the Department of Public Social Services process had been triggered by a magazine article, I thought that a positive story might lower the temperature. Robert Hilburn, the longtime music editor of the *Los Angeles Times*, was a champion of rock artists whom he admired (John Lennon and Bruce Springsteen among them), and as soon as *Nevermind* had been released he had asked me if he could interview Kurt. Now was the time.

Hilburn's piece appeared in the *Times* on September 11, two days after the VMAs, and it conveyed exactly the impression we were looking for particularly Kurt's final words to Hilburn, "I don't want my daughter to grow up and someday be hassled by kids at school . . . I don't want people telling her that her parents were junkies."

He also says in a quiet, but forceful way, that he is now drug-free. "'There's nothing better than having a baby,' says Cobain disarmingly. 'I've always loved children. I used to work summers at the YMCA and be in charge of like 30 preschool kids. Holding my baby is the best drug in the world.' He also doesn't want to be a bad role model for the group's teen-age fans." Hilburn interviewed me for the piece too.

> Danny Goldberg . . . confirmed in a separate interview that he's seen a dramatic change in Cobain since last spring.
>
> "Kurt is someone who had a hard time dealing with the unexpected intensity of the success," Goldberg said. "He came from a very difficult background, literally didn't have his own apartment when I first started managing him. Then, in a matter of a few months, he became an international ce-

lebrity. He got confused for a while, but last spring I saw a change when he had these ultrasound pictures of the fetus. He put it up on his wall at home. He is functioning the best I've ever seen him."

Ever mindful of his career, Kurt assured fans that more Nirvana music was coming but he did so in a way designed to reassure city officials of his commitment to parenthood.

"We could record and play shows once in a while, but to put myself in the physical strain of seven months of touring is too much for me. I would rather be healthy and alive. I don't want to sacrifice myself or my family."

The next day, while I was congratulating myself on the piece, Hilburn called me in an uncharacteristically bad mood. I hadn't told him that Kurt and Courtney were in the middle of a legal process that affected custody of their daughter but after the piece appeared another journalist spilled the beans to him. I had known and worked with Hilburn for almost twenty years and out of all the writers who covered rock and roll there was no one I respected more. "I feel I was used," he said in a hurt and angry voice, which had all the more impact because the writer was usually so congenial. He had me. My mind was racing to try to think of something to say, and I had nothing. After a long silence, Hilburn spoke again in a resigned tone: "Well I guess if I'm going to be used at least it's to help a genius." Years later, long after Kurt's death, I asked Hilburn if he still felt that way and he said, "Absolutely."

In their year-end issue *Spin* named Nirvana artist of the year; featured Kurt, Courtney, and Frances on the cover; and ran a positive article by Sub Pop's Jonathan Poneman that was head-lined "Family Values."

Somehow amid the rock-and-roll highs and the drug-created lows of the past year, Kurt had found the psychic energy to project political ideas that mattered to him into the ecosphere of rock culture. To many of his fans, these ideas were as important as his music.

ELEVEN

CITIZEN KURT

In retrospect, it is incredible to me how many intense things Kurt dealt with over the course of a few weeks in 1992. The *Vanity Fair* article came out on August 12. Frances was born on August 18. The Reading performance was on August 30 and the VMAs were on September 9.

The next day, on September 10, Nirvana flew to Portland, where they headlined a benefit to more than ten thousand people at an outdoor venue called Portland Meadows. The proceeds went to help fund the No on 9 campaign, which was an effort to defeat an antigay initiative on the Oregon ballot that coming November.

It had been a year since Kurt had asked me to have DGC change Nirvana's press kit to reduce the emphasis on politics. He didn't want the first impression new fans got of Nirvana to be that they were a political band like the Dead Kennedys or Fugazi, even though both bands had inspired him. Shortly after *Nevermind* was released he explicitly laid this concern out in an interview with a Malaysian journalist: "We're politically aware as individuals but we don't like to force our opinions down people's throats. Political bands haven't been very effective, you can't expect a rock and roll band to have a lot of political impact. First and foremost we're entertainers."

However, now that *Nevermind* had sold millions of albums he was ready to make a course correction. The persona Kurt created for himself balanced humor, music, and punk anger with progressive values. He embraced his inner dork, but he also hated cultural conservatism. With a sense of greater responsibility driven by his new fame, Kurt decided to be more outspoken on certain political issues, particularly those connected to feminism and gay rights.

In that new context, the benefit happened easily. A couple of months earlier I had gotten a call from Gus Van Sant, the director of the widely acclaimed films *Drugstore Cowboy* and *My Own Private Idaho*, who asked me if I would speak at a fund-raiser opposing the antigay initiative on the ballot in Oregon. It was going to be at his agent John Burnham's house, and Roseanne and Tom Arnold would speak (in those days, Roseanne was a lefty), but they wanted someone representing the ACLU as well. I readily agreed, and then Van Sant sprang his real agenda on me. What about Nirvana doing a benefit concert in Portland to raise money and visibility for the campaign? I knew that Kurt was a fan of his films and would be supportive of the issue, but given the level of commitment a concert involved I asked the director to make a personal pitch.

In due course Kurt and Courtney came over to our house for dinner with Van Sant and his boyfriend, Dirk-Jan Haanraadts (who called himself DJ). Kurt begged off attending the Hollywood fund-raiser, which was the next night, as he was never comfortable in that milieu, but he immediately agreed that Nirvana would play the benefit show.

DJ recalls Kurt and Courtney earnestly discussing how devastated they were to learn that a rapist had recently sung the lyrics of "Polly" to his victim. Van Sant's most vivid memory from the evening happened while the four of them were out in our garden smoking cigarettes. Courtney pulled out a music magazine featuring an interview with Pearl Jam. She read each Eddie Vedder quote out loud, followed by "several paragraphs of biting commentary, while Kurt just watched her, grinning." Despite the fact that Kurt had grown to like Vedder personally, he still saw him as a rival and "was obviously getting a big kick out of it." It was the only time that Van Sant ever met Kurt.

The offensive ballot initiative had been cooked up by a right-wing group called the Oregon Citizens Alliance. Oregon Ballot Measure 9, as it was officially called, would have added language to the state constitution saying, "All governments in Oregon may not use their monies or properties to promote, encourage or facilitate homosexuality, pedophilia, sadism or masochism. All levels of government including public education systems must assist in setting a standard for Oregon's youth which recognizes that these behaviors are abnormal, wrong, unnatural and perverse and they are to be discouraged and avoided." Among its many odious effects, passage of the bill would have prevented homosexuals from teaching in Oregon's public schools.

Oregon had a liberal reputation and a punk rock scene of its own, but the state also had a significant cohort of religious conservatives. Ballot initiatives are always nerve-wracking because a mobilized, impassioned minority can prevail if most voters aren't focused on the initiative and wind up leaving it blank when it comes time to cast their ballot.

Scot Nakagawa, the director of statewide development for the No on 9 campaign, explains, "The LGBT community in general was terrified. In 1988 the Oregon Citizens Alliance (OCA) was the sponsor of Ballot Measure 8, which attempted to roll back Governor Neil Goldschmidt's executive order banning discrimination in public employment against those perceived to be LGBT. Ballot Measure 8 won largely because of ads run by the OCA that propagated the idea that gay men are sexual predators and that sexual molestation at a young age is involved in the development of gay identity. A community that had been defamed, shamed, and defeated just four years before was now, once again, thrust into the spotlight. No on 9 became about redemption."

As far as I can tell, Kurt never had male lovers. He had, however, long identified with the gay community as an ally in the struggle against intolerance and bullying, and many of his artistic heroes were gay. Kurt described his hometown of Aberdeen to fanzine writers Jim Crotty and Michael Lane as "a very small community with a lot of people who have very small minds. Basically if you're not prepared to join the logging industry you're going to be beaten up or run out of town." Kurt added, "If I wasn't attracted to Courtney, I'd be bisexual." (The interview was in the couple's apartment and Courtney, overhearing this remark, jokingly yelled, "Faggot!")

Kurt told Azerrad that in high school he was "proud of *almost* being gay": "I had a gay friend who made a pass. I flatly told him I wasn't gay but said I'd still be his friend. I almost found my identity." Feminist music critic Ann Powers remembers being impressed by "the way Kurt presented himself to the world, the way that he performed queerness even though he himself was into women. In 2018 we have the term 'gender queer,' meaning that the way you present yourself is separate from your sexuality. That was him in the early nineties when there was no name for it."

Although Nirvana was the headliner of the No on 9 benefit, several other artists, including Poison Idea and Helmet, performed earlier. Jello Biafra was the emcee. He had been the lead singer of the Dead Kennedys, one of the bands that Kurt often cited as an exemplar of radical politics in the punk world. By 1992 Biafra had reinvented himself as a spoken-word artist and he was pleased to play a role at the benefit. He remembers, "It was quite a cool honor considering how big those bands were, and I was still way below the glass ceiling doing the underground thing. I had been pleasantly surprised by how outspoken and activist a lot of the key grunge bands turned out to be. It wasn't all seventies cock rock."

Biafra says, "The fact that Nirvana would even play a show like No on 9 over what was such a volatile topic, I thought, was great." In between sets, he wandered around the crowd and heard some kids saying stuff like, "I thought this was just a Nirvana show. I didn't know it was gonna be about faggots." Biafra believes that "the concert helped open some eyes, turned some people around."

Nirvana did one of their longer sets and there was little reference to politics until almost the end of the show. After performing "Blew," Kurt and Krist described the confrontation with Axl Rose the day before Kurt described sitting with Courtney at the MTV music awards, holding their three-week-old baby in his arms when Axl had walked by. They had shouted to him, "Axl, will you be godfather of our child?" He turned, and pointing at Courtney had said, "You better shut up, bitch, don't pitch me any shit tonight", then said to Kurt, "You better keep your wife's mouth shut or I'm gonna take you to the pavement." Kurt said that he was shaking, but challenged him, asking him if he was going to beat him up. Axl had then launched into a tirade about what an embarrassment Kurt was to everyone, including him.

At this point a boy who appeared to be in his late teens jumped onstage and tried to get Kurt's attention. Kurt waved security guys off and let the fan talk into the microphone. The kid nervously explained that he agreed that "no" on proposition 9 was the way to go, but he didn't understand why he had to choose between liking Guns N' Roses and liking Nirvana. "Man, I think you should let music be music, man."

I watched as Kurt carefully listened to the kid and then walked up to the mic, put his arm on the kid's shoulder, and spoke to him like a big brother. "But you can't like a rock star who obviously likes to beat up women and likes to control women and likes to tell women to shut up, who obviously is a racist and a homophobe. He does have the right to speak his mind—but so do we."

The kid sheepishly nodded in agreement and shook Kurt's hand, and the crowd roared. It seemed as if Kurt had changed the kid's mind in front of thousands of people. I thought it was one of the greatest rock-and-roll moments I'd ever witnessed. Then the band played "Rape Me," the song that MTV wouldn't let Kurt do the night before, after which they performed "All Apologies," which was also unreleased at the time. I hadn't been at Reading so it was the first time I'd heard the lyrics, including the line "What else could I say? Everyone is gay."

Biafra recalls that, "the feeling was Kurt is fragile. Is he really gonna wanna go and play? But that night it seemed like he was genuinely enjoying himself, really putting out and doing that primal thing that he did when Nirvana were really kicking ass at their best."

After Nirvana's performance I introduced him to Kurt. Biafra remembers, "He had gone through a lot of tabloid media bullshit, and you could see it in his face. He seemed kind of frazzled, nervous, waiting for the other shoe to drop. I really felt for him, but I couldn't resist making a joke, that I was bummed out that he hadn't named his child after me. He thought I was serious so I quickly walked *that* back and we chatted a bit more."

Kurt was happy to have met one of his heroes in such a positive way and gave me a little grin of satisfaction when I raved about the band's performance. For once he wasn't critical of a show he'd just done.

In an email decades later, Nakagawa referred to Nirvana's performance as a key inflection point in the campaign: "An evangelical right-wing group gathered enough signatures, in record time, to put a question on the ballot that was widely understood to be, in essence, 'Is this group fully human?' Donors to oppose the initiative weren't coming forward. We needed to change the story and the Nirvana concert helped to do so. Nirvana helped make the campaign magnetic. The number of volunteers soared, donor confidence rose, and many in the community felt redeemed. They felt less alone, less scared. It made us cool, and cool is more than a pair of sunglasses. Cool is current, culturally relevant, influential, and included." In November, Oregon Ballot Measure 9 was defeated by thirteen points.

Kurt's public commitment to gay rights made a strong impact in other parts of the gay community as well. Shortly after the benefit the band Pansy Division released a track called "Smells Like Queer Spirit" and on the cover sleeve wrote of Nirvana, "No superstar American rock band has ever before had the guts to take on such an overtly pro-gay stance."

Marco Collins, the program director of Seattle's leading alternative rock station, KNDD (known as "The End"), had taken the job shortly after *Nevermind* was released and at the time had not come out as gay. "I was in the closet. Kurt was the biggest rock star in the world. Knowing that he was pro-gay made me feel more comfortable."

A few months later Kurt was still milking the Axl Rose story, telling Patrick Chng of the Singapore magazine *Big O*, "I don't want to sound pretentious but it's a crusade to me. I think Guns N' Roses are promoting the wrong values, like sexism. What are they rebelling against? Rebellion is standing *up* to people like Guns N' Roses."

The night after the No on 9 show, Nirvana played another benefit, this one in Seattle for the anti-censorship Washington State Music Coalition, which had been created by the local ACLU and other groups to combat a piece of legislation called the Erotic Music Bill. The bill would have restricted kids under the age of eighteen from buying records or going to shows that had lyrics the government considered inappropriate, which would effectively make a lot of live music—especially punk rock—inaccessible to high school kids.

Washington governor Booth Gardner had recently boasted that Washington was "the home of Nirvana," so I called his office and identified myself as one of the band's managers. Although he took my call, the governor said he was going to sign the bill (presumably to mollify cultural conservatives) but told me to tell the band not to worry, the courts wouldn't allow it to be implemented. I was disgusted by his lack of political courage, but as Gardner predicted, the law was soon declared unconstitutional by a Washington State superior court judge.

Having saturated the media with interviews, Kurt was declining most requests, but he said yes to the LGBT magazine the *Advocate*. The interviewer, Kevin Allman, later wrote of

Kurt, "I found him smart, funny and sarcastic and not at all impressed with his status as the world's biggest rock star. In fact he was rather horrified, not only at being a corporate commodity, but also at being idolized by the same sort of meatheads he couldn't stand. He identified more with the misfits and the kids who were bullied. Kurt and Courtney wanted to know if I was a Beatles person or a Rolling Stones person. They said they were Beatles people."

Kurt reiterated his theory of subverting reactionary culture from the inside, saying that even if MTV was a corporate ogre, "it's played a part in raising consciousness." He added, "I think there's a new consciousness that's really positive among rock stars, like Rock the Vote [MTV's voter registration campaign]. . . . If Jello Biafra was a big international star it would be really cool. But he's not on a major label and doesn't write commercial enough music to use that as a tool."

Kurt told Allman that he had been called a "faggot" in high school and that he and Krist had spray-painted "HOMO SEX RULES" on the side of a bank when they were younger. "I thought I was gay for a while because I didn't find any of the girls in my high school attractive at all. They had really awful haircuts and fucked-up attitudes . . . but I'm just more sexually attracted to women. . . . I'm definitely gay in spirit, and I probably could be bisexual. But I'm married, and I'm more attracted to Courtney than I ever have been towards a person."

As the piece was about to come out, a New York gossip columnist wrote an item saying that in the interview both Kurt and Courtney were going to come out as gay, which wasn't true. Allman was terrified that they would think he had planted the item and called them to apologize, and Kurt just laughed and said, "Don't worry about it, this kind of thing happens all the time."

A year later, in a letter to the editor, Kurt wrote, "Of all the gut spilling and uh . . . whining I did in 1993, I never felt more relaxed than with *The Advocate*. What can I say? Thank you to the editors. I'll always be an advocate for fagdom."

Kurt's version of bringing political values to rock and roll was, like the rest of his art, distinctive. There were bands like R.E.M. and Pearl Jam who showed up for benefits but who rarely, if ever, included political ideas in their music. There were those like Rage Against the Machine, whose debut album was released a year after *Nevermind*, and who included left-wing and anarchist images and language in their graphics and lyrics. Kurt carved a middle path that seamlessly integrated his values into Nirvana's music without seeming to preach. He saw this kind of activism not as an adjunct of his art but as an integral part of it. In his journals he wrote, "There is a small percent of the population who were BORN with ability to detect injustice. They have Tendencies to question injustice and look for answers. These kids are usually hyperactive uncontrollable brats who never know when to quit."

That was the context in which Kurt made it his mission to broaden the idea of rock-and-roll masculinity. Just as the Beatles had made long hair sexy and David Bowie had done so with androgyny, Kurt embodied the idea that a cool guy could be snarling and powerful and also compassionate and sensitive.

Not long after they moved in together Courtney told me proudly, "You know, Kurt is going to feminize rock." He recognized that he was suddenly reaching audiences who also liked heavy metal and pop music, many of whom had no connection to the values that meant so much to him. At rock festivals Kurt and Krist sometimes fretted that some of the people cheering for the hit songs were the kinds of guys who'd kicked their asses in high school. Others were merely following the latest trend. (In 2017, Ivanka Trump would be quoted as saying she went through a "punk phase" and had "loved" Nirvana. Kurt would have been mortified.)

Ann Powers notes, "In my mind Kurt Cobain was the apotheosis of a certain arc in indie rock that was a corrective to the excesses of classic rock, on one level a little bit puritanical and negative, but on the other hand a necessary railing against the idea that women are just objects and that pleasure and exploitation for women are intertwined. It's clear from his work that this is something he felt deeply in his worldview, that women are equal as great creators, not just in the world in general but particularly in rock and roll. His personal relationships reflected that. He was involved with women musicians. On the cover of *Sassy*, Kurt and Courtney were wearing each other's sweaters. Kurt and Courtney presented a working artistic partnership to the world."

After Kurt died, Jessica Adams of the British magazine *Select* wrote, "Kurt was very kind to me when I interviewed Nirvana in Sydney. Wherever you are now, Kurt, know how loved you are and how important you are, especially to women, for whom you always took a stand."

Given that Nirvana only released three studio albums and Kurt's predisposition for nonlinear impressionistic lyrics, it's remarkable how many of his songs have a feminist subtext. Kurt underlined the meaning of the lyric to "In Bloom" in the interview he did for DGC a few months after *Nevermind* came out: "I don't like rednecks, I don't like macho men, I don't like abusive people." He told an Italian journalist about "Territorial Pissings," which was inspired in part by Kurt's feelings about the way Native Americans were treated in the areas around Aberdeen when he was growing up. "There are references to all those people living in North American reserves; people smashed by the raging Americans' attacks." Kurt explained that the song is also about sexism: "At the same time it's about appreciating women. I'm standing on their side because I hate the violence they suffer, the daily injustices resulting from belonging to a different sex."

After those news reports that an actual rapist had sung "Polly," Kurt became more explicit about the meanings of his songs and wrote "Rape Me." When he played it at the Halloween concert in Seattle he told the audience it was about, "hairy, sweaty, macho redneck men who rape."

Kurt still struggled with the balance between performing and proselytizing. He told Phil Sutcliffe of Britain's Q magazine that he had been disturbed at a New York concert when at one point "this girl was hoisted above everyone's heads and all these men in the audience started catcalling her and yelling— that really upset me but what am I supposed to do? Throw my guitar down and start yelling at them about it? It doesn't do any good. Fugazi do that all the time and they get nothing but shit for it."

However, near the end of the year in 1992, Nirvana did a short tour of Latin America. Kurt was furious when the crowd in Buenos Aires booed their opening act, Calamity Jane, a feminist punk band from Portland who were friends of Courtney's. Montgomery recalls that Kurt "took that pretty personally and he got a vibe from the crowd that was macho and misogynistic." The only way Kurt could think of to retaliate was to refuse to perform "Smells Like Teen Spirit." He played the opening chords to the famous song three times but wouldn't actually sing it. Afterward he told a local journalist, "The audience didn't deserve us playing it."

Unlike some of the anarchists in the punk world, Kurt had

no problem distinguishing between utopian ideals and electoral choices. He detested many Reagan and Bush administration policies and on more than one occasion told me, "Republicans are evil."

1992 was a presidential election year. Kurt was enthusiastic about once and future California governor Jerry Brown, who had exceeded expectations by beating Bill Clinton in a couple of Democratic presidential primaries. After hearing Brown on a radio broadcast, Kurt and Courtney called excitedly to tell me they had each contributed the $100 maximum to Brown's ultimately unsuccessful campaign. Kurt voted for Clinton in the general election but as far as I can tell only mentioned it publicly to a journalist in Argentina who asked if he had considered the third-party candidate Ross Perot. Kurt replied, "The guy sucks. He's rich. I don't trust him as president. I don't want to waste my vote. I prefer to make sure Bush doesn't continue."

One night in 1992 I debated conservative talk show host Dennis Prager about the separation of church and state. I enjoyed my avocation as an ACLU board officer, but I never mentioned things like this to the artists I worked with or even to the people in my office because I didn't want them to feel pressured to agree with me or to show up at any events, and this was a particularly nerdy one. I was flabbergasted to notice Kurt and Courtney sitting among the audience of a hundred or so people at the Hillel Center at UCLA. I'm not sure anyone in the crowd knew who was in their midst.

At one point, Prager asked a hypothetical question. If I was walking down a dark street at night and saw a group of people walking toward me, would I feel safer or less safe if I knew they were a religious group? I hesitated for a moment and during the pause Courtney loudly chimed in from her seat in the audience, "If I was going to get an abortion I'd feel a lot *less* safe if it were a bunch of antichoice Christians." Neither Prager nor anyone else in the audience had the nerve to disagree.

Afterward we went for dinner at Canter's Deli, a favorite haunt of Kurt's, not far from their apartment. I didn't think I'd done all that well against Prager, who is a formidable demagogue. Kurt reassured me with a beaming smile, "No, it was great. That was total entertainment." It was a touching role reversal. Normally it was my job to tell *him* things were okay.

Kurt was also a proponent of the progressive media group FAIR, which pointed out conservative bias in the mass media, and he always supported Krist's political interests. The bass player's family was Croatian, and Bob Guccione at *Spin* commissioned him to write a piece about the Balkan war. Krist donated the $3,000 fee to a charity that helped rape victims from the war, and Nirvana played a benefit at the Cow Palace in San Francisco for the same cause. When MTV asked Kurt beforehand why he wasn't planning to proselytize about the cause from the stage, he said, "I don't think it's going to be very effective to have a long-winded speech. I think the fact that we're doing this and the literature that people are going to be able to read is effective enough." Dave was supportive of all these efforts, and in interviews he added a pro-labor element to Nirvana's image and pointed out that his mother had been a public school teacher for several decades.

Kurt elaborated on his concept of activism in the *Advocate* interview: "I was helpless when I was 12, when Reagan got elected, and there was nothing I could do about that. But now this generation is growing up, and they're in their mid 20s; they're not putting up with it. . . . I would have rather had Jerry Brown . . . but I'm definitely happy that Clinton's in. . . . Chelsea seems like a pretty neat person—Birkenstock-wearing kid." He added, "Amy Carter's pretty cool too, from what I've heard. She's been seen at Butthole Surfers concerts!"

At the same time the part of Kurt's mind that was the archi-tect of his art never lost focus on the musical footprint he wanted Nirvana to leave.

TWELVE

INCESTICIDE

Several months after *Nevermind* was released, we found out that Sub Pop was planning to put out a compilation of early unreleased Nirvana material under the tongue-in-cheek name *Cash Cow*. At Kurt's request, we got Geffen to make a deal with Sub Pop whereby they would cancel their proposed album and instead license the rights to this earlier material to Geffen so that Kurt could do his own compilation. He initially referred to the album as *Throwaways* before coming up with the title *Incesticide*, and it was released on DGC shortly before Christmas 1992.

The previous year Bob Dylan had commercially released the first of his "official bootlegs," demonstrating that a curation of early material could be presented as a serious artistic effort and that there was a market for it. Although he would never publicly admit it, I knew that there was a part of Kurt that viewed his own canon in the same light even at this early stage of his career.

Incesticide was also a vehicle to super-serve the band's punk fans, who wanted more of the raw sound of *Bleach*, a mission that proved successful. In 2013, Nirvana historian Nick Soulsby devoted an entire book to the album, *Dark Slivers: Seeing Nirvana in the Shards of* Incesticide.

The album included several of the tracks that had appeared on the *Hormoaning* EP, which had only been released in Australia and Japan. Because many the recordings had been made over a period of years prior to *Nevermind*, there were four different drummers on the album, Chad Channing, Dale Crover, and Dan Peters in addition to Dave Grohl.

As Jenn Pelly would write in 2018 in a three-thousand-word elegy to the album on *Pitchfork*, "*Incesticide* embodies the free space of punk—part outsider visual art, part punk fanzine, thrillingly raw . . . Nirvana slid their fans a mixtape . . . Peel Sessions, covers, demos . . . vocal sounds like dying feral animals, unabashed feminism, and yeah, a devil-horn-saluting cock-rocker called 'Aero Zeppelin.'" (Discussing the idea behind that song in the album's press release, Kurt said, "Christ! Let's just throw together some heavy metal riffs in no particular order and give it a quirky name in homage to a couple of our favorite masturbatory '70s rock acts.")

For this release, Kurt once again zeroed in on the cover art. "I show up to work one day and Kurt was there with this picture," remembers Fisher as he describes Kurt's surreal and haunting painting of skeletal creatures from his imagination. For the back cover Fisher provided a photo of a rubber duck, one of many small toys and windups he had in a collection in his office.

Kurt asked Kerslake to do a music video of "Sliver." It was a stylized performance in a rehearsal space in which Kurt attacked the camera with wild eyes, adding intensity to the catchy chorus. Interspersed are several shots of a very cute baby Frances, another signal of "normalcy" in that part of his life. He also insisted that Kerslake include a close-up of the punk bible *Maximum Rocknroll,* a gesture of respect to the indie subculture. By 2018 the video had gotten more than thirty-three million plays on YouTube, not bad for a "throwaway."

There had been no liner notes on Nirvana's other albums, and I had no idea Kurt was writing them for *Incesticide* until he faxed them to the office shortly before the artwork deadline. He used them as a platform to speak directly to his fans without the intermediary of an interviewer.

The notes described how much it meant to Kurt to interact with artists he admired, including the Raincoats, Shonen Knife, and Sonic Youth ("totally being taken under their wing and being showed what dignity really means"). He also cited the Rock for Choice and No on 9 benefits as moments "that made life worth living," and then he wrote, "While all these things were very special, none were half as rewarding as having a baby with a person who is the supreme example of dignity, ethics, and honesty. My wife challenges injustice and the reason her character has been so severely attacked is because she chooses not to function the way the white corporate man insists." Kurt answered critics from Olympia, "I don't feel the least bit guilty for commercially exploiting a completely exhausted rock youth culture because, at this point in rock history, Punk Rock (while still sacred to some) is, to me, dead and gone."

Most memorably Kurt drew a line in the sand with the rock audience: "At this point I have a request for our fans. If any of you in any way hate homosexuals, people of different color, or women, please do this one favor for us—leave us the fuck alone! Don't come to our shows and don't buy our records."

He ended with "If it weren't for these people the world would suck eggs," followed by a list of names that began, "Danny

Goldberg, John Silva, Gary Gersh, Rosemary Carroll," and also included Janet Billig; Anton Brookes; Craig Montgomery; Mark Kates; John Rosenfelder; Ed Rosenblatt; David Geffen; Amy Finnerty; Jonathan Poneman; Bruce Pavitt and Nils Bernstein from Sub Pop; Everett True; *Spin* editor Bob Guccione Jr.; Lauren Spencer, who wrote the *Spin* cover story; European booking agent Russell Warby; and Nirvana road manager Alex MacLeod. *Pitchfork*'s Jenn Pelly writes, "The liner notes are the single most incisive document we have of the total intervention Nirvana staged on popular culture."

Three months after the *Vanity Fair* article had been published, Lynn Hirschberg continued to be a thorn in Kurt and Courtney's side. Rosemary responded to a hostile letter from Hirschberg's lawyer Richard Bernstein on November 19:

> Kurt Cobain and Courtney Love unequivocally deny having made repeatedly harassing and threatening phone calls to Lynn Hirschberg. They did not call Ms. Hirschberg at her hotel in California on the night of Oct 27, 1992, as you allege. They did not even know that she was in California . . . the only contact between either of them and Ms. Hirschberg occurred when Courtney left two messages on Ms. Hirschberg's answering machine shortly after the publication of the article. These messages which were left several months ago neither harassed nor threatened Ms. Hirschberg but merely sought an explanation for the libelous and defamatory contents of the article, a subject discussed with you at greater length in my letter to you of Sept 2, 1992.
>
> My clients asked me to request that you advise Ms. Hirschberg to leave them alone. They find her obsession with their family frightening and are annoyed that she continues to insinuate herself into their careers.

I have often tried to put myself in Hirschberg's head. Given her cultural bias, I guess Hirschberg talked herself into the idea that her portrayal of Courtney and Kurt was somehow righteous, but there is no excuse for how far she went. She dehumanized them and used unnamed sources who said things that could have cost Kurt and Courtney custody of their daughter. As if the article hadn't done enough damage, there were rumors that she bad-mouthed Kurt and Courtney to other journalists.

In January 2018, Hirschberg was working at *W* magazine as an editor and Courtney texted me in amazement that someone from the publication had invited Frances to an "it girl" luncheon with Hirschberg. It must have been sent by a young employee of the magazine who was unaware of their history, and of course Frances had her PR person inform them, "Lynn's invites definitely not welcome." Courtney reminded me that when Frances had gone to an acting camp in the Catskills as a teenager some bullies called her a "crack baby" because of the enduring ripples from the article.

Another drama unfolded in early 1993 that made Kurt and Courtney feel further under siege. Britt Collins and Victoria Clarke, two British journalists who wrote for the music magazine *Lime Lizard*, sold a book proposal about Nirvana to Hyperion, the publishing arm of Disney. The working title for the book was *Nirvana: Kitty Pettin', Baby Kissin', Corporate Rock Whores*, words that had been written on one of the Nirvana's early T-shirts. Initially the band decided to give them some access. Clarke was given a backstage pass for several dates on the European tour and interviewed Kurt briefly, but some of the questions she asked about Courtney made Kurt uncomfortable. It seemed like the Nirvana book was morphing into one about Kurt and Courtney and Clarke was asked to leave the tour.

Not long thereafter the writers interviewed Lynn Hirschberg

and went to Seattle for more research. As word got back to Courtney about the kinds of questions they were asking, focusing heavily on dirt and drug use, it felt to us that the book would be another character assassination. "They even called Kurt's aunt Judy!" Courtney told me as she worked herself into a rage about the project. Kurt was joined at the hip with Courtney on anything like this. He viewed an attack on his wife as an attack on him.

Janet made it clear to anyone who inquired that Nirvana was not cooperating with the book and most of Kurt's friends refused to talk to the writers, but Kurt and Courtney's level of anxiety about the book escalated to a level that seemed disproportionate to me. While Kurt had written that paranoids have real enemies, the converse was also true: just because they're out to get you doesn't mean that you're *not* paranoid. It was one of the few times when Kurt's usually brilliant instincts about the media failed him.

At one low point Kurt and Courtney took turns making angry and threatening phone calls that were recorded on Clarke's answering machine, which drew attention to the unauthorized book. An obviously very stoned Kurt was heard saying, "You parasitic little fucking cunts—if *anything* comes out in this book that hurts my wife I'll fucking hurt you. I don't care that this is a recorded threat. I'm at the end of my rope. I've never been more fucking serious in my life. . . . I suppose I could throw out a few thousand dollars to have you snuffed. Maybe I'll try the legal way first."

The would-be biographers gleefully played the recordings for any journalists who would listen, some of whom called me for comment. I lied to the *New York Times*, saying the messages were "either a prank that someone played on these women or this is something they are fabricating to publicize an unauthorized biography." I tried a similar tack with Steve Hochman from the *Los Angeles Times*, but he answered me in a pained voice, "I've spent time with both Kurt and Courtney and I recognize their voices." Hochman was a friend, a good guy, and a conscientious reporter, but I steeled myself and answered firmly, "I'm their manager and I'm denying that it's them and you have to print my denial." Hochman sighed with frustration but included my lie in his piece. I never had any regret about trying to cover up for them in this way. I wasn't under oath or responsible for government action; I was doing my job and standing up for my client. However, I was worried that Kurt and Courtney were out of control and were hurting themselves.

Courtney had heard that Clarke was telling people she (Clarke) had slept with Dave Grohl. On one of the websites where recordings of Kurt's and Courtney's phone messages are available there is a message attributed to Dave but that Courtney now says was actually left by Kurt pretending to be Dave. "Hi, Victoria, this is Dave Grohl from Nirvana. I've gotten word that you've told more than a few people that I've slept with you. . . . It's offensive and quite disgusting so I just wanted you to know that unless you let everyone realize that this is totally untrue that I'm gonna take some legal action against you."

At one point, Kurt and Courtney floated the idea of taking out an ad in the Seattle weekly the *Rocket* to announce that the book was unauthorized, but Janet and I persuaded them that this would have the opposite effect they wanted. I gave Kurt and Courtney a lecture suggesting they let Rosemary fight the battle legally and refrain from talking about it to the press and to please stop leaving messages on phone machines. A few days later Kurt called me to tattle on Courtney after she answered a call from a writer for *Entertainment Weekly* and reiterated her rage at Collins and Clarke. "I *told* her to hang up," he insisted. The magazine printed a transcript of the messages as well as the phone call between their reporter and Courtney.

Not long afterward, Kurt and Courtney visited the Holly-wood club Raji's to see a band, and Collins and Clarke were already sitting at a table there. In a 2011 blog entry (in which she said she now "forgave" Courtney) Clarke gave her version of what happened next: "I felt a sharp bang on my head, liquid poured down my face and I found myself on the floor, with Courtney grabbing me by the hair. She proceeded to drag me along the floor, while Kurt stood and watched. . . . I screamed for help, and a bouncer managed to rescue me."

I was not there and Courtney said that it was actually Clarke who physically attacked her first. It seemed to me that Clark used the "incident" as another excuse to generate publicity. She made a criminal claim and hired one of Axl Rose's lawyers to represent her. In February, after a preliminary hearing, the case was thrown out by the judge.

In her blog, Clarke, who has been the romantic partner of Shane MacGowan of the Pogues for many years, wrote that in retrospect she felt differently than she did at the time.

> Recently, Shane and I were sent a manuscript of a new Pogues biography. It was deeply unflattering, about both of us. After reading it, I was upset and angry for several days. Just the very thought that someone is scrutinizing your life and writing about you can be hurtful. I wondered what it must have been like for Kurt and Courtney, knowing that Britt and I could have been writing something that would affect their child, as well as them? Would I have been angry enough in their position to threaten the writers? Quite possibly!

At the time, although I had had little sympathy for the would-be biographers, I worried that Kurt and Courtney's over-reaction to them was counterproductive. Then a couple of weeks before *Incesticide* was released, Kurt faxed over additional liner notes about the evils of Lynn Hirschberg, Britt Collins, and Victoria Clarke, in particular, and the media in general. It was, thank God, too late to change the notes in the initial shipment, which was already in warehouses and heading shortly for stores, but Kurt demanded that they be included in future pressings of the record. The proposed addition was a venomous rant that sabotaged what Kurt had already written. It painted the media with a broad brush, as if everyone who wrote about music deserved to be in the same category as Hirschberg.

Janet prevailed upon me to try to stop the inclusion of the new notes. "You were the Kurt whisperer," she remembers. "You were older and knew more about the real world than any of us did." I too was worried that Kurt's diatribe would tip the scales of his image in a way that would be very hard to reverse and that he would later regret. However, I was demoralized that my phone conversations hadn't seemed to have gotten through, so I wrote him a letter. Except for budget memos and notes accompanying Christmas gifts, it was the only time that I conveyed my thoughts to Kurt in writing. The letter is dated November 23, 1992.

> *Dear Kurt,*
>
> *In general attacks on the press writ large do not help artists who make them and in your case it's particularly destructive because both Nirvana and Hole have been supported by the majority of writers despite some despicable sleaze elements that have caused you a lot of pain. "Media" includes all the writers and editors who did not repeat the* Vanity Fair *charges and who have praised and respected your music. Why alienate all of these innocent people by generalizing? People at* Newsweek, *the* LA Times, Spin,

The Rocket *etc. who have been allies in the past, will be much less sympathetic in the future. Even those who do not like Lynn Hirschberg or the slant of her story will be made very uncomfortable by continued attacks on her.*

The anger in the piece directly contradicts all of the attempts to portray you as a noncrazy responsible person. If, God forbid, there were ever another legal problem excerpts from it could look weird. Additionally, the same "inside sources" who informed much of Hirschberg's article are still out there and might be tempted to repeat their ugly comments on the record. This approach focuses attention on your enemies' version of reality rather than on the positive aspects of your life and career (like the Spin *cover).*

At a time when Rosemary very effectively wrote to urge Lynn Hirschberg to leave you alone and get a life, this will give Hirschberg an excuse to do another round of media calls and make it look like you are the one obsessed with her. Don't give her this weapon!

Victoria and Britt can only benefit by being publicly acknowledged by you. The more attention you give them, the more their book will sell. Courtney's original idea is still the best, to get someone you trust to write an authorized book, preferably a writer of some stature (Danny Sugerman, Everett True, Michael Azerrad etc.), and it will dwarf an unauthorized one written by amateurs.

Complaining while successful always looks bad in the press. For all the pain and trouble you have had in the last year the press looks on you as very fortunate.

MTV ran a retraction of Kurt Loder's original piece and you went to an enormous effort to win them over by doing the award show, an effort that completely succeeded to the point where not only are they committed to Nirvana but are very positively pre-disposed toward Hole. Although you will never totally control every single thing they say, they are allies. Why re-open this wound and undo what you have accomplished?

There was one more factor to take into consideration. Rosemary and Silva had been working on a renegotiation of the Geffen deal that would get the band a $4.5 million check within weeks and a royalty increase of several points.

The Geffen renegotiation has not been signed and the company has had a particularly bad year. This is the worst possible time to impose on them a packaging change that will cost them more money, time, and potential embarrassment. Even if you decide to go ahead with these new notes it is better to wait until you get the advance. They do not have any legal obligation to increase your royalty or advance you money except as called for in the current contract.

I deeply believe that through your music, through a clever approach to the media (such as the original liner notes, the LA Times and Spin pieces), good videos, significant benefits such as the Rock for Choice show, by being decent people, good friends and great parents—that you will totally marginalize people like Lynn, Victoria and Britt.

At times such as the statement you issued when Vanity Fair *came out and the recent letter to Hirschberg's lawyer a strong confrontational posture is necessary. But in general, by appearing to over-react to them—instead of weakening them, you empower them. Instead of submerging them, you elevate their visibility. Instead of looking strong, you look weak. By every standard you are much more important than they are. Things are going your way. Please don't hurt yourself unnecessarily.*

Having said that, I reiterate that you are the boss. If you
insist, Gold Mountain will send the revision out. I think you
know that I love you and Courtney and will support you in
any way I can and that the Gold Mountain people will as
well. But I would neither be a good friend or a good manager
if I didn't give you my thoughts.

I am not showing this letter to anyone else. It's between us.
Please let me know what you think,

Love Always, Danny

The fever finally broke. The next day Kurt and Courtney asked me over, and Kurt agreed to withdraw the inflammatory revision and called Michael Azerrad to ask him to do a book about Nirvana. Not long afterward, Rosemary got ahold of an early draft of Collins and Clarke's manuscript and wrote a detailed memo to Hyperion listing portions that she considered to be libelous. They canceled the book and no other publisher picked it up.

There was one more score to settle. In mid-January 1993 Courtney filed a lawsuit against Cedars-Sinai alleging that the hospital had violated Courtney's rights and cost her a lot of money and stress. Rosemary issued a statement that read, "The hospital and its staff reacted to a libelous article regarding my client which had appeared in a national magazine. Defendants ignored the medical realities of the Plaintiff's situation and falsified portions of her medical records to comport with the image of her conveyed by the article. They then violated her rights and her privacy by disclosing her medical records, including the falsified and inaccurate portions, to the media." The lawsuit alleged "wrongful disclosure of medical information, invasion of privacy, publicity placing false information in public eye and negligent infliction of emotional distress." Soon after it was filed the hospital made a confidential settlement with Courtney.

It is not possible to reflect on these dramas without acknowledging the role that drugs played. Junkies do crazy shit, and smart, talented, successful junkies do even crazier shit. During this same general time period Courtney also went on an extended rampage against Boston singer-songwriter Mary Lou Lord, who had a brief romantic relationship with Kurt before he was involved with Courtney. (Lord was also a close friend of Olympia's Slim Moon.)

There is no excuse for threatening people and everyone is accountable for their actions, even when they are high, but to me Kurt's and Courtney's behavior has to be viewed as a by-product of addiction. They both needed to stop using opiates. (Kurt, like many junkies, almost always insisted that he had stopped taking drugs, and when he wasn't stoned, he was very convincing. Much of the time I think he meant it when he said it.)

Yet it was impossible for me to ignore how well Kurt functioned most of the time. Thurston recalls speaking to Kurt during this period: "He was saying, 'I'm going to step back from this madness and try to get back into a place where I was happiest.' Which was before *Nevermind* came out and playing to the kind of audiences that they were playing with Sonic Youth, but at the same time I saw him walking off of arena stages playing to the enthusiastic crowds and he had a kind of swagger like, 'I'm doing good here.'"

Nonetheless Kurt knew that even the greatest success has a brief shelf life in rock and roll. *Nevermind* had run its course and to keep "doing good" Nirvana needed to make an album of new material.

THIRTEEN

IN UTERO

Kurt had started thinking about how to follow up *Nevermind* almost as soon as it came out. He was, as Krist says, "a planner," and some of the songs that ended up on *In Utero* had been developed by Kurt for years. "Dumb," "Pennyroyal Tea," and "All Apologies" were performed live by Nirvana as early as the UK tour at the end of 1991. However, to make an album, additional songs were needed. In January 1993, while the band had a day off in Rio de Janeiro, Montgomery recorded new demos that included "Heart-Shaped Box." Hole also used some of the studio time to record demos for songs that would appear on *Live Through This*.

When they got back to the States, Kurt and Courtney gave up the apartment in Hollywood and bought a house in Seattle where they felt more at home. However they came to Los Angeles frequently and would usually stay at the Four Seasons Hotel. On a couple of occasions Kurt invited Kaz over to hang out with him while Courtney was doing a workout in their room. "Kurt would come down and we'd have a drink or meal downstairs," Kaz recalls. "We would sit in a bar and he would give me demos to the songs that ended up on *In Utero*, which blew me away." Kurt saw Kaz as a connoisseur of rock songwriting and was encouraged by the emotional support, and he also enjoyed comparing notes with another father. Kaz's son was seven years old at the time. "I would say to spend as much time as possible with Frances before she started school. Till then it's all Daddy. After that, it's all about their friends."

Always wary of sounding pretentious, Kurt played down the *In Utero* lyrics to Azerrad: "They are sarcastic one minute and caring the next. That's how the songs come out. Every song is about things that piss me off, the conflict between good and evil. Some people do evil things to people for no reason, and I want to beat the shit out of them. All I can do is scream into a microphone instead."

Although the songs were written at different times, Kurt combined them into a holistic vision about the connections between birth, sickness, death, and rebirth. "Rape Me" appears on the album, and many of the other songs on *In Utero* were informed by Kurt's conviction that a lot of the negativity aimed at Courtney was misogynistic. "Pennyroyal Tea" is written from the point of view of a woman who wants to abort a fetus. Montgomery notes, "Some people accused Courtney's songwriting of being influenced by Kurt, but I think it was more the other way around."

That was true thematically but songwriting was something Kurt took very seriously as a core element of who he was as an artist. Courtney did a solo show at the Café Largo a few months after Frances was born where she performed "Pennyroyal Tea" acoustically and nailed it. The next day Kurt called me uncharacteristically agitated. Courtney had asked if she could record it on the next Hole album, and he wanted to make sure I didn't encourage the idea. "That's for the next Nirvana album. No way am I giving that song away!"

"Frances Farmer Will Have Her Revenge on Seattle" was inspired by William Arnold's biographical novel about Farmer, a film actress who was committed to a mental institution in Washington State for five years in the 1940s, where she was mistreated. The movie *Frances*, starring Jessica Lange, was heavily based on the book. Kurt made a point of telling the story of the protagonist's sad life in most of the interviews he did for *In Utero*.

Some of the songs were written after Frances Bean Cobain was born. Ann Powers points out that very few songwriters had previously addressed "the fear of being a parent. John Lennon did it in his last album but Kurt got at emotions that Lennon didn't get at. 'Heart-Shaped Box' evokes the limits of what a man can understand about a woman, and the album as a whole gives a very up-close consideration of becoming a parent, watching the person you love be pregnant and have a child, and the cover art is so much about a body changing." "Heart-Shaped Box" also has one of Kurt's most memorable melodies.

"Scentless Apprentice" is one of the few songs still credited to all three members of Nirvana because it evolved from a jam that Kurt, Krist, and Dave did. The lyrics were inspired by Patrick Süskind's *Perfume: The Story of a Murderer*, a historical horror novel that Kurt kept rereading.

Before recording *In Utero*, Kurt wanted to get his head around where he was financially. Once an artist is successful, there is a lot of pressure to plan a "cycle" in connection with a new album because many of the festivals and large venues are booked far in advance. Kurt had loved playing clubs when Nirvana was in a van, but the rock-star version of touring appealed to him a lot less. Whether it was because he felt more isolated at big venues, wanted to be home with Frances, was struggling with drug addiction, or wanted to write and draw more, Kurt was looking to be on the road a lot less in the coming year, but he also wanted to make sure that he wouldn't ever be broke again. His litigation bills and other expenses in the wake of the *Vanity Fair* piece had been significant, and notwithstanding the $1.5 million check from the record company that Kurt had gotten at the end of the prior year, he was stressed out about money as 1993 began.

Not long after the band got back from Latin America, Kurt asked me how much he would actually have left over "after taxes and after commissions," as he repeatedly said. He wanted a worst-case scenario. What would his finances look like if the next Nirvana album didn't do that well and if he only wanted to do a couple of months' worth of touring that would not include stadium shows or festivals? Would he be okay?

I assured him that even if he did no touring at all it would be fine, but afterward he pressed me for a more specific estimate in writing so that he and Courtney could really internalize it. I gave it a shot in a memo dated February 19, 1993, entitled "Projections for Nirvana Income Over the Next Year."

He had asked me to be conservative, so the projection I gave him was $2,190,000 after commissions and taxes. Only about $500,000, or less than one-fourth of the total amount, was from touring, based on the guidelines he gave me (forty shows worldwide and no arenas or stadiums). Kurt's insistence on making the lion's share of the songwriting money had achieved what he wanted. As long as he and Courtney didn't spend money in unexpected ways, he could do what he wanted and live very comfortably.

In theory this should have reduced the pressure on him, but Kurt had plenty of other ways of driving himself crazy, so the momentary equanimity the memo provided quickly dissipated.

Like most of the people who worked with him, I found that sometimes he was warm and easy to connect with, and at other times I felt a tense, unfathomable force field around him that kept me at bay. Over the next few months, continuing the pattern of the past two years, Kurt alternated between moments of depression and great creative work. Although some of the rock press had continued to suggest that Nirvana had burned out, the part of Kurt's mind that had inspired so many fans in the first place continued to function at a high level. As Krist says, when it came to creating art, Kurt was not lazy.

The only time he ever called me to complain about Geffen Records was when their international department was dragging its feet getting him some European video transferred to American standard so Kurt could watch it and make notes for a long-form home video. Several times when I visited him Kurt was feverishly working on it. He created a montage of the band smashing their instruments. He included a question from a TV interview where Krist was asked if Nirvana provoked their audience and the bass player answered, "No, they provoke us." When Kurt asked about Nirvana's influence, he answered, "If bands have been influenced by us I hope they've been influenced by the sincerity we try to put out."

He found a clip of Gersh saying, "This is not just a successful record, it's some sort of a phenomenon," and one of me debating a right-winger on CNN in which I said, "Entertainment makes people feel less alone, which is a positive thing." I can't imagine that any Nirvana fan cared about these moments. It was just Kurt's way of making each of us feel included in his version of Nirvana's ascent. After Kurt's death, Krist and Dave oversaw the video's completion with Kevin Kerslake as the director. It was released as *Nirvana: Live! Tonight! Sold Out!!* and is faithful to Kurt's vision as I understood it.

Kurt also designed a left-handed guitar that combined elements of Fender's Jaguar and Mustang models. He sent a mock-up of the concept to the company using combined Polaroid photos he took of each, and from that Fender created the "Jag-Stang." He was able to play a prototype of it a few times on Nirvana's last European tour.

Michael Azerrad was at work on *Come as You Are*, the Nirvana book we'd discussed, and Kurt sat down with him to do interviews, which were some of the most nuanced Kurt would ever give. As the book deadline loomed Kurt made up a list of fifty albums that had inspired Nirvana, but Azerrad told me, "Courtney convinced him to pull it. She thought it was too much of a pose."

Kurt's main focus, however, was on the new Nirvana album. He wanted to have a different sound on it to signal a return, at least symbolically, to the band's punk roots. Because the massive success of *Nevermind* had made its sound "mainstream," using Butch Vig or Andy Wallace again was out of the question.

Kurt had long admired Steve Albini, the indie-label purist who had taken Sonic Youth to task for signing with DGC a few years earlier. Albini had been a member of the band Big Black, which Kurt loved as a teenager. He never referred to himself a "producer" but instead used the word "recordist." He eschewed royalties on albums he worked on, but he received a $100,000 fee for his work on *In Utero*.

I cynically interpreted the selection of Albini as a PR move, but Janet insists that Kurt was a fan of many Albini-recorded albums. Courtney concurs: "Kurt really loved the P. J. Harvey record *Rid of Me* that Albini had just recorded."

Kurt explained to *Q* magazine's Phil Sutcliffe that he liked the way Albini captured Nirvana's sound. "I always wanted to record a record which has a very personal ambience to it, that sounded as though you were standing next to a band in a room. We used a lot of microphones. I thought if you positioned three or four microphones at the snare drum you'd be able to get the real sound of a snare drum. I've suggested it to Butch Vig and Jack Endino and they weren't willing to do it." He felt that was what Albini had done on the Pixies' *Surfer Rosa* and the Breeders' *Pod*, two of Kurt's favorite albums.

In Utero was recorded at Pachyderm Recording Studio in Cannon Falls, Minnesota, outside of Minneapolis, where the weather is very cold in February. Krist remembers, "Albini is very opinionated and he's got his perspectives. We showed up in rural Minnesota and there was this studio in this house that's, like, Frank Lloyd Wright meets Mike Brady." Despite the rustic setting Krist noticed that the studio had "the same board that AC/DC recorded *Back in Black* on. This big neat board."

When they were ready to record, there were at least thirty microphones taped to the walls, the floor, and the ceiling to capture the sound Kurt had in mind. Krist says, "Here's Albini and he had no idea what we were about. We rehearsed all the time. A lot of bands would have girls over or they party or whatever. We were just into playing. So, Albini's standing there next to the tape machine with his arms folded, like, 'Okay, let's do it.' And we're like, '*Sure*, press *record*.' Then we played that song 'Serve the Servants' and afterward we look at each other and said, 'Yeah, okay, Steve, that's a keeper. We're gonna do another song.' We were knocking these songs out first and second takes. I think we impressed him."

Kurt's lead vocals were done separately, but they were all recorded in a day over the course of around six hours. The whole album took ten days. At Albini's insistence no one from the label or Gold Mountain was there for any of it. Albini told Gillian Gaar, a journalist who had covered Nirvana from the beginning,

"I don't want to develop any relationships with any of these people, these administrative types, record label people. By and large these people are scum. I don't want to have anything to do with them."

After Albini mixed the album, Thurston recalls, "Krist and Dave took me to the studio. They played me some of *In Utero* and we actually jammed together as a trio waiting for Kurt to show up. He never showed up. Then they played me some songs. Some that didn't even get on the record, like 'Moist Vagina.' I remember saying, 'That should be your first song, because that song is insane. If you guys are gonna come out of the gate like crazy, come out of the gate really crazy. That's really good.'" Ultimately Kurt didn't include that song on the album but used it as the B-side of the "All Apologies" single. (Sonic Youth later covered the song for the B-side of *their* 1998 single "Sunday.")

Kurt got cassettes of the mixes to me, Janet, Silva, Gersh, and a few others. Notwithstanding Thurston's enthusiasm for the edgy side of Nirvana, Kurt still had his eye on the masses and he told me that "Heart-Shaped Box" was the first single. Montgomery says that the band had seen it as the lead single when they did the first demo of it months earlier.

I loved the songs right away but I was frustrated by how hard it was to hear Kurt's vocals, which were such a big part of Nirvana's identity. While I was wondering what to say to him about it, Courtney called and said that Kurt was worried that no one liked the album. I told her what I thought and she said, "You've got to tell Kurt!" She asked me if I had played the new record for Katie, and I laughed and admitted that in the car my daughter had said, "I don't want to hear the new Nirvana—I want to hear the *old* Nirvana." Courtney again said, "Tell Kurt!"

I wasn't gonna tell him what a three-year-old said, but I called and assured Kurt that the songs were incredible but said that I thought the mixes were weird and I missed being able to hear his vocals clearly. Gersh evidently gave Kurt similar feedback. Kurt told me that Albini had rushed through the mixes, doing an average of one per hour. (Typically for bands at that time, especially a band for which the recording budget was no problem, the average was one or two mixes a *day*.) Azerrad quips, "It's as if Kurt was in love with the *idea* of the low-budget philosophy but not its actuality."

Courtney, who knew that Kurt cared as much about how the punk community would feel about the record as he did about having radio hits, also asked Thurston to talk to Kurt. The Sonic Youth guitarist reassured him, "Everybody has an agenda here. You guys are super big shots now. You made a great record. Just stay strong."

Around this same time, David Geffen called me and said that Nirvana had been the label's biggest artist last year, adding, "It's a little embarrassing to me that I've never met Kurt." Kurt was worried that some kind of label pressure was in the offing, but it sounded to me like David had a friend who wanted to know what Kurt was like.

I was sure that there was no chance that David Geffen would personally criticize the new record. In 1983, after Neil Young followed up *Trans*, his commercially unsuccessful electronic album, with a rockabilly record, Geffen had sued Young for delivering records that were "unrepresentative" of the style that had made him successful. In the wake of bad press and the legal reality that Young's contract gave him creative control, the suit was withdrawn. David apologized, and Young recorded and promoted two more albums for Geffen Records.

Ten years later, David was a billionaire and one of the most admired people in the entertainment business. The last thing he would want was a public argument with a high-profile artist to remind people of one of his rare missteps.

I drove Kurt out to David's house on the beach in Malibu, where we ate lunch and spent a very pleasant hour in which David charmed Kurt with his candor about his own ups and downs over the years. Not a word was uttered about the new Nirvana album. As we were leaving Kurt asked David if he'd heard that there were some at the label who thought he should change the record, and David said emphatically, "Don't pay any attention to anything anyone else says; just make the record you want to make." Despite my previous assurances to Kurt that he shouldn't worry, he was relieved, and on the ride back to Hollywood he happily told me, "He was so different from what I expected."

Soon thereafter, Kurt decided that he wanted to remix "Heart-Shaped Box" and "All Apologies," which he expected to be the second single. I asked him why he didn't want to remix the whole album, and he said he could fix a lot of the problems with the vocal level in the mastering. I realized that Kurt was trying to find a middle ground and avoid totally burning the bridge with Albini while making sure that there were hits.

As Kurt was figuring things out, Albini did an interview with the *Chicago Tribune*'s Greg Kot that was headlined "Record Label Finds Little Bliss in Nirvana's Latest." He was quoted as saying, "Geffen and the band's management hate this record," and claimed that a source at the label said it was "un-releasable." I wasn't on the phone when Gersh spoke to Kurt, and Gersh has chosen not to talk much about Nirvana publicly since Kurt's death, but it is inconceivable to me that he would have used language like "un-releasable" or said he "hated" the record. Needless to say neither Silva, Janet, nor I said anything remotely like that to Kurt nor did we feel that way. Silva, who rarely spoke to the media, gave a diplomatic but pointed quote: "If the band says the record's ready, then it's ready. But as of now there is no Nirvana record to release."

Despite Albini's outrage, the situation really wasn't complicated. Kurt had absolute control of the album, not just legally but also emotionally. He had the only vote and he came to a rational conclusion. As he told Jon Savage, "Steve is a good recording engineer but he's terrible at mixing as far as I'm concerned. Every Albini record I've ever heard the vocals were too quiet." The songs were great. The recording was what Kurt had wanted. The mix was disappointing to anyone who liked to hear Kurt sing. The problem was easy to fix.

I felt at the time that Albini cynically invented the story demonizing Geffen to depict himself as a purist fighting showbiz philistines. However, Janet says that it was almost certainly Kurt himself who told Albini that there was pressure from the label "because *he* didn't want to take the hit. If he could lay it off on Courtney or the label or us, he was gonna do it." Courtney concurs: "Kurt didn't like confrontation."

The obvious choice to do the remix was Scott Litt, who had produced the last four R.E.M. albums, which were also their most successful. Although those records had put him on the A list in the record business, Litt, then in his late thirties, had spent a decade before that laboring as an engineer and mixer for a wide variety of artists, and he was sensitive and soft-spoken, without a hint of record-business swagger. When Gersh and Kurt had discussed producers for *Nevermind*, Litt had been on their short list, but he was just about to get married and took himself out of contention, a decision that he regrets to this day. When I called to ask him if he wanted to remix a couple of songs on *In Utero* he jumped at the chance.

They did the remixes at Bad Animals studio in Seattle, which was owned by Ann and Nancy Wilson of Heart. Litt remembers that when Kurt, Krist, and Dave first met him "all three of them felt the mixes had been rushed and were bothered by the fact that Albini had refused to redo any of them." Litt says that once he listened to the tracks he realized that "the recordings were dynamite. They were great."

Although Litt had heard the drug rumors, Kurt seemed straight to him at that moment. He was definitely focused. "Kurt was so savvy in the studio. He was a perfectionist and he knew exactly what he wanted. He had no problem making decisions." Kurt gave Litt a few hours to start working on a remix of "All Apologies," and when he walked into the studio Kurt loved what he was hearing and felt comfortable enough that he suggested doing a harmony vocal on the verse. "He sang one take, boom boom boom, and it was done," says Litt, still marveling at it a quarter of a century later.

Kurt was euphoric when he called me afterward. Not only was he happy and relieved with the new mix, he felt good about the process. "Scott is such a nice guy! No wonder R.E.M. likes working with him!" The next day Litt remixed "Heart-Shaped Box," and Kurt had his two singles.

The PR dance of trying to balance punk credibility while releasing a record that would achieve all of what Kurt wanted became more difficult after Jeff Giles wrote a story with Albini's spin in it for *Newsweek*, which had a much bigger national footprint than the *Chicago Tribune*. The usually unflappable Eddie Rosenblatt was incensed by the suggestion that his company was unsupportive to one of their artists. It was a particularly sensitive moment because Gersh had just decided to leave Geffen to become president of Capitol Records and it was important to Rosenblatt to make it clear to the music business that the label was still unambiguous in its support of Nirvana's creative wishes.

Kurt was offended that anyone would think he would be involved with a work of art he did not control. This was Nirvana's record, not Albini's. Just as important he did not want to be at war with his label just as they were about to release the album. The band took out a full-page ad in *Billboard* reiterating that they and they alone controlled the new album. Additionally, at Kurt's insistence, Janet and I worked with him on a letter to *Newsweek* that ran in their May 17 issue.

> *To the Editor:*
>
> *Jeff Giles has written an article on our band Nirvana which was not based on the band's view nor on information provided by our representatives. He pulled together quotes from "un-named sources and music industry insiders." . . . He quotes Albini at length and never approached our management company to speak to us at all. After stating that Albini will not speak about "the Nirvana fracas" Giles quotes him ranting about Geffen Records (our label) in the very same paragraph. How balanced can any reporting be if the center of "the fracas" cannot respond?*
>
> *Most damaging to us is that Giles ridiculed our relationship with our label based on totally erroneous information. Geffen Records has supported our efforts all along in making this record.*
>
> *We hope in the future information provided by us will be taken literally and gossip will be taken for what it is.*
>
> *Kurt Cobain, Dave Grohl, Krist Novoselic*

Despite this, several journalists around the world who were aficionados of punk culture repeated Albini's invention of record company and management interference with the supposedly true wishes of the band. That myth has persisted and was still being repeated by some rock critics when the album was rereleased twenty years later.

The interview Kurt did for *Q* makes it clear that once the controversy became public, he was willing to pay the price of dissing the punk recordist. "The truth is that Steve Albini is very paranoid and I've never worked with so many people who I respect. I've had a lot of co-workers who do their jobs and at this point I do have to consider that this is my job. It's how I create my income. Everyone at DGC has been nothing but supportive and truthful to us. We could disprove the myth about them wanting to not put the album out by making copies of the contract we have with DGC because we have 100% artistic freedom and control."

As he reflects on the intensity of the time, Litt is still impressed by Kurt's ability to have functioned at such a high level and to have borne so much of the pressure. "I don't think there was ever anything like Nirvana in rock and roll except the Beatles. R.E.M. was great and successful and I love them, but the tumultuous effect of when Nirvana came on the scene and the anticipation for that second record and everything going on around Kurt and Courtney, the fervor of their fans, was on a different level. How do you deal with that? At least with the Beatles, they had four guys."

There was a period right after the recording when Kurt wanted to call the album *I Hate Myself and I Want to Die*. I wasn't alone in hoping that he would change it. Krist told Kurt that a title like that could be used against the band if a Nirvana fan ever killed themself. In 1990, the British metal band Judas Priest had been sued by the parents of a boy who had shot himself. The suit claimed he had done so because of "subliminal messages" in their music. Kurt rechristened the album *In Utero*, after a line from a poem Courtney had written while she was pregnant.

With the album title decided, Kurt turned to the cover design. In general, the art that most inspired him was abstract or impressionistic, but he wanted this cover to reflect his fascination with birth and death. Fisher designed the front cover based on ideas from Kurt, who insisted that the cover figure, a transparent anatomical mannequin, have wings. The back cover features a collage of Kurt's artwork, including several depictions of fetuses. In the photo booklet inside, Kurt made sure to include a picture of him in a Flipper T-shirt.

When *Nevermind* had come out we'd anticipated that there might be some resistance to the visibility of the baby's penis on the album cover, but despite a handful of consumer complaints, no retailer declined to carry it. However, the *In Utero* artwork immediately triggered resistance from Walmart, the giant retail chain, which was at the time the single biggest outlet for mass-appeal albums. They told the Geffen sales department they would not sell it with that cover, and I was asked if the band could come up with an alternative.

I felt that Walmart's position was absurd. There was nothing violent, erotic, or profane in the artwork. Any medical textbook has similar images of body parts. Nirvana had been acclaimed by critics all over the world and had won the biggest music awards. I assumed that the resistance was politically rooted in the anti-abortion movement, for which the fetus was an object of veneration.

Bursting with free speech and pro-choice indignation, I told Kurt about the problem and proudly let him know I'd be more than happy to tell the label to back the fuck off. After all, N.W.A's recent album hadn't been carried by Walmart and it was still one of the biggest records of the year. To my surprise Kurt disagreed with me. He explained that when he was growing up the only place he could get records was Walmart, and he wanted kids like him to be able to get Nirvana's new album, so I was to ask Geffen to tell us what changes were needed to get *In Utero* into their stores.

Thus, for their shipments to Walmart (as well as Kmart, another big retail chain that rejected the original cover), Geffen, with the band's approval, simplified the back cover and eliminated the fetuses. The mass retailers also had balked at the song title "Rape Me" being listed on the back cover. Kurt jokingly suggested they change it to "Sexually Assault Me," but to make a quick graphic change he knew they needed to replace one four-letter word with another, so he came up with the meaningless "Waif Me."

I later learned that the "control" Nirvana had did not extend to places in the world where they ignored contracts. In a 2018 piece for Discogs, Ben Blackwell described acquiring a Saudi Arabian cassette of *In Utero* "that completely censored the musculature of the female body depicted on the front cover, almost as if to partially appropriate the chador worn by some Muslim women . . . the face, arms, feet and wings were exposed, but everything in between was blacked out." Blackwell also found a Saudi cassette of *Nevermind* in which the local label had airbrushed a white diaper over the baby's penis. I suspect that Kurt would have been more amused than upset by these releases and happy that some Saudi teenagers were able to hear his music.

Unbeknownst to me at the time, Kurt had slipped back into heroin addiction at some point in the early spring. I was commuting between New York and Los Angeles, so most of my contact was by phone. My memory of that period is shaky, but there is no shortage of documentation of several events. On May 2, 1993, Courtney called the Seattle paramedics because Kurt had overdosed. By the time they got there she had given him pharmaceuticals that stabilized his condition, so he didn't need to go to the hospital. A month later, on June 4, the couple had a

loud enough fight that a neighbor called the cops, and thanks
to a legally mandated procedure in Seattle at the time requiring
someone to be taken to jail when there was a domestic violence
complaint, Kurt was brought to the police station. Charges were
dropped immediately and both Courtney and Kurt played down
the incident. In the weeks that followed Courtney said that she
was attending NA meetings again but Kurt still hated the idea
of group therapy of any kind.

Yet Kurt had his addiction sufficiently under control and it
was not apparent to many of the people around him. The *In Utero*
tour was well received, particularly the show in New York at the
Roseland Ballroom, although later there were reports that he'd
been fucked up earlier in the day. Despite his inner struggles,
Kurt was still pushing Nirvana to keep evolving. For this cycle
the band added guitarist Pat Smear and, for some shows, cellist
Lori Goldston. During the Roseland performance Kurt experi-
mented with a twenty-minute acoustic set in the middle that went
over pretty well, a harbinger of what he would do a few months
later with *Unplugged*. Jim Merlis, a Geffen publicist who had recently started working with the band, remembers, "He was in a
good mood afterward and talking a lot about the guitar that
supposedly had been played by Lead Belly that was being offered
for sale."

Given the level of intensity of everything going on in Kurt's
life, it shouldn't have been a surprise that there was also drama
and a lawsuit over the music video for "Heart-Shaped Box," but
it still blows my mind how stressful Kurt's world had become.

In the previous decade, when MTV had become the dominant exposure medium for many musicians, there had been ever-
shifting relationships between artists, record companies, and video
directors. A few of the latter, such as Bob Giraldi, who directed Michael Jackson's "Beat It," and David Fincher, who directed

Madonna's "Express Yourself," were able to parlay their MTV visibility into careers as feature film directors and were treated like auteurs. However, for some video directors the gig was bittersweet, more like directing a commercial than a movie, except that the clients were artists with creative ideas of their own, who viewed the videos as *their* self-expression and a tool to sell records.

Everyone who was associated with Nirvana in the early nineties was the beneficiary of an ambient glow that made others treat us as if we had suddenly gotten smarter and more glamorous. Kevin Kerslake, who had directed three of the videos for songs off of *Nevermind* as well as the one for "Sliver," was no exception.

My opinion is that as with previous videos the images and ideas for "Heart-Shaped Box" were Kurt's but I was not present when Kerslake and Kurt discussed the video and obviously I am completely biased. Robin Sloane went to Seattle to meet with Kurt and discuss plans for the marketing of the album. She remembers, "Kurt had a whole storyboard written out. The field of poppies he had drawn out beautifully." Shortly afterward, Kurt and Courtney asked me and Rosemary if Katie, then three years old, could be the blond girl in a Ku Klux Klan outfit. (We declined.)

Kerslake submitted what Sloane still calls "an outrageous budget" that was close to $500,000. I reminded Kurt that half of the video budget would be recoupable, meaning it would be deducted from royalties otherwise payable to the band. Kurt felt taken advantage of and decided not to use Kerslake, and asked Sloane to hire Anton Corbijn, a Dutch photographer who had taken pictures of Nirvana and who had made videos for Echo and the Bunnymen that Kurt liked. Corbijn directed the video for "Heart-Shaped Box" for a little more than half of Kerslake's budget.

Sloane suggested that they should try to replicate the Technicolor style of fifties movies for the video and Kurt loved that idea. Actual Technicolor was not doable, but Corbijn found a lab that came very close to duplicating its lush look. The director recalls, "Kurt Cobain was a really sweet man. He had made drawings for the whole video—they were so detailed. I've never seen a treatment that detailed." "Heart-Shaped Box" became MTV's most-played video for many weeks, and it went on to win two awards at the VMAs.

Apparently Kerslake had copyrighted the treatment and he sued the band. Kurt was devestated by the claim, which he viewed as totally unfair and as an insult to him as an artist. The lawsuit was eventually settled after Kurt died on terms that were not disclosed publicly.

Separate and apart from all of the distractions, *In Utero* was about to come out, and the focus went back to the music. Anton Brookes says, "For me it's a better album than *Nevermind*. It's stronger lyrically. The artwork is so amazing. It took them to the next stratosphere. You listen to 'Pennyroyal Tea' and it's just breathtaking." Litt says, "I remember hearing 'Heart-Shaped Box' on KROQ with my niece at a birthday party and people went ballistic. They had been waiting for the next Nirvana song and here's the record and it was so great."

Perhaps as an olive branch to Dave in the wake of changing the songwriting payments, Kurt selected "Marigold," a song Dave wrote and sang lead on, as the B-side of the "Heart-Shaped Box" single. "Heart-Shaped Box" achieved the pop success Kurt envisioned for it, going to number 4 on the U.S. singles charts and to number 5 in the UK.

Jim Merlis had joined the Geffen Records publicity department shortly after the Albini drama played out. Kurt took an immediate liking to him, in part because earlier in his life the publicist had played in an indie band that got to Seattle in the summer of 1990. They had even slept on the floor of Kurt's friend Charles Peterson, the legendary local photographer who documented the Seattle rock culture. Kurt asked for Merlis to accompany him on a press day for European journalists, and that went well enough that Merlis became the label person overseeing the American press for *In Utero*.

Kurt was friendly and unguarded with Merlis, but by this time Kurt and Courtney were much more wary of journalists than they had been pre-Hirschberg. Janet insisted that he "had to fax Kurt and Courtney copies of several pieces from each writer that wanted to talk to them, even Jon Pareles of the *New York Times*, who had already been there for ten years and who had never printed any kind of gossip." Kurt also wanted Merlis to be present for all the interviews and make his own recording of them as a precaution against being misquoted.

Even in this defensive period, Kurt's sophistication in dealing with the media was undiminished. When Pareles flew out to Seattle the publicist was impressed that "the interview was at the Space Needle, the most touristy place possible." Afterward Kurt and Dave rode a roller coaster together with Pareles and Merlis.

Kurt took his time deciding on whether or not to talk to David Fricke, the music editor of *Rolling Stone*, but then he called the writer and seductively said, "I'm gonna tell you the stuff I'm not telling anybody else." They eventually did the interview in Chicago while Nirvana played two gigs on the *In Utero* tour. "The first night was the best show I ever saw them play," says Merlis, "and then there was a day off and then that second show the following night was one of the worst." That was when Fricke's interview was scheduled, and Merlis was worried that after the bad performance Kurt might want to postpone it. However, when the publicist went backstage, Kurt was in a great mood and was holding Frances. "That whole thing about him being depressed all the time often wasn't the case. He was playing with her and beaming."

When Merlis asked if he was still up for the *Rolling Stone* interview, Kurt looked at him like he was crazy and said, "Where's David Fricke? Go get him. Why wouldn't I want to do it?" The interview was in the publicist's hotel suite, and as per the new policy, he brought out his own tape recorder. Kurt acted shocked and told the publicist, "Jim, it's David Fricke! We don't have to record this." Merlis laughs appreciatively as he reflects on it. "It was an intentionally staged thing. Fricke knew that but he appreciated it too. They spoke for six hours. I fell asleep."

Merlis marvels, "Kurt was painting a portrait of himself in media." But Kurt was still hypersensitive. "The reviews for *In Utero* were almost all fantastic. I'd fax Kurt and Courtney all the clippings when they came in but once there was one negative review from the *Boston Herald*. One out of a hundred." Janet called and complained to Merlis, "Did you send a negative review? They're obsessed with the negative review!"

Kurt did an interview with his favorite French journalist, Youri Lenquette, who came to Seattle along with the winner of a *Best* magazine contest whose prize was getting to meet the band. The interview was at a restaurant in Seattle, where Kurt ate a cheeseburger "dripping with grease and surrounded by fries." The writer asked Kurt if that was good for his stomach and Kurt said he no longer had stomach pain.

In Utero was released on September 21, 1993, two years after *Nevermind*. Domestically, 180,000 copies were sold in the first week, making it number 1 on the *Billboard* sales chart—and this was without Walmart and Kmart. (Because of the lead time required for manufacturing album jackets, the version with the "censored" cover wouldn't be available for sale by those mass merchants for two more months.) Although it would never be as big as *Nevermind, In Utero* eventually sold more than five million albums in the U.S. and another five million in the rest of the world. In 2011, the *Guardian* conducted a poll on their website asking fans to name their favorite Nirvana album, and *In Utero* came in first with 43 percent. It's my favorite Nirvana album too.

In Utero's sales were dwarfed the following month by Pearl Jam's album *Vs.*, which scanned more than nine hundred thousand albums in *its* first week. Two years after *Nevermind* had changed the rock-and-roll world, the ultimate establishment magazine, *Time*, was belatedly working on a cover story about the "new" wave of popular, punk-influenced rock and roll. Kurt didn't want to do an interview, and I vaguely remember encouraging him not to. The last thing I wanted was for him to feel he was being pushed into something mainstream he didn't like, and as a practical matter *Time* covers had been a mixed blessing to rock artists over the years.

However, I later learned that Kurt had second thoughts about having blown it off. Courtney heard that Eddie Vedder initially agreed to do an interview and then, after *Time* was fully committed to a Pearl Jam cover, Vedder changed his mind, having his cake and eating it too. The cover of the issue featured a photo of him singing live with the caption "All The Rage: Angry young rockers like Pearl Jam give voice to the passions and fears of a generation." Twenty-five years later Courtney told me with a sigh, "Kurt was pissed. He ranted for a day about it, calling Eddie a poseur. Kelly Curtis [Pearl Jam's manager] played that chess move better than we did."

Michael Azerrad's *Come as You Are* had been published the same week that *In Utero* was released. I felt it was an elegant document of the band's origins and of *Nevermind*, and more importantly Courtney and Kurt were happy with it. The writer lived in New York, and when Kurt was in town for an MTV interview promoting the new album Azerrad, knowing that Kurt loved paintings, suggested Kurt meet him at the Museum of Modern Art. Kurt brought Amy Finnerty along and insisted on paying for everyone's ticket. "I don't think he had ever been there before," says Azerrad, "and there was a big exhibition of Robert Ryman, who painted these large white canvases, and Kurt wasn't into them." However Kurt lit up when they went to the floors of the museum that held classics. "He particularly loved seeing Van Gogh up close," remembers Azerrad fondly. "If I accomplish nothing else in my life, at least I made sure that Kurt Cobain saw *The Starry Night.*" On that same New York trip Kurt finally got to perform "Rape Me" on television, insisting on doing that song in addition to "Heart-Shaped Box" for the band's last appearance on *Saturday Night Live,* the weekend after the album came out.

One of the tools that helped market an artist was an "electronic press kit" with interview and other video footage that could be disseminated worldwide to TV outlets in lieu of individual interviews. Nirvana shot one with comedian Bobcat Goldthwait at Fairfax High in Hollywood. Kurt had first met the comedian during the *Bleach* cycle when they were both at a college radio station in Ann Arbor. "He said he was a fan of mine," Goldthwait recalled later, "which was like hearing that Jimi Hendrix had been a fan of Buddy Hackett." They ended up with a gag video in which Goldthwait pretended to coach Krist, Dave, and Kurt through birth.

Before the *In Utero* tour started, Craig Montgomery was fired as the sound engineer. The band's tour manager Alex MacLeod delivered the news and no one ever told Montgomery what the reason was. I can't remember what triggered it and neither can Courtney, who says of Montgomery, "He was a class act." Some people around the band told the soundman that Kurt had been very unhappy with the sound on *Saturday Night Live.* That wouldn't make sense since the NBC people ultimately controlled the sound on the broadcast, but logic does not always dictate rock-and-roll decisions.

Montgomery got a job working for Juliana Hatfield and then Courtney hired him to work for Hole as she prepared to release *Live Through This*. While he was visiting her at the Seattle house to discuss plans, she put him on the phone with Kurt, who was in New York doing promo. It was a short conversation but friendly, and the last one Montgomery would have with Kurt.

Kurt asked Goldthwait to perform as the opening act for Nirvana on several dates of the American tour, and he stood on the side of the stage every night cracking up as Goldthwait did his routines. The first night was in Chicago and the comedian did a joke about Michael Jordan's father, who had recently been shot to death. The audience booed, but Kurt thought it was hilarious. Goldthwait brainstormed one night about doing a video for "All Apologies" that was a takeoff on the JFK assassination with Kurt as Lee Harvey Oswald, an idea that even Kurt knew was a nonstarter.

In October 1993 in Atlanta, Hole recorded *Live Through This*, their first album for DGC. Kurt missed the initial days of recording because he was busy doing *In Utero* promo but arrived in time to hang out for several days till Hole was finished. For the mix, Kurt recommended Scott Litt, who did it in Los Angeles at Ocean Way Recording. Litt recalls, "Kurt and Courtney were getting along fine. The moments that were fun were fun. I never saw them argumentative in any way but you could feel the press and world around them—there was no escaping it. I couldn't understand how he could keep sober and sane." While they were there Kurt also asked Scott to do a remix of "Pennyroyal Tea" so it would be ready to go if there was going to be a third single from the album.

The label was hoping for more promotion such as radio interviews or live broadcasts from Nirvana, and it was Mark Kates's job to try to get them done. He knew Kurt was stressed out, so he tried broaching the subject with other members of the band, but he hit a brick wall. "Dave would say, 'I'm just the drummer,' and Krist would say, 'Talk to Kurt.'" At this moment, Kurt wanted to back away from media and insisted on not doing any more interviews or radio shows for a while. I got it. Anything to reduce the pressure he was feeling seemed like a good idea.

Kates was also tasked with trying to get another music video done so that MTV would have something to play after "Heart-Shaped Box" ran its course. He recalls, "At this time, Kurt was quiet and intense. I didn't particularly relish walking into a room with the goal of talking him into something he didn't want to do. He knew what I was there to ask him. I knew what he was going to say. He knew that I knew, but he understood I had to go through the motions. He was nice about it." But the answer was negative, as Kates had anticipated. Even though Kurt knew that "All Apologies" was the next single, he just didn't see a way of following the elaborate "Heart-Shaped Box" video. Later, Kurt played around with video ideas for both "Rape Me" and "Pennyroyal Tea," but Nirvana would never make another music video.

For the last group of American dates following the release of *In Utero*, Kurt asked the Meat Puppets to be the support act. Originally from Phoenix, Arizona, the Meat Puppets had made their first records on SST and Kurt had seen them open for Black Flag when he was a teenager. Meat Puppets drummer Derrick Bostrom remembers, "Dave Grohl gave me a rose to welcome me to the tour. Courtney and Frances were on the road and the only sign of stress I noticed was that the catering was so bland because of Kurt's stomach problems. Nirvana shows had a feeling of excitement—not just because they were big—we'd opened for other big bands—but there was that magic about Nirvana, a sense that risks were being taken."

The first of this group of shows was on Halloween 1993 at the University of Akron in a sold-out arena that held six thousand people. Kurt came out onstage completely covered by a purple Barney costume; the dinosaur's kids' show was then at its peak. He also carried a bottle of Jack Daniel's, which he periodically poured into the giant mouth of the Barney head. Pat Smear was dressed up as Slash from Guns N' Roses, and in keeping with Nirvana's rock parody tradition, "Slash" and "Barney" at one point did a guitar duel. Dave was dressed as a mummy and Krist wore whiteface and had the letters PC, for "politically correct," written on his forehead, a reference to a recent contretemps about blackface worn by the actor Ted Danson, who was Whoopi Goldberg's boyfriend at the time.

Bostrom remembers, "It was full of joy and fun. The costumes, the joking, the interaction with the audience. In hindsight it's amazing that a band that big could put on shows that large that had that grassroots kind of small-club feel and have a good time."

In addition to his use of the opening act slot on Nirvana dates, over the preceding year, even while he was immersed in *In Utero*, Kurt had also made time to support other artists he admired in other ways.

FOURTEEN

KURT AND THE MACHINE

When they still lived in Hollywood, Kurt and Courtney would often visit our house, which was in the Hancock Park neighborhood, a five-minute drive away from their place. Kurt liked playing with Katie, who by the summer of 1992 was a very verbal two-year-old who adored him. One night when my new boss, Atlantic cochairman Doug Morris, was in town, Kurt and Courtney joined us for dinner. Afterward Kurt got up from his seat and shook Doug's hand and said earnestly, "I don't really know what you do but you are a very nice person and it's been great to meet you." Of course Kurt knew exactly what he did.

Somehow I felt it was okay for me to lean on Kurt to help me do my new job and that at the same time I was giving him another outlet in his mission to help musicians he cared about. As soon as I had started at Atlantic, I'd asked Kurt who his favorite artist unsigned by a major was. Without hesitating he said

Captain America, which is what motivated the Eugenius signing. The name change mandated by Marvel Comics robbed the band of the visibility Kurt had created for them, but Eugene Kelly was still a significant talent and, more importantly, I wanted to show Kurt I was there for him. Steve Greenberg, a young A & R guy at Atlantic, had a relationship with Kelly, and we quickly signed the band.

Overall it usually seemed like Kurt did more for me than I did for him. Juliana Hatfield was the most successful artist on a label called Mammoth Records, which I had Atlantic acquire. Her song "My Sister" got a decent amount of alternative rock radio and MTV play, and she also wrote a song called "Nirvana," about how much the band meant to her.

Juliana's album was produced by Scott Litt shortly after he remixed the *In Utero* singles. When Nirvana played in New York, Litt brought her backstage but Kurt was frazzled and barely said hello. The next day she got a fax from him saying how much he liked her new album and apologizing for the way he had been backstage: "I was just disoriented because of all the classic after show meet and greet grossness that goes on. We are very lucky to know Danny Goldberg. He's the most honest man in show biz and as long as we know him we'll be in good hands. I wish you all the best.... Love Kurt." I was unaware of this until after Kurt died and Juliana sent me a copy of it. I've kept it framed ever since.

I have mixed feelings about Kurt's production of the Melvins' album *Houdini*, which was Kurt's biggest interaction with Atlantic. From the time I got to the label I was determined to sign the band, which had such a big influence on Kurt, and I thought it might mean a lot to Kurt to produce their first album for us. Of course, I also knew that his name on the record would guarantee some extra media attention. *Houdini* turned out to be the only album that Kurt ever officially produced and Atlantic is the only major label that ever released a Melvins record.

I assigned the project to Al Smith, a young A & R guy at Atlantic, who was already a fan of the Melvins. Smith remembers being impressed, as Kurt and Krist had been as young men, by the charisma of lead singer Buzz Osborne. "I saw them open for Gwar. Buzz played one note for the whole time. He had his back to the audience. They were so defiant and so knew who they were and they had such a unique sound. I knew I wanted to work with them."

Recording was in San Francisco and it was a pivotal time in Smith's career. "Kurt is arguably the biggest rock star on the planet. I'm transporting him back and forth in a rent-a-car from his hotel to a little hole-in-the-wall studio in the Mission District. I thought that Kurt was a fucking genius, the John Lennon of our generation. He did more in a very short period of time than most people do in lifetime."

At first Kurt said little to Smith. When Nirvana recorded there had been no A & R person around and Kurt didn't like the idea of someone looking over his shoulder. One day a writer sent by the Atlantic publicity department appeared in the studio, ostensibly to do a piece on the Melvins. Instead, he started asking Kurt and Courtney questions, which made both of them very uncomfortable. Al promptly called me and explained the situation and I told him it was fine to throw the writer out. After Kurt saw that Al had stuck up for him he warmed to the young A & R guy and gave him his personal phone number.

One day Smith asked Kurt what it was like to be so beloved. He answered, "Al, I just am into the music. The rest of the stuff I don't like. Fame is not that much fun." Kurt then suggested they go out for tacos. While they were walking down the street they passed "a kid who was obviously trying to look like Kurt

Cobain. He had long blond hair, ripped jeans, Converse shoes, and a striped sweater. He had no idea that he was walking by the real Kurt Cobain. Kurt just looked at me and said, 'See?'"

Smith says that as veterans of many previous albums the Melvins knew what they were doing in the studio, so Kurt didn't get involved with most takes, but every once in a while he'd take Buzz into a corner and the two of them would strum guitars. "Kurt was a genius at choruses and his main contribution was to focus on them. We'd listen to takes going back to the hotel in the rent-a-car." For the first few days the vibe was great. "Kurt and Buzz really liked each other. Buzz was one of the few people who had known Kurt before he was famous. Buzz was not at all impressed by the rock-star thing. Kurt also loved [Melvins drummer] Dale Crover."

Encouraged by the early reports, I hoped that Kurt would write a song for the album and encouraged Buzz to ask him for one. A couple of days later Kurt called me and said, "Buzz asked me to write a song for the Melvins. I'm not gonna do that. I'm going to save any good songs for Nirvana." I felt terrible. It was clear from the tone in Kurt's voice that the project was stressing him out and I had only added to the stress.

The recording took a total of three weeks. Smith says, "I realized that Kurt was the smartest guy in the room and I wanted some of that on the record. After a while he thought I was pushing him." Kurt called me one day and was bummed out that Smith was pressuring him to be more involved in the arrangements. I screamed at the young A & R guy to lay off. He was inexperienced and thought that in that situation his job was to "do" something to help make the record better. I couldn't bear for anyone associated with me to upset Kurt. Plus I knew that in trying to influence Kurt, less was more. The only way he was going to get more engaged was if he felt more confident, so in this situation, criticism was counterproductive. Smith backed off, and a couple of days later when he picked up Kurt, Kurt "was in a good mood because the night before he'd written a song for the next Nirvana album. He was truly excited about it."

One night after recording, Kurt, Courtney, Dale Crover and his girlfriend, and Smith went to a P. J. Harvey show at Slim's. Their names were on the guest list, but there was a big line out front. Courtney wanted to go to the front. Kurt insisted on standing in line like everybody else, but they were soon recognized and someone from the club ran out and ushered them inside. Smith says, "Kurt and Courtney's dynamic was great. She did almost all of the talking. She was like a Twitter feed. He would communicate with looks and she always knew what he meant."

The good mood was short-lived because Kurt was back on heroin. Smith recalls, "Kurt was only there for the first ten days. He had good days and bad days—more bad days. Some days in the studio he was engaged and other times he would be passed out on a couch while the Melvins recorded. I'd never been around heroin before so I didn't know what it looked like. Sometimes he was cloudy and sleeping in the corner. On any given day we didn't know which Kurt we would get."

After half a dozen songs were done, Kurt left the studio. He was too strung out, and the Melvins finished the album without him. In an interview for *Kerrang!*, done years after Kurt's death, Buzz described the recording of *Houdini*. He acknowledged that it was the Melvins' bestselling album but said that after the first several sessions with Kurt, "It got to the point where he was so out of control that we basically fired him and went our separate ways."

Courtney's view is a little different: "Kurt was excited to produce the album, but Buzz was so dark."

Many people in Kurt's life knew they couldn't control him,

but they tried to encourage him to help himself. Buddy Arnold kept trying to get Kurt into a twelve-step program, but as much as Kurt liked the old jazz player, he wasn't having it.

There are other spiritual paths besides twelve-step's formulation of a "higher power," and at Christmas I gave Kurt and Courtney statues of the Hindu deities Ganesha and Durga. I had found the connection to such images extremely helpful to me over the years, and I hoped maybe in the privacy of his own mind Kurt would find such a connection. However, without a leap of faith (and/or grace) they were just statues.

Kurt was never disrespectful of my hippie-influenced connection to Eastern spirituality, or of Courtney's and Eric's proactive Buddhist chanting, or even of the twelve-step language about a higher power, but he seemed to have decided that none of these notions of the universe applied to *him*. It was one thing for him to empathize with other people but quite another thing for him to believe that anyone or any force in the universe could understand him.

Over the next several months Kurt talked frequently to interviewers about the Melvins album, which was released on September 21, 1993, the same day that *In Utero* came out. Kurt came to the record release party that Atlantic threw for it as part of a showcase they did at the New Music Seminar in New York. Smith recalls, "Atlantic had several bands, including the Melvins, the Lemonheads, and Surgery, play acoustically in a hotel. Dave Grohl and Kim Deal of the Pixies were there and so was Courtney. Kurt came after Nirvana's Coliseum show wearing the same red-and-black-striped sweater he wore during the recording." Courtney says, "He was proud of the Melvins record."

As of this writing, the Melvins are in their thirty-sixth year. In some ways *Houdini* was just a blip in a long career defined by artistic integrity, but Smith says, "I meet Melvins fans today and most of them feel *Houdini* was one of their high points." As of early 2018, Spotify offered listeners twenty-six studio albums by the Melvins covering a period from 1989 to 2017. By far the most popular track is "Honey Bucket" from *Houdini* at 3.8 million streams, and five of six of the most streamed tracks by the Melvins are from that album that Kurt produced.

Another one of Kurt's favorite artists was Daniel Johnston, a singer-songwriter who had struggled with mental illness. One of the T-shirts Kurt wore when he knew he was going to be photographed featured the cover of Johnston's indie cassette *Hi, How Are You*. Yves Beauvais, an Atlantic A & R person who usually dealt with jazz artists, was obsessed with Johnston. With Kurt's encouragement, I green-lit the signing. Atlantic released *Fun* in the fall of 1994, after Kurt's death and at a time when Johnston was back in a mental institution. It was his only major-label release; after I left Atlantic they dropped him and he resumed making indie records.

Kurt also encouraged me to have Atlantic acquire half of the indie label Matador Records, which released albums by Pavement and Liz Phair, among others. Matador was one of the indie labels Kurt sent letters and cassettes to before he got Sub Pop to sign Nirvana.

My time at Atlantic was during a period when all the major record companies were in the quixotic pursuit of "the next Nirvana." I knew that there was no such thing, but I had no qualms about finding ways to make money for my company with bands that were addressing the post-*Nevermind* rock audience. Even though he was not a fan of Stone Temple Pilots and some of the other artists I signed, Kurt never gave me shit about them, nor did he ever publicly disparage them.

On a personal level, though, Kurt was only interested in music that he considered to be art. He had mentioned the British art-rock band the Raincoats in the *Incesticide* liner notes, and in the spring of 1993 he wrote notes for a Raincoats compilation that was released in the UK. He began by reiterating what they meant to him: "I don't really know anything about the Raincoats except that they recorded some music that has affected me so much that whenever I hear it I'm reminded of a particular time in my life when I was (shall we say) extremely un-happy, lonely and bored. If it weren't for the luxury of putting on that scratchy copy of the Raincoats' first record, I would have had very few moments of peace."

Kurt ended those notes by writing of the Raincoats, "They're playing their music for themselves," and when I read this I felt there was a tinge of melancholy as he contemplated the road not taken. From his earliest days as a performer, Kurt had decided that his path required connecting to a large audience. Yet he had also long been fascinated by that kind of intimacy in music. Having honored his punk roots by releasing *Incesticide* and recording *In Utero* with Albini, he was almost immediately drawn to the sounds of acoustic instruments, and he figured out how to express himself in a new way while also adding another dimension to Nirvana's career.

FIFTEEN

UNPLUGGED

K urt still cared a lot about MTV, and in December 1993 he called Amy Finnerty and asked her to bring Kurt Loder to a tour date in St. Paul to erase any ill will left over from the anger that Kurt and Courtney had about Loder's reporting on the *Vanity Fair* piece. Loder says that he only spent a few minutes with Kurt and that all he wanted to talk about was Lead Belly.

Since 1989, MTV had been airing a series of "unplugged" performances in which rock artists performed their songs with acoustic instruments. Some of these were later released as albums, most notably Eric Clapton's *Unplugged*, which won the 1992 Grammy for album of the year.

Nirvana: MTV Unplugged in New York became a big deal because the album came out after Kurt's death. However, it was taped less than two months after *In Utero* had been released, and initially Kurt saw it as a way to continue Nirvana's visibility on

MTV without making a new video, while also giving him a platform to further experiment with a new creative direction.

Finnerty remembers, "He was staying at the Paramount Hotel near MTV Studios and asked me to come over and told me he was worried that it wasn't going to work. Dave was playing too hard." That problem was solved when Dave agreed to play the drums only with brushes and Kurt scheduled an extra rehearsal to refine some of the arrangements with the softer percussive sound.

It was hard for me to tell Kurt that I was not going to be able to come to the taping in New York on November 18, 1993. Although I had just been made president of Atlantic, which was based in New York, I was still commuting from Los Angeles because Rosemary was eight and a half months pregnant. There was no way I was going to be three thousand miles away from her at that point. Our son, Max, was born twelve days later.

Janet remembers, "Up until the actual performance it was not a great day physically for Kurt." (Her tactful way of saying he was high.) At sound check Janet was focusing on schmoozing the MTV people until Kurt insisted she stop and sit and pay attention to the run-through. She says, "That's when I realized this was going to be something different than anything he'd done before."

Kurt asked Scott Litt to mix the *Unplugged* sound for the taping, which was done "live" in the sound truck. Litt recalls MTV's Alex Coletti asking for acoustic versions of the hits from *Nevermind*, in keeping with the way most other artists had performed on the series. On previous occasions Kurt had agreed to feed the MTV beast without insisting on fidelity to his creative vision. He had agreed to do "Lithium" instead of "Rape Me" at the VMAs, but to Kurt *that* was MTV's show. The acoustic concert was a *Nirvana* performance. Kurt saw it as art, not as promo, and no one was going to tell him what to do with his art. Other than "Come as You Are," in Kurt's mind none of Nirvana's hits from *Nevermind* lent themselves to acoustic arrangements, and he had no interest in rearranging "Heart-Shaped Box" either.

MTV backed off, and they also acquiesced when Janet rejected the network's push for special guests who were known to their viewers, like Eddie Vedder or Tori Amos, ideas that Janet didn't even convey to Kurt, knowing how tone-deaf such notions were relative to where his head was at. Instead Kurt invited Cris and Curt Kirkwood of the Meat Puppets to participate. Janet recalls, "He added them a day or two before. MTV didn't get it," but they did agree to it. Kurt ended up singing three Meat Puppets songs that he had never performed publicly before and gave them a life that even an indie rock connoisseur like Janet had never realized was there. "How did he know they would sound like masterpieces?"

In a documentary that MTV made years later about the making of Nirvana's *Unplugged*, a couple of the network's execs were still bitching about the lack of hits and famous guests. This is typical of the difference in perspective between a media company that is focused on the current sensibilities of a mass audience and a visionary artist who is creating for the future. Like David Bowie when he jettisoned Ziggy Stardust, or John Lennon when he sang, "The dream is over," after leaving the Beatles, or Dylan at numerous junctures in his career, Kurt, at that moment, was deconstructing the character that made him famous in order to keep his inner artist alive.

Kurt told Coletti that he wanted stargazer lilies and candles for the onstage set. "Like a funeral?" the producer asked. "Yes, like a funeral." After Kurt died, a mere five months later, many writers noted this fact and mentioned that five of the six songs that were broadcast referred to death, but at the time the set and set list just seemed like the kind of dark aesthetic choices Kurt usually made.

He was a nervous wreck in the days leading up to it. Having obsessively rehearsed every previous record for months before recording, Kurt was debuting a new chapter of Nirvana's music with only three days of rehearsal before taping a show that would be seen by millions of people.

Finnerty describes Kurt's state of mind before the show: "I knew how fragile Kurt was that day so I remained upstairs with him. Then Kurt went into the bathroom and would not come out." She figured that Kurt had shot up and passed out. "It was very scary. People were asking me, 'Do they have anything to perk him up? Is he gonna be sick?' I don't know if people were aware how dangerously close we were to not having that show. We didn't know if he was gonna come out of it." After a few more minutes Kurt found his way out and came downstairs with Finnerty. "He wanted to make sure that some of his friends, especially Janet, were in the front row." Then he asked Finnerty to accompany him to the lobby so he could see members of the audience up close. They walked to the line of people waiting to be seated. "People were jumping all over him, and he needed that. He wanted to hug the fans."

Even in his stressed-out state, Kurt was mindful of his young ally. On his way backstage, Kurt pulled MTV president Judy McGrath aside. The company had just given Finnerty a promotion and a raise, and Kurt told McGrath, "I just wanted to thank you for moving Amy up."

Kurt wore a T-shirt for the feminist punk band Frightwig, which could be seen under his unbuttoned light green cardigan. Once the performance started with "About a Girl," Kurt again rose to the occasion. "You could hear a pin drop, which wasn't anything you'd expect at a Nirvana show," remembers Finnerty.

Since the *Unplugged* performances on MTV were taped, many artists did second or third takes of songs to correct errors or tweak the arrangements, but Nirvana's was live without any retakes. When it came time to cover David Bowie's "The Man Who Sold the World," Kurt told the audience, "I'm sure I'll screw this song up," but of course he didn't.

Kurt ended with a cover of Lead Belly's "Where Did You Sleep Last Night?" A few years earlier Kurt and Krist had played on a recording of the song by their friend Mark Lanegan, the singer of the Seattle band The Screaming Trees. Litt was blindsided by its inclusion because Nirvana hadn't done the song in any of the rehearsals, but he still captured Kurt's extraordinary vocal performance.

When Neil Young first watched the performance, he described the final note of Cobain's as "unearthly, like a werewolf, unbelievable." An MTV exec asked if the band would do an encore and Kurt refused.

Right afterward, when Janet told him it had been amazing, Kurt insisted, "We fucking sucked. I'm a shitty guitar player." He asked Finnerty why the crowd had been so quiet and lamented, "I don't think anybody liked it." Janet and Finnerty told him how wrong he was. The quietness was because of the intimacy. People had been moved to tears.

By the next day when he called me Kurt had finally internalized the fact that the show had worked and was exuberant about it. "I can't wait for you to see it. I think it's really going to change the way people see our band." I thought it was so typical of Kurt to feel he *still* had something to prove.

The *Unplugged* performance operated on many levels. It showed the quality of his songwriting (eight of the fourteen songs were ones that Kurt had written) and his singing. He also used the platform to draw attention, yet again, to more obscure artists that he admired. In addition to the relatively unknown Meat Puppets songs, he also included an old favorite of his, Eugene Kelly's "Jesus Don't Want Me for a Sunbeam," originally recorded by the Vaselines.

For Litt, the highlight was the Bowie song: "It always gets to me as touching me in a weird way. The way that they played it, it kind of gave me chills. That was when I knew we were onto something special." My favorite is "Pennyroyal Tea," which Kurt performed by himself on acoustic guitar. The show aired on MTV on December 16, and the week before a clip of the *Unplugged* version of "All Apologies" went into regular rotation on the channel.

To further compensate for not doing another music video, and to remind fans of the aggressive side of Nirvana, Kurt agreed for the band to do one more performance for MTV. On December 13 they taped a live performance in Seattle of a version of the show that the band had been doing for the *In Utero* tour.

Although the *Unplugged* album would not be released until seven months after Kurt's death, he knew right away that the concept was what he wanted for Nirvana's next release. Kurt contemplated rerecording it all in a studio, not because of any creative concerns but to save money. Litt remembers, "When he found out that MTV got a [royalty] point on *Unplugged* albums he said to me, 'Let's just go into a studio and do it again. Now that we know it works it will be easy.'" Of course the rerecording never happened.

Shortly after taping *Unplugged*, Kurt asked me if I thought Nirvana should be part of the Lollapalooza tour the following summer. I had always felt that Nirvana should avoid that tour, not because I didn't respect its cultural power but because it would place them inside someone else's musical vision, which, in my mind, contradicted Nirvana's unique status. I was also worried that even though Lollapalooza had offered the band $6 million, which was more than they would make on their own tour, there would be much more liability in canceling performances on a Lollapalooza tour than on a Nirvana tour. Given the number of shows Kurt had canceled in the last couple of years, this was a significant financial downside. He sounded relieved to hear a dissenting view and asked, "Can you tell that to Courtney?"

After Hole finished *Live Through This*, some DGC execs came up to Seattle to discuss promotion with Courtney. Among them was Merlis, who remembers, "The last time I saw Kurt was at that meeting. He was holding Frances and looked surprised and asked me, 'What are you doing here?' He was totally friendly and he walked me down to the basement, where Frances immediately starting banging on drums. It was beautiful. If there had to be a last moment, this was a good one." During Christmas week Kurt and Courtney made another attempt at tending to their health and went to the Canyon Ranch spa in Tucson.

In February 1994 Nirvana went on a European tour and Courtney missed the first month of it. She was doing setup for the Hole album, so she and Frances arrived near the end. French promoter Gérard Drouot reminded me that Kurt was nowhere to be found when it was time for the band to play a sold-out show at the Zénith theater in Paris, where they were headlining. "He had an argument with Courtney in the limo and left the car," Drouot recalls. "There were no cell phones in France in those days. Finally, just as I was worrying that I'd have to tell six thousand people that Nirvana would not play, Kurt arrived in a normal Parisian taxi and went onstage and then did a good show." The last French show was in Toulon, near Marseilles. "We did around four thousand tickets," says Drouot, "and that was a lot in the French provinces. I stood in the balcony and watched the entire concert and it was another amazing show."

It would be Nirvana's final show in France. After that the band went to Italy and the Melvins opened for them for seven shows, all in Europe. They would be the last performances Nirvana would ever give.

SIXTEEN

THE DOWNWARD SPIRAL

On March 4, 1994, Courtney called me and said that Kurt had OD'd on Rohypnol in Rome and was in a hospital unconscious, hovering between life and death. She was crying and the two of us prayed together on the phone for him. I was freaked out, but I didn't believe or didn't want to believe that he was going to die. News of Kurt's condition hit the wire services and I got several calls over the next few hours from concerned friends. I got periodic updates from Janet, who was in frequent touch with Courtney. Finally word came that he was conscious. Kurt was going to pull through.

Because he died a month later, the OD in Rome has become intertwined in the narrative of Kurt's life and his actual suicide, but at the time I breathed a sigh of relief. He was okay! I foolishly believed that this horrible close call would somehow awaken in him the need to change his behavior. As I was selling myself this fairy tale, David Geffen called and began the conversation somberly, saying, "Well, there are some people who just can't be helped no matter what you do." I was giving him the rap I'd been disseminating to others, that Courtney was with him and that he would probably be fine, when David interrupted and said in a tone that indicated I was delusional, "Danny, he's dead. Courtney just called me and told me he's dead." I felt a shiver of horror followed by a shadow of doubt. I told him that while it was certainly possible that Kurt had died and I hadn't been told yet, it also was possible that the call was a hoax. It seemed unlikely to me that Courtney would have called him but not shared the supposed news with Janet, Rosemary, or me, although in the insane moment and knowing that Geffen had a totemic role in Courtney's mind, it wasn't completely impossible. Geffen was understandably incensed by the uncertainty and the idea that someone would prank him about such a serious matter and asked me to please get back to him as soon as I knew anything more.

It took twenty agonizing minutes for Janet to get ahold of Courtney and confirm that Kurt was indeed still alive, and I called Geffen and confirmed that whoever called him was an imposter. I never figured out who the asshole was or why they did it. It's the sort of weird thing that happens sometimes around famous people.

When I finally spoke to Kurt on the phone a few days later he sounded sweet but weak. Back in Seattle two weeks later, and unbeknownst to me at the time, Courtney called the Seattle police because Kurt was locked in a room at their house with guns and she was terrified that he would hurt himself. The cops confiscated four guns and several boxes of ammunition.

A few days after that, on March 24, Courtney prevailed upon me to join a few people in Seattle and be part of an intervention the next day. She said that Kurt was the worst she'd ever seen him and that for the first time since Frances had been born even being with his daughter wasn't making him smile. Over the last couple of years I'd lived through some tough times with Courtney. I'd witnessed her in despair, in a rage, and stoned, but this was the first time I'd ever heard fear in her voice.

Early the next morning at Kennedy Airport, I met Janet and a drug counselor she had hastily found named David Burr, and the three of us boarded a plane to Seattle. Burr had a beard and an avuncular manner and appeared to be in his late thirties. He wasn't trying to be cool or impress us with the people he'd worked with like the guy a couple of years earlier, but I was doubtful that any stranger would have an ability to communicate with Kurt in a meaningful way. Nevertheless I understood that his presence could add gravity to the upcoming confrontation, which presumably was why Courtney had asked Janet to get someone to play that role.

Around midday we got to the big house Kurt and Courtney had bought at 171 Lake Washington Boulevard. Several people from Los Angeles arrived around the same time. Kurt was sitting on the floor of the big living room next to his longtime friend Dylan Carlson, the guitarist and singer in an indie rock group called Earth. Carlson and Kurt had briefly been roommates in Olympia back in the day. They were both glassy eyed and exuded an odious junkie smugness, as if they were the only two members of some special club.

Kurt was defensive, which didn't surprise me. No one likes to be pressured by a group of people in his own home without any warning. Some accounts of the afternoon describe a conventional intervention in which each person confronted him and suggested they wouldn't be involved with him if he kept doing drugs. That's not the way it was. What I recall is a lot of us just begging him to stop for his own good. Still, it must have seemed like an invasion to Kurt, and I can see why Courtney later said she regretted having suggested it because "Kurt felt ganged up on."

My message was simple. I can see that you're really unhappy. Whatever it is that is bothering you, you can't deal with it effectively until you get clean. Kurt gave me a rap about how he felt trapped because everywhere he went he was recognized while Dylan nodded sympathetically. I was irritated by this dubious excuse for being a junkie and also kind of insulted that he would give me such a generic response, but I knew he was feeling embattled, so I took a deep breath and tried to take his remark at face value. I reminded him that he'd been famous for more than a couple of years and had rarely had a problem blending into the background in public when he just altered his appearance slightly. What did being famous have to do with getting off heroin?

Changing tacks, Kurt asked me indignantly, "Why are you talking to me about this? You should talk to Courtney!" I felt at least now he was being a bit more honest with his emotions. I assured him that I had said the same thing to her and that she had told me she that she was prepared to go to rehab.

I felt so impotent. Just a few months earlier he had told a journalist that I was like a "second father" to him in the most loving tone. Now I could barely reach him. At one point, Janet went upstairs into Kurt's bathroom and started throwing pills into the toilet. Kurt figured out what she was doing and ran upstairs after her, yelling that Janet had no right to do that with his personal property and demanding my support in his outrage. I joined them in the bathroom and Janet looked mortified. I felt bad for both of them. Kurt felt violated but obviously Janet was just trying to do the right thing. After Rome she was freaked out by the prospect of another pharmaceutical OD. It was also a dramatic way to convey to Kurt the depth of her concern. I told Kurt that I understood why he was upset by the intrusion but asked him to please understand that we were all terrified that he was going to harm himself.

When we went downstairs, Burr, the counselor, decided to weigh in, to give a sentence or two about his own struggles with addiction and try to appeal to Kurt as a father. The notion of a stranger lecturing him infuriated Kurt, who bitterly said, "You don't know anything about me." Now roused into high dudgeon, Kurt said that he didn't need rehab, he needed a therapist. He added that because he couldn't trust the motivations of people around him, he would find one in the Yellow Pages. Kurt actually grabbed a copy of the large book that phone companies gave out in those days and started manically leafing through the pages, as if that were a good way to find a shrink.

Vainly trying to stick to the point, I said that any therapist he found would only be able to help him if he got clean first. I had no idea what had triggered the last few weeks of Kurt's despair. Maybe it was an intense crystallization of the depressions that had long tormented him.

Maybe it was something at home. Maybe it was related to his career. (Kurt, who had musical ideas he didn't think were right for Nirvana, had, in the prior months, asked me a couple of times if I thought he could have a career outside of the band. I told him he definitely could but that he didn't need to choose one or the other. For example, Neil Young did solo albums and he also periodically reunited with Crosby, Stills and Nash, but only when he felt like it.)

I reiterated that whatever his issues were with the band, or for that matter with Courtney, or with the demons in his head I couldn't access, no matter what he wanted to do artistically or personally, he would be able to think more clearly and make better decisions if he detoxed. I just couldn't think of anything else to say.

Kurt wasn't having it. He insisted that William Burroughs had been able to function for decades as a junkie and Kurt didn't see any reason why he couldn't have a life like that. For some reason this annoyed me more than anything else he had said and I showed it in my tone. I told him that I wanted to get home to see my own kids. I had just come because I was worried about him and I had a plane to catch. I implored him again to get clean so he could make better decisions. I would support him in any way I could after that no matter what he wanted to do but I was heading for the airport.

When I got home to L.A. a few hours later I felt terrible about the exasperation that had crept into my voice before I left and I immediately called Kurt and apologized if I'd come off in a lecturing way. I told Kurt that I respected him and loved him and was just upset because I was worried about him. He sounded depressed and was probably stoned, but even in that state Kurt had a gentle sweetness and said, "I know that."

Katie wandered into the room while I was talking to him and said she had something she'd been meaning to tell him. I hoped that her voice would cheer him up so I put her on the phone. She talked to Kurt for a minute or two, informing him indignantly that Frances had pinched her the last time they were together. She paused to listen to his response and then said, "Kurt, you sound a little grumpy. Don't be grumpy!" and said she loved him and handed the phone back to me. I told him I loved him again. Kurt and I said goodbye to each other and his despair sounded undiminished. I felt helpless. It was the last time we spoke.

Over the next couple of days both Kurt and Courtney came down to L.A. to get into rehab, and I hoped this time it would finally have a more lasting impact. There were lots of stories of addicts who had to go in several times before finally turning a corner. I thought this might be his moment.

Two weeks later, on Friday, April 8, I was back in New York in a meeting with Atlantic general manager Val Azzoli and Stevie Nicks about a new record she was planning for the label when my assistant told me that Rosemary was on the phone and that it was urgent. She was calling from her car on her way to see Courtney, who was still in rehab, and said she had to tell her what happened. I said that I had no idea what she was talking about and she replied, "Oh my God. Of course you don't know yet either. Kurt killed himself." I will never completely get over the sadness and anguish I felt at that moment.

Pain was soon replaced by shock and the need to "function." I flew back to L.A. and the following day, I, Rosemary, Katie, and four-and-a-half-month-old Max flew to Seattle, where we were met by a female limo driver. She quickly figured out that we were in town for Kurt's funeral. "You know, I drove him a few months ago. He was so nice. I told him that my fourteen-year-old son was a big fan of his and he asked where we lived, and when he realized that it was on the way to his house he suggested we stop there so he could say hello." She continued, "Kurt shook my son's hand and looked him in the eyes and said, 'You know, your mom is a really great driver.'" She was sobbing by the time she got to the end of the story and so were we. After she regained her composure the driver said, "My son is so upset at people who are criticizing Kurt now. He says they just don't understand what Kurt was going through."

Janet was tasked with figuring out where to have a funeral. Because it was a suicide, most churches wouldn't allow it. "I was at the Four Seasons cold-calling from the Yellow Pages. Finally, [Soundgarden manager] Susan Silver suggested trying the Unitarians."

At some point later we were all at Courtney's house. There were dozens of people milling around in different rooms but a few of us sat with Courtney and Kurt's mother, Wendy, in one of the bedrooms. Kat Bjelland from Babes in Toyland arrived. Courtney had feuded with her frequently in the press, but they meant a lot to each other.

At one point Courtney told us that she'd found a suicide note. I don't know if she'd been holding on to it for a while or had just discovered it. In the years that followed, the note has been published dozens of times and subject to various interpretations, but to hear her read it at that moment was heartbreaking. She started, "'To Boddah: Speaking from the tongue of an experienced simpleton who would rather be an emasculated, infantile complain-ee—'" At this point she interjected, "Fucking Kurt didn't even spell the name Buddha right." Wendy gasped and told us that Boddah had been the name of an imaginary friend Kurt had when he was a little kid. We were all stunned into silence.

Later that night Courtney took me aside and tearfully said, "Kurt and I wanted to be like Danny and Rosemary but the problem was—we both wanted to be Rosemary."

She asked if I would speak at the funeral service and I started looking around the house for a Bible. I had recently been at a funeral at which a rabbi read from the Book of Ecclesiastes ("To everything there is a season . . . a time to be born and a time to die"), and it had touched me. Courtney wanted to have a song played when the service was over and I suggested John Lennon's "In My Life."

At the place Janet secured, the Unity Church of Truth, various people spoke who knew Kurt when he was growing up, and then it was my turn. I did not write out my remarks and as far as I know no recording exists, so my memory of what I said is spotty. I know that I quoted the Ecclesiastes verse and added the idea of

Kurt's being a special soul who brought light to earth, the stuff that Everett True complained about in his book. I believed it then and I believe it now.

I didn't want the people who had met him in the last few years to feel excluded. Eddie Rosenblatt said that the only Geffen people who should come were those who knew Kurt personally, but that still meant that he, Gary Gersh, Mark Kates, John Rosenfelder, Ray Farrell, and Robin Sloane were in the church mourning with us. My mind was on them and on Silva and the other Gold Mountain people. I talked about what it was like to work with him after he came to Los Angeles, how he wanted to maintain his artistic integrity and yet also cared about reaching a lot of people. I was thinking about Rosemary, so I told the story of the two of us talking to Kurt when he was trying to make up his mind about whether or not to do the MTV Video Music Awards. And I was thinking about Kurt's wife. *Rolling Stone* printed the one quote from my remarks that survives: "I believe he would have left the world years ago if he hadn't met Courtney."

I have only fragmentary memories of the moments afterward as the Lennon song played. When I saw Eddie Rosenblatt I hugged him and started sobbing uncontrollably in his arms. A couple of minutes later a man came over to me and shook my hand and introduced himself as Kurt's dad, Don Cobain. Later I told Krist that I had never met the elder Cobain before and he said, "Yeah. Kurt had a hard time forgiving him," and then added wistfully, "I'm a forgiver."

The media coverage of Kurt's death was massive. It made all of the network news shows, and MTV's Judy McGrath told me, "I told my people to find every minute we had of him and run it." The *New York Times* ran an obituary on their front page with a headline that called him a "hesitant poet of grunge rock." Of course he wasn't particularly hesitant, didn't consider himself a poet, and rarely used the word "grunge," but somehow the story had a dignity that I felt was appropriate.

Not everyone agreed. On the CBS show *60 Minutes*, commentator Andy Rooney expressed outrage at the outpouring of emotion over the suicide of a drug addict. He wondered of such artists, "Are they contributing anything to the world they are taking so much from?"

Several days later, *New York Times* columnist Frank Rich described his teenage sons' outrage at Rooney and also at the mainstream media cliché that Kurt was the voice of his generation: "To label Mr. Cobain . . . as a symbolic victim of success or drugs or rock nihilism is to tune him out . . . his primal screams of sheer pain, unsweetened by showmanship or sentimentality . . . demanded a more direct and passionate response. Without prompting by hype, millions of Americans made that intimate connection."

The next day, a satirical fax circulated in the punk rock world purporting to be a memo I'd send Silva a year later morbidly celebrating the money we supposedly would have made from exploiting Kurt's death. Putting aside the disgusting and unfair implication about our motivations, the trope about a musical artist being worth more dead than alive was untrue. Then, as now, rock artists made more money from touring than from any other source. Although there is often a spurt of record sales right after a death, the fact that there will be no future albums or tours is far more of a financial negative than a positive. No one with any experience in the music business, no matter how venal or stupid, would conclude that an artist is worth more dead than alive. More to the point, of course, we were every bit as devastated at Kurt's death as anyone from Washington State was. The satirical "letter" cruelly ended with "me" writing, "Without Kurt's meddling interference we have finally built the career we always wanted."

For reasons that were never clear to me, Courtney initially believed that Slim Moon was the source of the fax. She excoriated Moon on an AOL message board called the Velvet Rope, which was a precursor to social networking: "I CAN'T BELIEVE YOU AUTHORED THAT FAX ABOUT DANNY'S SPEECH AT THE FUNERAL. Kurt was *in* that church and all he heard coming out of Danny Goldberg's mouth was love sincerity compassion and EMPATHY, the very empathy that killed him, the pained fucking truth beauty which he could not live with and which you could not have a fucking piece of." Moon emphatically denied writing the fax, and he and I developed a polite relationship via email in the aftermath.

When I talked to Moon recently he disavowed any knowledge of the fax's origin but explained to me that he and his indie friends were offended by my story about Rosemary and I speaking to Kurt about doing the MTV awards. "The Olympia contingent felt that the juxtaposition of Kurt's regret at the major-label route and management bragging about manipulating him was tone-deaf when some people felt that he is dead 'cause he had been manipulated."

Carrie Brownstein wrote in her memoir that one of the reasons that her band Sleater-Kinney signed to Moon's Kill Rock Stars label instead of a major was because of Kurt's death. "The simplified version of his story could be reduced to a guy who signed to a major label, got so famous that he felt alienated from his audience and then killed himself . . . this tragedy was now in the figurative guidebook—it functioned as a cautionary tale."

I thought it was pretty lame for people to use Kurt's death as a talking point in their self-serving arguments about the supposed moral superiority of their own choices in life. My own "cautionary tale" is: Don't do heroin. Don't become a fucking junkie. And if you are a junkie, do whatever it takes to stop. But even the junkie factor isn't dispositive. There are mysteries of the mind and spirit. With the possible exception of saints, human beings simply aren't designed to understand everything about life and death.

Even at the time I realized that whoever wrote that fax and those amused by it were in anguish over Kurt's death. They wanted to lash out at someone, to create some sort of explanation for a dreadful tragedy. They loved him, or at least they loved the part of him that they knew, just as I and the rest of us from L.A. loved the part of him that we knew. I had worked for Albert Grossman when Janis Joplin died of an overdose, and even though he was my boss, a piece of me wondered at the time if Grossman couldn't have somehow done something to prevent her death. It wasn't rational, and in retrospect I see how unfair it was, but I understand the impulse to place blame on anyone whose name is associated with an artist who kills themself. Part of the karma of having been able to work with Kurt was becoming the recipient of the rage of others who loved him.

For weeks I would scan the Velvet Rope for comments about Kurt's death. When fans blamed me or my colleagues I would respond that we had lost someone whom we loved and that we only wished we had known how to stop him from killing himself. Most wrote back apologetically once they realized that we too were actual human beings who were also grieving.

I had less sympathy for a few rock journalists who wrote self-righteous articles suggesting that if only those of us who worked with Kurt had been more honest with the press about his drug problems, somehow this candor would have magically saved his life. For one thing, our obligation to him included confidentiality. Moreover, there is no viable theory I am aware of that suggests that media coverage of addiction helps the addict.

A couple of weeks after the funeral Rosemary told me about a private detective Courtney had hired when Kurt left rehab. In the past she had not shared her professional conversations with Kurt or Courtney with me because the role of attorney required confidentiality, but she made an exception because of the intense pressure being brought to bear by the detective, whose name was Tom Grant.

Evidently Courtney shared Kurt's notion that the only way to get help without the risk of being manipulated was to look in the Yellow Pages, which is how she found Grant. After Kurt left the Exodus rehab center in Marina del Rey and Courtney couldn't get ahold of him for a day or two, she had a sense of foreboding and retained the detective to try to track Kurt down via credit card records and other tricks of the trade. Rosemary remembers, "She asked me to cooperate with him completely and follow his instructions."

When Courtney first hired him, the detective had traveled to Seattle and spent time with Dylan Carlson, who was apparently the last person to see Kurt alive. Dylan had gone with Kurt to Stan Baker Sports and bought a shotgun for him because Kurt couldn't buy one himself after the recent fights with Courtney where the police got involved.

Observing the extraordinary amount of media attention that Kurt's death received, Grant decided to keep "investigating" on his own. Rosemary asked if I could meet the detective so I could give her my thoughts about his current point of view. I visited him in what appeared to be a one-man office in a seedy section of Hollywood. He laid out some of his theories, which he would later make public in a series of interviews and documentaries. Grant said that the amount of heroin found in Kurt's body was much higher than most people could absorb and remain conscious. If he had passed out, the detective said, Kurt couldn't have pulled the trigger on the shotgun himself. I reminded him that Kurt was a rock star who'd had access to high-quality heroin over a long period of time and probably had a much higher tolerance for the drug than an average person.

Grant then asked me if I thought that the handwriting on the suicide note was really Kurt's. I told him that I had just glanced at it once and I wasn't a handwriting expert, but it looked similar to other handwritten notes of his I'd seen.

After a few more minutes it became clear to me that the detective was suggesting that Kurt had been murdered. I asked him what motivation anyone would have had to do it. Grant smiled with feigned sophistication and said, "He would be worth more dead than alive," the same myth that the writer of the anonymous fax had conjured up. I explained to him that the opposite was true.

I asked Grant why, if the evidence cast so much doubt on suicide, the Seattle police weren't investigating. Weren't they the ones with the forensic tools and legal mandate to find out what happened? Didn't they have a big incentive to get to the truth on such a high-profile matter? In a tone dripping with contempt, Grant said he had worked for the L.A. sheriff's department and he knew how a police department could be corrupted. I had been trying to give him the benefit of the doubt, thinking that perhaps he was a sincere if misguided truth seeker. Now I believed he was a nut.

It was, and is, inconceivable to me that Courtney would have been involved in killing her husband. Nothing Grant said then or in future years has changed my conviction that his theory is wrong. Moreover, the notion that Courtney, struggling with her own drug problems at the time, could have somehow executed a cover-up inside the Seattle Police Department is laughable.

When I got back home I told Rosemary in no uncertain terms that I thought Grant was a bullshitter and publicity seeker, intoxicated by his first experience with a case that made headlines, and that his theories made no sense to me. She told him to stop contacting her, and Grant creepily suggested that her refusal to cooperate with him could jeopardize her career.

Twenty years later, Grant still maintained a website promoting his theories, and over the course of time a few misguided writers and filmmakers were seduced by the murder conspiracy theory. Some of them preposterously tried to make the case that Kurt was not depressed, was not a drug addict, or no longer had stomach pain. Another conspiracy theorist claims that "government officials" killed Kurt.

From time to time the Seattle Police Department has released more details to try to address the pressure from the tiny cult of conspiracy buffs who cling to the murder theory, but a few of them remain convinced that Kurt was murdered.

Krist agrees with me that such theories are absurd. He feels that his friend was never the same after the OD in Rome and that "something affected his brain." He sees a lot of forethought in Kurt's final days, even including his choice of a small-gauge shotgun. "It wasn't the kind of gun you'd get to protect yourself, it's what you should use for killing birds. He didn't want to make a big mess." Using a phrase he had employed previously to describe Kurt relative to his art, Krist concluded bitterly, "Kurt was a planner."

SEVENTEEN

AFTERMATH

It is likely that if Kurt had lived his next project would have included different musicians and had a more acoustic feel to it. He was thinking about collaborating with one of his heroes, Michael Stipe of R.E.M. Stipe wrote me that for many years he has chosen not to talk about Kurt except in private to Frances but referred me to an interview he did shortly after Kurt's death in which he said that near the end of his life Kurt talked to him "about what direction he was heading in." Stipe said, "I know what the next Nirvana recording was gonna sound like. It was gonna be very quiet and acoustic with lots of stringed instruments. He and I were gonna record a trial run of the album—a demo tape. It was all set up. He had a plane ticket. He had a car picking him up. And at the last minute he called and said, 'I can't come.'"

Despite my fatalistic attitude about Kurt's suicide at this point, my emotions make me wonder from time to time if things might have been different if I had spent more time with Kurt over the last few months of his life, if I had adopted a different tone at the intervention, if I had asked him to stay with us for a few days, or if I had been more imaginative in trying to find someone else to help him.

In 2016, there were 44,965 recorded suicides in the United States. More than three-quarters of them were men, and half of them killed themselves with guns. Suicide is also a global phenomenon. More than 800,000 people killed themselves around the world in 2015.

Eric Erlandson researched suicide for his book *Letters to Kurt* in part because of his added anguish when, a couple of months after Kurt killed himself, Hole's bass player Kristen Pfaff fatally overdosed. Eric lists some of the risk factors that increase the likelihood of suicide as failed belongingness, isolation, and numbing oneself to pain.

Another factor that some people believe increases the odds of suicide is a genetic predisposition. Kurt often talked of having "suicide genes." He said that his great-uncle Burle and great-uncle Kenneth both shot themselves, and he also thought he had a great-grandfather who stabbed himself.

Eric emailed me, "I'm not a big fan of the suicide gene theory. Depression maybe, but I believe that if you hear someone chose that way out, and you have some mental illness, you are given the idea that it's an option. Families having mental illness passed down through generations yes, but a gene that compels one to go against one's survival instincts, I don't buy it. Like many suffering from depression, Kurt would conveniently use anything he could as an excuse for his problems rather than focusing on the responsibility of breaking the cycle."

Eric is not the only person who was close to Kurt who is mad at him for taking his life. After all this time Krist is still pissed.

"He just gave up! How could he do that to his daughter? And having Dylan buy the gun. How could he do that to Dylan? He could have done anything he wanted to. He was a master of the world and to go crawl off and do that! Why the hell did he do that? He should have stuck around just for his daughter's sake."

I respect these emotions but see it differently. It's morally essential to do everything possible to prevent and discourage suicide, but I still keep coming back to the idea that Kurt had a disease that no one knew how to cure and that he died from it when he was twenty-seven. It's the only formulation that feels right to me, but the reality is that no one knows.

Kurt's last words to Courtney were "Whatever happens, remember you made a good album." Hole's *Live Through This* was released on April 12, one week after Kurt's death. The juxtaposition was a mind-fuck. The album's title had been decided long before Kurt's death and referred to so many obstacles in Courtney's earlier life, but when the album was released it eerily seemed to refer to Kurt's suicide.

I cannot imagine how Courtney handled the conflicting pressures inside her head on the Hole tour following the release of the album. She now recalls, "I was grieving in public to ten thousand people a night. I didn't really think I had a choice—it was like, the show must go on. I had my band and my baby."

That year *Live Through This* was named best album of the year by critics at both *Spin* and *Rolling Stone,* and Courtney was named best female rock singer in readers' polls in both magazines. Hole had a platinum album. Many women were inspired to become artists because they saw Courtney do it so effectively.

In addition to having influenced virtually every rock artist who came after him, Kurt's persona is part of hip-hop's lexicon. Lil Wayne told *MTV News* in 2011 that he was a fan of "Smells Like Teen Spirit" as a kid. "I probably felt at that time

I was rebelling, and I can associate myself with that, and relate to things he was talking about." New York rapper A$AP Rocky says, "Growing up, I was aware of Kurt Cobain and Nirvana's 'Smells Like Teen Spirit' and not just the usual stuff you'd expect growing up in Harlem."

In 2011, Kid Cudi visited Kurt's home and released a video entitled "Kid Cudi Pays His Respects to Kurt Cobain," in which the rapper and his friends discuss Cobain's death and music while "Smells Like Teen Spirit" plays in the background. In 2018 Cudi and Kanye West sampled Kurt's song "Burn the Rain" on "Cudi Montage," the final song on their *Kids See Ghosts* collaboration.

In hip-hop lyrics, the suicide looms large. "Holy Grail" by Jay Z and Justin Timberlake includes the words "I know nobody to blame / Kurt Cobain, I did it to myself." In Eminem's song "Cum On Everybody" he refers to "Kurt Cobain's head when he shot himself dead."

However Kurt's larger legacy is not his death but his music. In 2017 in *May It Last*, an HBO documentary about the Avett Brothers, Seth Avett says his two role models are Doc Watson and Kurt Cobain. In 2013 Lana Del Rey covered "Heart-Shaped Box." The YouTube clip of her performance has been played more than seven million times. In March 2018, HBO debuted the trailer for the second season of *Westworld*, the score of which was an instrumental piano arrangement of the same song. The show's composer, Ramin Djawadi, said, "Even without lyrics and just the melody. . . . it's actually quite incredible."

In 2018, poet Michael Wasson, author of the award-winning anthology *This American Ghost*, spoke of his childhood to the online magazine *Literary Hub*: "Back then, being way confused, I gravitated to Nirvana. I saw gut instinct, sketches in journals, and literary juxtapositions. Kurt drew anatomy and turtles. I loved

'Drain You.' In it there is a baby speaking unabashedly to another baby about gratitude as if to say *I'm so glad I was alive to meet you."*

Kurt's life and death have also been the subject of several films. I have a cameo appearance at the end of Nick Broomfield's 1998 documentary *Kurt & Courtney,* a film that has a negative take on Courtney. At an ACLU dinner in 1997, Courtney presented Miloš Forman with a free-speech award for having directed *The People vs. Larry Flynt,* in which she costarred. Broomfield jumped onstage uninvited and started ranting about Courtney's understandable refusal to answer questions for his conspiracy-friendly film. I demanded that he leave the stage and Broomfield promptly did, knowing that a cameraperson was filming the moment of his ejection, which, to his acolytes, was censorship.

Nick Hornby's wonderful novel *About a Boy* describes an alienated British teenager who finds an identity and some friends when he becomes a Kurt Cobain fan and is devastated by Kurt's death. The producers of the film version starring Hugh Grant evidently didn't have a budget to license any of Nirvana's music, but Kurt's spirit hovers over it anyway.

In 2005, Gus Van Sant released *Last Days,* a work of fiction he wrote and directed about a character who is obviously based on Kurt. Although Michael Pitt's portrayal of "Blake" has an uncanny physical similarity to Kurt, there is no other resemblance. Van Sant told me that the story was not meant as any kind of docudrama but was more a "response to the publicity about his death."

Blake lives in a big house in Seattle. Van Sant told me that a lot of what goes on there was based on his own experience after early success, not Kurt's: "I had a big Victorian house in Portland and sometimes people would be there and I'd avoid them." There is a detective who somehow figures into the plot. Kim Gordon plays a record executive who vainly tries to dissuade Blake from self-destructiveness. In her memoir *Girl in a Band,* Gordon writes that she used Rosemary as the model for her portrayal of a compassionate businessperson. Despite these superficial echoes of reality, the story bears little relation to what was going on at the end of Kurt's life.

I was not involved with the documentary *Montage of Heck,* which HBO aired in 2015, and have mixed feelings about it. It's a subjective portrait by filmmaker Brett Morgen, who didn't know Kurt, and it is a much darker view of his life than the one I have. I think it's a sincere work of art and I honor the fact that Frances and Courtney signed off on it, but a lot of the Kurt I remember is absent from it.

Other than the excellent concert documentaries that have been released, my favorite film connected to Kurt is A. J. Schnack's 2006 film *Kurt Cobain: About a Son,* which revolves around audio interviews Michael Azerrad did with Kurt.

There are a handful of crazy fans, like the guy from Australia who used to leave messages on my voice mail saying he was the reincarnation of Kurt, but the vast majority of those who feel deeply connected to Kurt are passionate aficionados whom I believe Kurt would appreciate.

When he was alive, Kurt hated bootlegs, not so much because of their financial impact on him but because he hated the idea of not having the final approval over any version of his art. However, he has no ability to make decisions from beyond the grave. I have respect for superfans who created bootlegs such as *Outcesticide* that include an assortment of song demos, outtakes, live recordings, and broadcast appearances unavailable elsewhere. However when *Outcesticide 2* came out someone involved in the packaging wrote, "The genius of Kurt Cobain should not be left to rot in record company vaults," a sentiment that is delusional. Neither Krist, Dave, Courtney, nor anyone at any record company has any interest in suppressing any of Kurt's music. Quite the opposite. There simply are no other great or even good Kurt Cobain songs that exist. He gave us quite a lot in a short time. John Lennon had seventeen years of access to recording studios. Prince had thirty-eight; David Bowie had forty-nine. Kurt had only five.

As I was approaching the deadline for this book in July 2018, an exhibition of Kurt's belongings was about to open in New-bridge, Ireland. Jeff Gold of Recordmecca, the leading broker of rock memorabilia, says, "For Generation X, Kurt Cobain is the Jimi Hendrix or Bob Dylan of their generation. Nirvana is by far the most collectible act of the 90s, and there is a huge demand for Kurt Cobain memorabilia." Among his examples: in 2017 the MTV Video Music Award for the "Heart-Shaped Box" video sold for $40,000, and in 2015 the sweater Kurt wore on *Unplugged* was sold for $140,000.

Of course most fans can't afford such things, but thousands have shown their devotion over the last twenty-five years by post-ing comments on the sites NirvanaClub.com and LiveNirvana .com.

Among my favorites is: "I think that Kurt Cobain was the greatest man to ever live. He is the reason I am the way I am. He has inspired me to do what I want not what other people want me to do. I believe he is still with all of us and that he never died."

Another fan wrote: "I used to be really angsty when I was younger. I wanted revenge because I was bullied my whole life, never seen as a person, only a joke. I was depressed and suicidal and pissed off basically, and Kurt was the one person who made me feel safe, someone who would never hurt me, but was always there to listen to my problems by relating to me through his lyr-ics. He made me feel like everything is ok, even when I was on the verge of going insane."

Thurston reflects, "Kurt wanted to be Neil Young. And in a

sense he was. He couldn't stay alive long enough to keep doing it. It's a fucking drag." It *is* a fucking drag that Kurt died so young, especially for Courtney and Frances. But it's *not* a drag that he lived. The darkness of his suicide is awful. Much of the drama that was a by-product of drug abuse is mortifying. The sadness and anger that many people saw in him was real. But so were his smile and his kindness and, most of all, his extraordinary music. He was the last rock artist who was also a pop figure. The man who wrote of being "stupid and contagious" in 1991 was as famous then as Drake or Rihanna are a quarter of a century later. He gave the world so much in twenty-seven years.

Kurt told a journalist a few weeks after *Nevermind* was released, "People think of life as being so sacred and they feel like this is their only chance and they have to do something with their life and make an impact. As far as I'm concerned, it's just a pit-stop for an afterlife. It's just a little test to see how you can handle reality."

Everett True told me that his favorite piece among the many he published about the band is the introduction to a book of photos published in England in 2001 called *Nirvana*, in which he wrote, "Here is my take on history books. I hate them. I fucking hate them. I hate anything that means something has ceased to exist. I don't want to let it go. I don't like the idea that a moment in time can be captured, stilled, become, in other words, a moment in time. What was Nirvana? A celebration of much that was glorious about our lives."

For all that Kurt inspired and for all that he gave, I believe there was a significant part of him that was a mystery even to those who were closest to him. I am so glad to have had a few glimpses and so glad that so much of his legacy still inspires so many people.

Notwithstanding Kurt's dark side, I keep returning to the

last chorus of "All Apologies," where Kurt sang, "In the sun I feel as one / All in all is all we are," and to these lines from his journals: "No True Talent is fully organic, yet the obviously superior talented have, not only control of study, but that extra special little gift at birth, fueled by passion. A built in totally unexplainable, New Age, fucking cosmic energy bursting love."

NOTE ON SOURCES

To help my memory and fill in gaps, I leaned particularly heavily on Michael Azerrad's books *Come as You Are: The Story of Nirvana* and *Our Band Could Be Your Life*.

Also indispensable were *Nirvana: The Biography* by Everett True, *Heavier Than Heaven* and *Here We Are Now: The Lasting Impact of Kurt Cobain* by Charles Cross, *Dark Slivers: Seeing Nirvana in the Shards of* Incesticide and *Cobain on Cobain: Interviews and Encounters* by Nick Soulsby, and *Nirvana: A Day by Day Eyewitness Chronicle* by Carrie Borzillo.

Other titles that were helpful include: *Nirvana: A Tour Diary* by Andy Bollen, *Journals* by Kurt Cobain, *Cobain* by the editors of *Rolling Stone, Dead Kennedys: Fresh Fruit for Rotting Vegetables: The Early Years* by Alex Ogg, *Get in the Van: On the Road with Black Flag* by Henry Rollins, *Girls to the Front: The True Story of the Riot Grrrl Revolution* by Sara Marcus, *Hit So Hard* by Patty Schemel, *Letters to Kurt* by Eric Erlandson, *Love Rock Revolution: K Records and the Rise of Independent Music* by Mark Baumgarten, *Of Grunge and Government: Let's Fix This Broken Democracy!* by Krist Novoselic, and *Spray Paint the Walls: The Story of Black Flag* by Stevie Chick.

In addition, reporting in the following publications was extremely valuable: the *Advocate*, *Bay Area Music*, Discogs, *GQ*, the *Los Angeles Times*, *Melody Maker*, *New Musical Express*, the *New Yorker*, the *New York Times*, *Newsweek*, *Pitchfork*, *Rolling Stone*, and *Spin*. As were the websites LiveNirvana.com, NirvanaClub.com, and MyBackPages.com.

Also helpful were numerous YouTube clips and the following films: *1991: The Year Punk Broke*, directed by Dave Markey; *Kurt and Courtney*, directed by Nick Broomfield; *Soaked in Bleach*, directed by Benjamin Statler; *Hype!*, directed by Doug Pray; *Last Days*, directed by Gus Van Sant; and *Kurt Cobain: About a Son*, directed by A. J. Schnack.

ACKNOWLEDGMENTS

Thanks to my editor, Denise Oswald, at Ecco Books, who believed in this book and who guided me through it with clarity and support. Thanks also to Emma Janaskie and Trina Hunn at Ecco, to copyeditor Aja Pollock, and to Anna Valentine at Trapeze in the UK.

My agent Laura Nolan at Aevitas held my hand at every stage of this process with patience and wisdom, for which I am deeply grateful. Thanks also to Chelsey Heller at Aevitas for overseeing the international rights.

Courtney Love has gone in and out of my life like the phases of the moon over the last quarter of a century. Her encouragement and help while I was writing this book mean the world to me.

Rosemary Carroll and I lived through many of the experiences recounted in this book together, and I cannot thank her enough for generously sharing her memories with me. Our children, Katie and Max, were very young when Kurt died, but they grew up in a world he helped create and I appreciate their emotional support.

Krist Novoselic's openhearted willingness to go over his memories one more time was inspiring and indispensable.

Michael Azerrad was one of the first people I spoke to about this undertaking and was repeatedly helpful; his friendship during the process was of incalculable value to me.

I also want to thank the following people who spoke to me: Jello Biafra, Jennie Boddy, Derrick Bostrom, Anton Brookes, Gérard Drouot, Eric Erlandson, Ray Farrell, Amy Finnerty, Robert Fisher, Leslie Fram, Jeff Gold, Steve Greenberg, Dirk-Jan Haanraadts, Mark Kates, Kenny Laguna, Scott Litt, Craig Marks, Ben Merlis, Jim Merlis, Chris Monlus, Thurston Moore, Scot Nakagawa, Andrew Loog Oldham, Ann Powers, Janet Billig Rich, John Rosenfelder, Robin Sloane Seibert, Al Smith, Robert Smith, Tim Sommer, Mark Spector, Susie Tennant, Everett True, Kaz Utsunomiya, Gus Van Sant, Butch Vig, and Greg Werckman.

I am grateful for feedback at various stages to Eric Alterman, Michael Azerrad, Eric Erlandson, and Michael Simmons.

Thanks to Benjamin Hafetz for research and to Stuart Coupe, Tim Sommer, Adam Sticklor, Katie Sticklor, and Cyndy Villano for valuable advice.

Thanks to Jesse Bauer and Shelby McElrath, my colleagues at Gold Village, for their patience with me during the last year, to Steve Earle for his brilliance and friendship, to my former assistant Robin Klein for organizing my files with so much care, and to Warren Grant and Lori Ichimura, my longtime business managers, for steadfast support.

As was the case with my last book, Karen Greenberg read every version of this one, and helped, nurtured, and inspired me in countless ways that words cannot describe.

INDEX